Hogarty

Tempest-Tossed

Isabella, circa 1896–1906. *Courtesy of the Harriet Beecher Stowe Center, Hartford, Connecticut.*

Susan Campbell

Tempest-Tossed

THE SPIRIT OF

ISABELLA BEECHER HOOKER

Wesleyan University Press   Middletown, Connecticut

Wesleyan University Press
Middletown CT 06459
www.wesleyan.edu/wespress
© 2014 Susan Campbell
All rights reserved
Manufactured in the
United States of America
Designed by Mindy Basinger Hill
Typeset in Fanwood

Library of Congress
Cataloging-in-Publication Data

Campbell, Susan, 1959–
Tempest-tossed : The spirit of Isabella
Beecher Hooker / Susan Campbell.
        pages   cm.—(Garnet books)
Includes bibliographical references
and index.
ISBN 978-0-8195-7340-7
(cloth: alk. paper)—
ISBN 978-0-8195-7388-9 (ebook)
1. Hooker, Isabella Beecher, 1822–1907.
2. Feminists—United States—Biography.
3. Women social reformers—United
States—Biography. I. Title.
HQ1413.H65C36 2013
305.42092—dc23
[B]   2013028419

5   4   3   2   1

CONTENTS

Preface

WHY A BOOK ABOUT

ISABELLA BEECHER HOOKER?

There it is, on page 57 of *Connecticut Curiosities: Quirky Characters, Road-side Oddities & Other Offbeat Stuff,* a book I cowrote with my friend Bill Heald some time back. *Curiosities* was a book about the interesting and weird things in Connecticut — a state not known for its frivolity — and that thin volume contained a short entry on Isabella Beecher Hooker, a complicated Hartford woman, written by me. In three snarky paragraphs, I called her "the more eccentric sister of author Harriet Beecher Stowe." I dismissed decades of hard work in a parenthetical phrase: "Isabella, a suffragist, was also a spiritualist"— because Spiritualism is a grabber, and "suffragist" is not.

It is not my best work.

Like most every American child, I read *Uncle Tom's Cabin.* I learned that Harriet Beecher Stowe opposed slavery, and that mid-1850s English is really hard to read. Beyond that, I knew nothing — not how disappointed some abolitionists were when Harriet pulled her punches and promoted colonization of freed slaves, not of Harriet's illustrious family, not anything about her life and times other than that women wore hoopskirts and curls and the wealthier ones had fainting couches.

I may have made up the fainting couches, but still.

And then a little more than ten years ago, Valerie Finholm, a former colleague at the *Hartford Courant,* suggested three of us journalists explore Harriet and two of her sisters, Catharine and Isabella. I did not know Harriet even had sisters (there was a fourth, Mary, who was staunchly private), nor did I know Harriet was from a family once known as the Fabulous Beechers for their far-reaching influence in religion, in politics, in issues of the day such as abolition and women's suffrage.

Think the Kennedys, but bigger, said Valerie.

I do not remember why I was assigned to Isabella, but Valerie began researching the older sister, Catharine, while another colleague, Kathy Megan, began researching Harriet. I felt sorry for them — Valerie, because she was writing about a woman I came to consider vaguely unlikable, and Kathy, because she was writing about someone who'd been written about to death — and quite well, actually. Connecticut's own Joan D. Hedrick had already written a Pulitzer Prize–winning biography of Harriet in *Harriet Beecher Stowe: A Life.*

It is hard to improve upon a Pulitzer.

I figured I had the best of the three. If I hadn't heard of Isabella Beecher, surely no one else had either and the possibilities were limitless. There'd be no ancient scholar calling from some dusty library correcting my characterization of this long-dead woman. Yay!

But there was something more. As we made our way — individually and as a group — to Hartford's Harriet Beecher Stowe Center, I became entranced. Isabella kept showing up with bold-faced suffragists such as Elizabeth Cady Stanton and Susan B. Anthony. Why had we lost track of her? Why had history not included her? She lobbied, spoke, and wrote laws, yet all I knew was she was the half-sister of one of the better-known authors of all time.

The people at the Stowe Center were incredibly kind. We were allowed — carefully — to handle family letters, which were the lifeline of the Beecher family. Someone would start a conversation and send it on, and the next sibling would add a few lines, and send it on again. Eventually, the pages were covered with spidery handwriting from some of the smartest people of their time. It was like reading the transcript from an intellectual salon — with a few barbed sibling-digs thrown in.

And oh! What siblings. The family included Harriet Beecher Stowe, who more than any other author brought slavery to the forefront of America's psyche; Henry Ward Beecher, a minister who was considered, at one point, the most famous man in America; and William, Edward, George, Charles, Thomas, and James — ministers who lacked the world renown of their brother, but who wielded immeasurable influence in their day. Add to them the eldest child, Catharine, who was dedicated to the education of women, and was perhaps the most outspoken of her siblings.

The lone holdout to public life, the private Mary Beecher, immersed herself in her family in Hartford. We know little about her other than through her involvement with her siblings, yet her influence — particularly on Isa-bella — was acute. Even so, that influence paled in comparison to the sway their father, Lyman, held over his children.

We came to know this family well, and over time — or so we joked — we each began to emulate our subjects. Valerie got bossy, Kathy became the accommodator, and I took on the mantle of the moderately difficult little sister who would not be moved.

There. I did it again. Even that short description doesn't do Isabella justice. There's a fine line between "difficult" and "resolute."

In my research, I came across a few attempts in the 1970s at capturing her life, when feminist historians began to look at figures who'd been pushed to the sidelines. One product of that effort was Anne Throne Margolis and Margaret Granville Mair's rather remarkable *The Isabella Beecher Hooker Project,* a 126-page compilation of the woman's life and correspondence. Much of what was written in that 1979 work forms the backbone of this book. I am deeply in the authors' debt.

I rather quickly learned that most (male) biographers had long ago dismissed Isabella as something between eccentric and crazy, with slightly more votes for crazy. Joseph S. Van Why, former director of the Stowe-Day Foundation, the precursor of the Stowe Center, wrote in his 1975 book, *Nook Farm,* that no other resident of this storied Hartford neighborhood lived under such "criti-cism and censure." Chalk some of that up to the rules of her day. A woman's place was in the home, and popular literature tried to romanticize just how keen that could be. Motherhood was wrapped up in lacy lavender ribbons, and here was Isabella furiously untying them — or trying to. Many women might have privately railed against their prescribed roles, but Isabella recorded her dissatisfaction over decades in blunt letters and journals. She wanted a voice, and she wanted an existence separate from her beloved husband, John Hooker, who preceded her into abolitionism and then followed her into the suffrage movement. She felt called by God to be more than a wife and mother, and she struggled with the guilt that this calling engendered. Her half-sister, Catharine, made a career of encouraging women to wrap their arms around their babies (the first anchor babies!) and stay home. They could, wrote the never-married Catharine, rule the world by rocking the cradle.

We may have left the hoopskirts behind, but Catharine's writing remains the foundation of our Woman Canon, the one we can recite from memory. Catharine's motivation to push for women's education was to train women to run a more godly home. Even today, her notion about a woman's highest calling has its passionate adherents, and its — vocal — opponents.

Count me among the latter. I am on Team Isabella.

Meanwhile, Isabella mingled with the great (Elizabeth Cady Stanton, Susan B. Anthony, Frederick Douglass) and the notorious (Victoria Wood-hull), and when the pressure became too much, she slipped off for water cures in New York and Massachusetts. This was common among women of her class, but Isabella freely admitted that her frequent trips away were mostly an escape from household drudgery. Much as she loved her husband and children, she could not contain herself within the expression of that love. The world was too big.

Can I get an amen?

In her era, that big vision was reason enough for public condemnation, but then Isabella sided against her powerful family when her famous preacher brother, Henry Ward Beecher (stop thinking Kennedys and start thinking Billy Graham in Rev. Graham's heyday), was accused of infidelity. Some of her siblings — older sister, Mary, chief among them — never forgave her that disloyalty to the family. Though it would have been easier to go along with the thunderous voting bloc that was the Beechers, Isabella clung to the truth, as she saw it. Henry had sinned. Henry needed to repent.

Is that crazy? Or is that resolute?

It is a dicey thing, analyzing someone's mental state from beyond the grave, and I wouldn't have the credentials to analyze her if she were alive, but consider the facts of Isabella's life: She lost her mother — who'd mostly been absent because of illness — just as she entered her teens. She watched her older sisters move into public life and suffer both success and condemnation. She also, as the much-shuttled younger sister, saw her siblings' marriages up close, and came away with a distinct fear of the all-encompassing and some-times stifling nature of that bond for women of the 1800s. She was hesitant to marry for fear she'd lose herself. In an 1831 letter to her intended, she called herself "tempest-tossed" and offered to end the engagement should either of them have second thoughts. She filled pages with her second thoughts — but then she married John Hooker anyway. She lost an infant son early in her marriage, and later she lost a beloved adult daughter. She talked to spirits and toward the end of her life, she seemed more comfortable talking to the dead than to the living. Her neighbor Mark Twain was a little frightened of and a lot annoyed with her. Word got around, and the editor of her local paper eventually refused to print her letters and articles about suffrage.

And still she soldiered on.

I did not do a wonderful job boiling all that down into a newspaper story, though the series Valerie, Kathy, and I wrote was well received and reprinted for distribution in classrooms around Connecticut. That felt good, but it wasn't enough, and that felt strange. Ask any journalist. Once you've spent time with a topic and the story is published, by necessity you move on. There are countless other topics that need your attention, and paying attention to already-published pieces is like dragging an anchor behind a boat.

But there I was, dragging Isabella. Maybe it was my guilt over writing a bland piece about an interesting woman. Maybe there was something else about this early feminist that caught in my net. Maybe it was a little bit of both. Any woman who lives her life in even a semipublic fashion runs the risk of being misunderstood, misrepresented, or cast to the side because no one takes the time to figure her out. As a dedicated chronicler of history in a hurry, I was keenly aware of the vagaries of who gets remembered, and who gets forgotten, and who becomes the butt of history's jokes.

So I kept coming back to Isabella. I inserted her — inelegantly — into the travel book. I wrote newspaper columns about her. I began to write essays about her — for what or whom, I haven't a clue. A couple of times, I dreamed about her and — metaphor alert! — she was always shrouded in the foggy distance. Maybe this is what a girl-crush looks like, and lucky me to have chosen a dead woman who could never love me back.

But I kept thinking how hard it is to swim against the tide, and how much harder still to do so in crinoline and pin curls. And yet she did, with her rage and humor intact.

For however much history has ignored her, Isabella Beecher Hooker lived and loved. She worked tirelessly for votes for women. She stood up and spoke up, often at great personal cost.

I am tempted to say she haunted me, but given Isabella's tendency to embrace spirits that wouldn't lie fallow, I don't want to encourage that kind of thing. Then again, I kind of do. "Do you have a feeling for her?" a medium asked, before she agreed to help me try to contact her. Well, yeah. I do.

And so I wrote this book — well, not this book, but one very much like it. The first manuscript I handed in was a rather perfunctory retelling of the facts: "And then in 1863, the family . . . ," that sort of thing. It was a fine book, and a thick book, a book packed with footnotes, but it was not the right book. With the blessing of my editor, Suzanna Tamminen (thanks, Suzanna!), I tore back into it. I do not know if anyone else will ever take a stab at Isabella. I only know I had this one shot, and if I wrote a boring book, I'd deserve a visit from the grave from an angry shade who was never, ever boring.

I still don't know if I've done justice to Isabella. I only know I tried.

For all the time I've spent with her journals, her speeches, and her letters, Isabella seems to me to be the closest thing we have to a modern woman. With her worries about juggling home-time and me-time and work-time, she would have fit in well today. Though society was telling her to settle for less, she wanted it all, and she wanted it all at once. She was prickly and difficult to like sometimes, but in the time I have spent plumbing her depths, I have been confused sometimes, and frustrated at others, but I have never been bored. I do not expect anyone to search through my own letters and journals, but if they do, my fondest wish is that they'd be every bit as delighted as I have been with Isabella.

About the use of first names: the Beechers were fond of naming their children after one another. There is an abundance of Lymans and Thomases and Harriets and several derivations of Isabella. When appropriate, I refer to them by their first names — and, if necessary for identification, their middle or last names. Some of the letters contain misspellings, or abbreviations. As much as possible, I have retained the original spellings, and I haven't inserted a note when something is misspelled. I am in no way Isabella's editor. I wouldn't want to tell her — even a long-dead her — a thing about how to get her point across. Misspellings and abbreviations aside, I prefer to let Isabella Beecher Hooker speak for herself.

In addition to the encouragement and editing I got from Suzanna, I could not have written this without the support of Joan D. Hedrick, and Debby Applegate, who wrote *The Most Famous Man in America: The Biography of Henry Ward Beecher*, the Pulitzer Prize winner for biography in 2007. It is a daunting thing to have two Pulitzer-winning biographies at your elbow as you make your own attempt at pinning down a Beecher. Early on, Joan offered to meet and chat and listen to my fumbling attempts to contain a life within a book. When I contacted her about Isabella, Debby (I'd never met her, but I hounded her electronically, so I felt I'd earned the right to call her by her first name) said she had a few notes she hadn't used in her book about Henry Ward Beecher, and then she sent me some two hundred pages' worth. And then, when I lost those notes, she sent them again, and apologized for not having placed them in chronological order. Sisterhood is not dead. It's alive and well and living among Pulitzer-winning authors who have a lot on their plate but cheerfully offered to help me pick through mine.

I must thank, as well, Katherine Kane, executive director of the Harriet Beecher Stowe Center, who was supportive and encouraging from the first moment — and Elizabeth Burgess, collections manager/goddess of research, who managed to say precisely the right thing every time I wandered in, dazed but convinced I would never be able to do this woman justice, no matter how many pages I wrote. And of course, thank you to Valerie and Kathy. Valerie, if you hadn't had the idea in the first place, I'd have never met Isabella, and then what would my obsession have been?

Thank you, as well, to my husband, Frank Schiavone, who has endured years of Isabella-inspired non sequiturs. We'd be walking around a village and come across a house marked by a dated commemorative plaque (a common thing in New England), and I'd volunteer that that, 1853, was the same year the Hookers finished their Hartford mansion. I have worked Isabella into conversations about stir-fry, tire balancing, and trees. Perhaps you can imagine the restraint it takes to politely listen to years of this. Frank finally suggested I write a book in the hopes that I'd stop talking about Isabella already. That has not turned out to be the case, but I appreciate the encouragement, and appreciate even more having found my very own John Hooker — patient, steadfast, and fiery in his convictions, all at once.

And finally — and I admit this is odd — I want to thank Isabella herself. As difficult as it is for women to defy cultural norms today, it was harder then. A woman who said "No, thank you" to bone corsets that made teeny-tiny waists to inhabit teeny-tiny lives could lose everything.

Yet Isabella did it anyway, and even when it was clear the world could not quite catch up with her on this side of the grave, she never stopped pushing. How can you not love a woman like that?

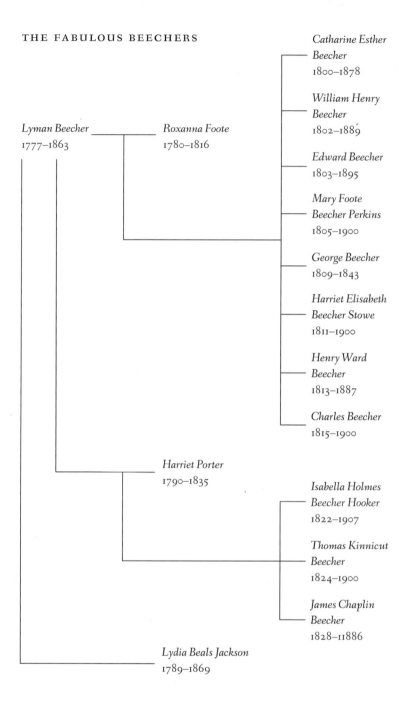

Lyman Beecher
1777–1863

Roxanna Foote
1780–1816

Catharine Esther
Beecher
1800–1878

William Henry
Beecher
1802–1889

Edward Beecher
1803–1895

Mary Foote
Beecher Perkins
1805–1900

George Beecher
1809–1843

Harriet Elisabeth
Beecher Stowe
1811–1900

Henry Ward
Beecher
1813–1887

Charles Beecher
1815–1900

Harriet Porter
1790–1835

Isabella Holmes
Beecher Hooker
1822–1907

Thomas Kinnicut
Beecher
1824–1900

James Chaplin
Beecher
1828–11886

Lydia Beals Jackson
1789–1869

THE CHILDREN OF JOHN HOOKER AND
ISABELLA BEECHER HOOKER

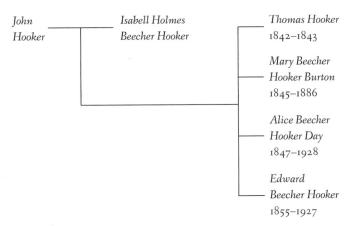

John
Hooker

Isabell Holmes
Beecher Hooker

Thomas Hooker
1842–1843

Mary Beecher
Hooker Burton
1845–1886

Alice Beecher
Hooker Day
1847–1928

Edward
Beecher Hooker
1855–1927

*Created by the author with substantial input
from the Harriet Beecher Stowe Center, Hartford, Connecticut*

Tempest-Tossed

1

THE WORLD THAT

AWAITED BELLE

Understanding Isabella Beecher Hooker means first understanding her family — the large, dynamic New England Beecher clan. Isabella was born in 1822, the first child of her father's second wife, with eight older half-siblings to welcome her. Her father was the noted early American minister Lyman Beecher, and her siblings included a world-famous author, a world-famous minister, and an internationally recognized advocate for women's education. "Lyman Beecher," wrote one biographer, "gave us queens as well as kings among men."[1]

Certainly he held an unparalleled position of authority in early-1800s America. From a 1904 biography: "Perhaps no one during the first half of the nineteenth century was more closely connected with the better life of America, both in its religious and in its reformatory aspects."[2]

If Lyman Beecher had not existed, someone would have invented him. He was thunderous in the pulpit, and rough-hewn away from it. Even though his children did not cleave to his brand of fundamentalist theology, they worshipped him for all his charismatic, sometimes coarse ways. But at his core, Lyman was a storyteller, and one of his favorite stories involved his own birth. How he came to this story one can only guess, as one can only guess if it's accurate. But it's a good story.

As so often happened with marrying men in the 1700s, Lyman's father, a blacksmith named David, was widowed and married five times — to Mary Austin, Lydia Morris, Esther Lyman, Elizabeth Hoadly, and Mary Lewis Elliott. He had twelve children with his wives, though eight of the children died in infancy. This, too, was common in a time of infant mortality that ranged, depending on the year and location, from 10 to 30 percent.[3] Lyman, born October 12, 1775, in Guilford, Connecticut, was the product of David's third and best-loved wife, Esther. She was from Middletown, Connecticut, and of Scottish descent. She possessed, said her son, "a joyous, sparkling, hopeful temperament."[4]

This characterization is conjecture on his part, or it is a description based on information gathered from his relatives. Lyman Beecher was born in the seventh month of his mother's pregnancy, and she died of consumption — the "great white plague"— two days after his birth.[5] Her illness had weakened her to the point that the midwives had little hope for the baby, and, wrote Beecher, wrapped his tiny body and laid him aside to die, until one of the women attending his mother thought to check him, and found him alive. She cleaned him and properly ushered him into the world.

"So you see it was but by a hair's-breadth I got a foothold in this world," Lyman wrote.[6] That early brush with death — or, at least, the family stories he heard about it — helped set Lyman Beecher on the road to a lifetime of conquering — starting with his weak infant nature and branching out to conquer his adult sinful nature and that of sinners who refused to hear the gospel. The story paints Lyman as stronger than mere mortals — a view his children, including Isabella, all seemed to share.

He entered Yale College, then nearly a hundred years old, in 1793.[7] His education was interrupted in its first year when he contracted scarlet fever. An epidemic swept through Connecticut and peaked in New Haven in January 1794 with some seven hundred cases reported.[8] Lyman recovered, only to discover during his second year that he was abysmal at mathematics. During his third year, he became heavily involved in gambling — so much so that he ended the year in debt. Frightened at the hold gambling had on him, he took a leave of absence for a week and cured himself of "that mania."[9]

A degree from Yale — a school with a theology far more orthodox than that of the other premier New England school, Harvard — gave graduates two career choices, law or the ministry. By Lyman's junior year, the thought of entering law — with its "little quirks, and turns and janglings — disgusted me," wrote Lyman.[10] He graduated in 1797 with a class of thirty-one, sixteen of whom became lawyers, fifteen of whom entered the ministry.[11]

As he was completing his education, Lyman met the woman who would be the love of his life, Roxanna Foote. Roxanna traced her family back to the early congregation of Thomas Hooker, who settled Connecticut and was known as the first American democrat.[12] The men of her family fought in the French and Indian and Revolutionary Wars.

Roxanna Foote was every bit as intellectually curious as her young swain. As a girl, she'd learned French by propping her lesson books on her distaff so that she could read them as she spun flax. Her grandfather once described his three eldest granddaughters by guessing what each girl would say upon rising from bed. Harriet, the eldest, would encourage everyone to start a fire and sweep. Betsy would wonder which ribbon to wear to a party. And Roxanna would say, "Which do you think was the greater general, Hannibal or Alexander?"[13] Neighbors shared books with one another, and when one much-awaited volume was published, a neighbor rode on horseback to bring it to Roxanna, and "a great treat they had of it."[14]

~records~

Lyman had sworn he'd never marry a weak woman, though Roxanna's Episcopal religion — against which Lyman waged a lifelong war — must have given him pause. After a brief courtship, Lyman asked if she would marry him. In response, she mentioned their religious differences and the fact that he was still in school. Undeterred, he told her he intended to continue his visits with an eye on marriage, and Roxana — as she told him later — consented because she never thought the relationship would amount to much. At one point, Lyman seems to have agreed with her, and he came to the family's Guilford home, Nut Plains, prepared to end the problematic relationship. But Roxanna, perhaps sensing a breakup, began to cry and he wasn't able to tell her why he'd come — and he never did. He did, however, send her books to read that might convince her of the errors of her theology. In turn, Roxanna wrote impassioned letters asking for her beloved's help in finding the defects in her prayer life.[15]

Later, as Lyman aged and began to slip into dementia, his son Charles read him snippets of the letters he'd written to Roxanna so long ago and saved. As Charles read, occasionally Lyman interrupted him and said, "Who is that fellow? He's all wrong." When Charles told his father he was reading Lyman's love letters to Roxanna, Lyman stopped a moment, then said, "Well, I was an ignoramus, but if I had him and her in one of my inquiry meetings, I could have set them all right in half an hour."[16]

They married on a rainy September 19, 1799, and with Roxanna at his side, Lyman Beecher set out to spread his influence by writing sermons that lit on the topics of the day. A series of sermons against dueling in 1806 was delivered in response to the death-by-dueling of former secretary of treasury Alexander Hamilton at the hand of Vice President Aaron Burr.[16]

But it was a sermon Lyman gave in 1807 in East Hampton, New York, and later delivered at a larger church meeting in Newark, that placed him firmly in the public eye. Remember, this was a time when the leading thinkers of the day were not politicians, but ministers, and sermons were reprinted as booklets and in newspapers and circulated widely. Beecher's first popular sermon, "The Government of God Desirable," was favorably compared with the work of the storied Jonathan Edwards, whose 1741 sermon "Sinners in the Hands of an Angry God" was supposed to have moved his congregation to "tears and convulsions."[17] Printed, Lyman's sermon ran twenty-seven pages and ended with the warning, "But rebel, and still he will reign, still he will bless his kingdom, but he will exclude you, forever, from its holy joys."[18]

It's not a modern-day page-turner, but this was Christian orthodoxy at its most raw, and it would make Lyman Beecher as much a household name as possible in the days before mass communication — "a Puritan of the Puritans," according to his son Henry Ward.[19]

But Lyman was restless, and he and Roxanna and their growing family — Catharine born in 1800, William Henry in 1802, Edward a year later, and Mary two years after him — could not live on Lyman's $400 a year. Roxanna would prove a practical balance to the high-strung Lyman by taking in boarders, but when that didn't meet the family's financial needs, she opened a school and taught English and French. Lyman's growing influence caught the attention of Congregationalists in Litchfield, Connecticut, and the family soon settled in the Litchfield Hills in a large and drafty home that was the frequent stop of wayfarers and teachers intent on taking advantage of a poor minister's largesse.

The move's timing could not have been better. With world-class educational institutions, Litchfield was a vibrant, changeable town. For a short time between 1790 and 1830, all roads passed — or seemed to — through Litchfield.

The two main educational institutions in Litchfield — one a law school and the other one of the country's rare schools for young women — were part of a shift in America from an agrarian culture to one centered in urban areas and small towns. The shift to a mercantile society helped spread capital to families that heretofore had scant opportunity — other than marrying into it — to amass wealth. You either owned a farm or you didn't.

The shift also broadened the opportunities for education, making books and the advancement of knowledge not so much the enclave of the wealthy and the clergy but also open to anyone with access to a newspaper or book.[20] At the same time, the shift to a more mechanized society and a more urban environment made the enforcement of the country's slave economy more difficult.[21]

Those were the positive results of the modernization of the U.S. economy, but for every winner, there is a loser. Railroads might make travel more convenient, but they destroyed previously untouched vistas. Factories increased productivity, but they polluted the streams. Material wealth that had been unimagined outside of royal families rewarded a choice few — and consigned the losers to slums equally unimaginable.

With the shift came an even sharper division between the worlds of women and men. On a farm, chores were unending, and rare was the family that would begrudge an extra pair of hands in the fields — whether those hands were male or female. Not so in a mercantile society. To fulfill economic roles, the world was splitting in two, with, in general, women assigned the indoor tasks and men assigned the rest. That is not as much an overstatement as it might appear. The attitude of taming a wilderness — the new country of America — was being replaced by a desire for more order, starting with the home front. For the first time in the country's short history, the feminine role was shrinking.

Lyman's spiritual ancestors had come to the colonies with a mania for salvation equaled only by their disdain for royal rule. Their love of a heavenly king far trumped their embrace of an earthly one — and their worship began with discipline of self.[22] The same way women of Isabella's generation would be told they could rule the world by ruling their homes, the Puritans believed they could usher in a godly world by focusing on eradicating their own foibles. This rigorous self-examination shows up in the austerity in paintings and sculptures that portrayed the Puritans as possessing "rock-ribbed integrity."[23] Throughout Isabella's life, the imagined simplicity and integrity of Puritan family life would be recalled with fondness — if not complete accuracy. Ironically, the same theology that would condemn modernity was a healthy backdrop for industrialization, because Puritanism rewarded those who worked hard and those who treated idleness as a sin. Puritanism rewarded thrift as well — so families living on meager resources found theological support for their scrimping.[24] Salvation could be found in the lesser cut of meat — or in no meat at all. If life on earth was difficult, a reward in heaven could be gained by working hard.

With that foundation of a binary gender world, Lyman Beecher did not pursue the formal education of his daughters beyond a certain age, but he at least saw the wisdom of sending them to Miss Sarah Pierce's Litchfield Female Academy. Miss Pierce adhered to the radical notion that women and men were intellectual equals. Her rigorous curriculum included logic, chemistry, botany, and mathematics — not a common course of study for women in the early 1800s. Townsfolk who worried that their daughters were being taught dangerous topics could rest assured that Pierce's classes also included painting, singing, and dancing.[25] Catharine and Harriet — and, for a while, Henry Ward — were students. The fit was not a comfortable one for Henry Ward. As the only boy, he once laughed out of turn in class, and as punishment was tied to a bench.[26]

Tuition was $5 per quarter for writing, history, grammar, rhetoric, and arithmetic and an additional $6 per quarter for French. Board was offered with "respectable families" for anywhere from $1.75 to $2 a week — a substantial sum at a time when median wages were roughly $10 a month.[27] The fee did not include laundry.[28] By teaching religion at Miss Pierce's, Lyman Beecher earned his daughters a tuition discount. Given their close proximity to the school, the Beecher sisters would have avoided paying board, and of course they'd do their own laundry, so the family could just afford a world-class education for the young women — for a few years, at least.

When the Beechers entered the school, women were being encouraged to enter into lives of domesticity,[29] and most of that was in class-specific terms.[30] In fact, modern domesticity in America — think Food Network and mommy blogs — had its birth in the late eighteenth century.[31] If the halls of power were closed to them, women "had a special role to play in promoting civic virtue. As 'republican mothers,' they should educate themselves and take an interest in political affairs, in order to raise their sons to be virtuous citizens and their daughters to become republican mothers in the next generation."[32] The British notion of "fashionable womanhood"— characterized by later marriage and more education — had all but been erased.[33] Replacing it was the notion of the hearth as a haven and a sanctuary.[34]

Miss Pierce's school became a focal point of the family's activities. The school drew students from around the country, and during Miss Pierce's forty years as a superintendent, the school educated some three thousand students in the Litchfield Hills, where "the country was preferred as most suitable for females' improvement away from the frivolities and dissipations of fashionable life."[35]

While the Beecher girls were getting an education, Lyman Beecher was throwing himself into church life. Writing in the 1860s, Henry Ward Beecher said that his father had no life separate from the church, that he "entered the church briskly, walked nimbly down the aisle, ascended the pulpit stairs with a springy step that threatened to throw him up two stairs at a time . . . he looked around the church as familiarly as if it was his own parlor."

As God demanded Lyman's energies, God also demanded the family's support.[36] Lyman's enthusiasm was further fueled by his belief that his brand of American Christianity was exceptional, that it was the one true faith, and that it would be the salvation of the world. This led rather handily into a firm belief in American exceptionalism. Though there is some disagreement among modern-day scholars, for years, historians and theologians said that Jonathan Edwards — who framed early American Calvinism and whom Lyman Beecher held in great esteem — had predicted that the millennium would begin in America.[37] The millennium, said Edwards, would involve a thousand-year reign of Jesus on earth, and when Beecher first heard that supposition, he'd dismissed it. Over time, though, he began to see the new country as the starting point of a new religious age, one that would hasten Jesus' subsequent return to earth. "What nation," he said, in a series of speeches given in 1834 as he toured the East Coast as head of Cincinnati's Lane Seminary, "is blessed with such experimental knowledge of free institutions, with such facilities and resources of communication, obstructed by so few obstacles, as our own? There is not a nation upon earth which, in 50 years, can by all possible reformation place itself in circumstances so favorable as our own for the free unembarrassed application of physical effort and pecuniary and moral power to evangelize the world."[38]

Before Jesus' arrival — which at the time was thought to be imminent — the people would need to be made ready through rigorous policing of not just their actions but their thoughts and emotions as well. This notion would embed itself in Isabella's psyche: only through rigorous self-examination could she aspire heavenward. Though her father would not have recognized her theology as she grew older, even when she was at the height of her political power, her letters and journals are full of self-condemnation in which she agonizes that she never measured up to the Christian ideal. For Isabella, there was no life but a simple striving toward the holy, however one defined holy.

"Hundreds of times," wrote Charles of his father, "have we heard him 'hew down' antagonists, 'wring their necks off,' 'hang them on their own gallows,' and do other sanguinary things too dreadful to mention. But there was always something in his eye and manner which told that he was speaking in a highly figurative sense of the logical demolition of error."[39]

At home, Roxanna Beecher, the exquisite mother and brilliant wife, had borne eight children in fifteen years: Catharine, William, Edward, Mary, George, Harriet, Henry Ward, and Charles. She had imprinted upon her children the notion of Perfect Motherhood — and no woman would ever compare. Catharine would later transform it into "a public mission fired with the passion and preeminence of the ministry."[40] But ill health dogged Roxanna, and in 1816, at age forty-one, she died of consumption.[41] Her youngest child was just one, and the next oldest — Henry Ward — was not yet three. Her oldest, Catharine, was sixteen.

Lyman Beecher stood in a tub pulpit with Roxanna's coffin below, and preached her funeral service.[42] The rest of the family quickly began to turn the accomplished woman into a saint. Later, Henry Ward, although he was still a toddler when she died, would tell his congregation that his mother meant to him what the Virgin Mary meant to a devout Roman Catholic.[43]

As mournful as was the family — particularly Lyman, who had lost both an intellectual partner and a Christian wife — it would not do for a man of the cloth, and the father of eight, to go unwed. So Lyman Beecher followed in his father's footsteps of rapid wife replacement and, nearly a year to the day of Roxanna's death, traveled to the Park Street Church in Boston to give a sermon titled "The Bible, a Code of Laws." For both Litchfield and Boston Congregationalists, the reason for his trip was clear. According to the supposition of the girls he taught at Miss Pierce's school, Lyman had gone to Boston to seek a wife and a mother for his children.[44]

And he was successful. He returned to Boston a month later to retrieve twenty-seven-year-old Harriet Porter, the daughter of a prominent doctor from Portland, Maine, who counted among her family a Maine governor, a congressman, and a member of the Continental Congress.[45] Her family members did not approve of the union of their fair Harriet with the older firebrand who had, as he'd done with his first wife, proved to be a persuasive suitor in his letters. Lyman Beecher may have had a growing influence on the country's theology, but he would never earn a decent living, and what did Harriet Porter know of raising children?

Harriet Porter was beautiful, and hardly equipped for the rigors of parish life or ministerial poverty that was not always so genteel.[46] Catharine, who was just ten years younger than Harriet Porter, wrote a letter that sought to alert her soon-to-be stepmother of the welcome that awaited her. Catharine said she and her siblings "promise to make it our constant study to render you the affection, obedience, and all the kind offices which we should wish to pay our own mother were she now restored to us from the grave. The sacred name of mother, so bound up in our hearts, would alone entitle you to the most undeviating affection and respect."[47]

Despite the Porter family's trepidations, from all indications, everyone's first impressions were favorable. Harriet Porter Beecher, who was every bit as committed to orthodoxy in her religion as was her new husband, seemed pleased with the relative sophistication of her new home.[48] On first meeting his stepmother after he'd already gone to bed for the night, Henry Ward Beecher wrote, "I remember well how happy I was. I felt that I had a mother. I felt her kiss, and I heard her voice. I could not distinguish her features, but I knew that she was my mother."[49]

Of that first meeting, his sister Harriet wrote:

> I was about six years old and slept in the nursery with my two younger brothers. We knew Father was going away somewhere on a journey, and was expected home, and thus the sound of a bustle or disturbance in the

house more easily awoke us. We heard Father's voice in the entry, and started up, crying out as he entered our room, "Why, here's pa!" A cheerful voice called out from behind him, "And here's ma!"

A beautiful lady, very fair, with bright blue eyes and soft auburn hair bound round with a black velvet bandeau, came into the room, smiling, eager, and happy-looking, and coming up to our beds, kissed us and told us she loved little children and would be our mother. We wanted forthwith to get up and dressed, but she pacified us with the promise that we should find her in the morning.[50]

That next morning, Harriet Beecher wrote, "We looked at her with awe."[51]

She seemed to us so fair, so delicate, so elegant, that we were almost afraid to go near her. We must have been rough, red-cheeked, hearty country children, honest, obedient, and bashful. She was peculiarly dainty and neat in all her ways and arrangements; and I remember I used to feel breezy and rough and rude in her presence. We felt a little in awe of her, as if she were a strange princess rather than our own mamma; but her voice was very sweet, her ways of speaking and moving very graceful, and she took us up in her lap and let us play with her beautiful hands, which seemed wonderful things, made of pearl, and ornamented with strange rings.[52]

As for her impression of her new family, Harriet Porter Beecher wrote to her sister: "I never saw so many rosy cheeks and laughing eyes. They began all, the first thing, to tell their dreams, for it seems they have dreamed of nothing else but father's coming home; and some dreamed he came without me, and some that he brought two mothers."[53] She would write subsequent letters extolling the family's cheerfulness and health, and the "uncommon intellect" shown by even the smallest of the brood. She was particularly taken with Edward, the third child, and suggested he would one day be a great scholar. She would also express thanks that the children were so self-sufficient. Being without a mother — even for just a year — had pushed Catharine and Mary into the role, and both seemed willing and capable of continuing their motherly duties even after the arrival of their new stepmother. The new Mrs. Beecher found herself called upon only a little, and she displayed her sensitive nature early when her husband tried to read to her Edwards's "Angry God" sermon. As Lyman read, she stormed from the room, saying, "Dr. Beecher, I shall not listen to another word of that slander on my Heavenly Father!"[54]

Church life, as well, required little of Harriet Porter. She described in letters church services that relied heavily on singing and reading scriptures aloud. She was impressed with the relationship between Harriet and Henry, sister and brother just two years apart, who were "always hand-in-hand."[55] She did, however, travel with her husband to visit the flock, and she held church teas. She also tried to start a women's committee. She was heartily impressed with her husband's stamina.

The family was on the verge of scattering — the boys to college, the girls to marriage — and they held on to one another through their letters. In one, Catharine wrote to Edward of the death of a family cat, Tom Junior, and noted that their sister Harriet was "our chief mourner always at their [the cats'] funerals," to which Lyman added his concern that "soon none but letters so solid and weighty as to earn their postage will be passing to and fro." An addition from Catharine reminded Edward that "papa loves to laugh as well as any of us, and is quite as much tickled at nonsense as we are!"[56]

Soon after he was joined by his new wife, Lyman Beecher's prodigious energy failed him, and he stepped away from the pulpit to spend a year working the farmland around his Litchfield homestead. The diagnosis was "nervous dyspepsia," or an upset stomach caused by stress or exhaustion. After a year's sojourn in the fields, he was back in the pulpit, and traveling at the same hectic pace as before.

About the same time Lyman stepped back into his ministerial duties, Harriet Porter Beecher began having babies, starting in 1818 with Frederick C. Beecher, who would live not quite two years. On June 20, 1820, Catharine wrote brother Edward, then a student at Yale:

"We are all anxious and troubled at home. Frederick had the canker, or scarlet fever, very badly. For two of three days we have despaired of his life."[57]

On June 23, Catharine wrote family at Nut Plains that "little Freddy had breathed his last" and that:

were it not for religion, I think mamma would sink, but she is a most eminent Christian, and feels resignation and comfort from above. I wish you could see how beautiful he looks even in death. I think I never beheld any thing earthly so perfect and lovely as his little corpse. His hair curls in beautiful ringlets all over his head, and he looks so natural and unaltered, one would think him in a peaceful slumber. I can not bear to think he must be laid in the grave.[58]

Harriet, the younger, was taken with the same illness but she recovered.

In January 1822, the house had four boarders, and even with the extra income, the family budget was stretched.[59] With the birth of Lyman Beecher's eighth child imminent, the family sent ten-year-old Harriet Beecher to Nut Plains, to her mother's homestead. From a family letter describing Roxanna's family:

These Footes are a people by themselves in their literary accomplishments, their good sense and fine breeding. Their homestead almost talks to you from its very walls of the days gone by. I never felt more sure of spirit companionship of the highest order, and your father thinks few parlors in all the land have gathered a more noble company.[60]

And while she wintered there, her ever-vigilant big sister Catharine wrote her:

I suppose you will be very glad to hear you have a little sister at home. We have no name for her yet. We all want you at home very much, but hope you are now where you will learn to stand and sit straight, and hear what people say to you, and sit still in your chair, and learn to sew and knit well, and be a good girl in every particular; and if you don't learn while you are with Aunt Harriet, I am afraid you never will.[61]

Eventually, the family would settle on the name Isabella — consecrated to God. So tagged, the baby girl entered the frantic, intellectually challenging, and curious world of the Fabulous Beechers.

2

TRAINING TO BE

A BEECHER

Childbirth in early America was a dangerous thing. Women gave birth anywhere from five to eight times, and a new mother's chance of dying during the process was between 1 and 1.5 percent. Extrapolating for the non–math majors, that meant a woman's chances of dying over the course of her childbearing years could be as high as one in eight.[1] If she survived, her child might not. In the early 1800s, there wasn't the language for birth control.[2] You can perhaps see why pregnancy was approached with no small amount of dread.

We know nothing about Isabella's actual birth, other than it took place on February 22, 1822, but we can take a few educated guesses. Unattended births were rare among people with any kind of social standing. A woman of Harriet Porter's position might have opted to give birth in the presence of a physician.[3] However, with her marriage to Lyman Beecher, Harriet Porter had slipped a few rungs down the socioeconomic ladder, and Isabella's birth most likely was attended — if it was attended at all — by a house servant or a trusted family member such as the ever-present Aunt Esther Beecher, Lyman's unmarried sister who frequently cared for the children. As Harriet Porter had had one child previously — little doomed Frederick — she would have at least known what to expect.

Meanwhile, the joys of child-rearing were being codified in a slew of parenting books that began hitting the markets in the 1820s. Previously, childhood was considered an event best navigated quickly, but in the early part of the nineteenth century, writers began to devote more time to essays and books on child-rearing, and on parental (read: maternal) involvement. By mid-decade, the relatively new genre focused most intently on the authority of the parent, and the need for the child to acquiesce.[4] The books stressed self-discipline "over physical and moral faculties"— which dovetailed nicely with the Beecher family religion of rigorous self-examination.[5]

Two more children followed Isabella: Thomas Kinnicut Beecher in 1824 and James Chaplin Beecher in 1828. With each new child, Harriet's sojourns in her bedroom grew longer and longer, and her time with her children — both step- and birth — grew increasingly short. Mary and Catharine proved themselves capable of helping run the household and manage the children, and Isabella most likely learned to look to her sisters for what mothering she needed.

Catharine, a generation older than baby sister Isabella, was engaged to be married and soon to leave the nest when word reached Litchfield that her fiancé, Alexander Metcalf Fisher, a brilliant mathematician from Yale, had been killed in a shipwreck off the coast of Ireland just two months after Isabella was born. For as much as he could move people from the pulpit, Lyman Beecher lacked the ability to comfort his grieving eldest daughter. He believed that her beloved had died in a state of sin, because although Fisher had studied religion at Yale, he was not a member of the Congregational Church. If the young mathematician had had a religious conversion — to Lyman's brand of Christianity, as none other would do — he left no record of such a conversion.[6] Instead of comfort, Lyman spoke to his daughter about how God tests his children, and he urged her to turn to God for comfort.

Being told by your father that your fiancé is burning in hell is not a motivator to draw nigh unto the Lord. Catharine, who had seemed likely to be the Beecher who would cling to the old rugged cross so adored by her father, suffered a crisis of faith from which she never quite recovered. Why should she give fealty to a God who took her beloved? An anguished father-daughter debate carried on for months, and was sometimes joined by Edward, three years Catharine's junior and one of the family's earliest abolitionists.

Catharine inherited Fisher's library, which she began to rigorously explore. With study and debate within the family, Catharine became an ambassador of a new theology, and the family's first break from their father's brand of Calvinism had begun.[7] And those family debates formed the foundation of Isabella's instruction — that she should be as well-read as her brothers in order to create a home environment that would serve as a springboard for her future husband's son's success in the world.

At home, the family scene was dynamic. There was the ever-rotating crew of boarders and the continual addition of new babes, while older children rotated in and out, subject to the school calendar.

Not long after the death of her fiancé, Catharine founded the Hartford Female Seminary in a rented room over a harness shop, with two teachers and a student body of seven. The school was funded mostly by the women of Hartford, after their husbands balked at educating girls in mathematics and other topics that had been restricted to boys. One father wrote a worried letter to the local paper, the *Courant*: "I would rather my daughters to go to school and sit down and do nothing, than to study philosophy. . . . These branches fill young Misses with vanity to the degree that they are above attending to the more useful parts of an education."[8] If this gentleman had sat in on any of Catharine's classes, he would have been even more concerned, for Catharine used her school to explore her own evolving notions about theology and women's roles. Her father's Calvinist theology insisted that salvation came from the grace of God. Instead, Catharine emphasized the importance of good works.[9] She began to concentrate on raising funds for her school in 1826 and was able to move to a larger facility in a church basement at Main and Morgan in Hartford's downtown, though the school was still confined to just one room. Catharine's sister Harriet began teaching there soon after, and after another round of fundraising, Catharine moved into a neoclassical building on Pratt Street.[10] When prospective student Angelina Grimké, who would later be an outspoken abolitionist and suffragist, visited from South Carolina in 1831, she found that Catharine wanted students "to feel that they had no right to spend their time in idleness, fashion and folly, but they as individuals were bound to be useful in Society after they had finished their education, and that as teachers single women could be more useful in this than in any other way."[11]

In addition to running her classes, Catharine began to hold revival services in a house she rented in Hartford, though her father cautioned against that, given her gender. Universal education was not yet embraced in Hartford or elsewhere, and funding was always an issue. In 1832, when the family left for Cincinnati, Catharine would eventually join them.[12]

Catharine's campaign for education for females, her notions about a woman's place in the world, and her spiritual fluctuations affected her peers in ways great and small. While all around her women were confining themselves to the hearth, Catharine and later Harriet were making their way with their own careers. In family conversations, Isabella would have heard what was then the radical notion about education for females. Later, Isabella would take that notion further and insist a woman's place was out in the world. Perhaps she was only building on her sister's early lessons.

Throughout her life, Isabella clung to an idealized notion of a mother who offered unconditional support and love, and she would even, as a Spiritualist, believe that her mother crossed back into the world to give her advice and love when she acutely needed it. In the real world, her "mothers" included Catharine, Harriet, Mary, and Aunt Esther.

Other than snippets from family letters, not much is known about Aunt Esther. According to Catharine, Aunt Esther was a home economist in the truest sense of the word. She abhorred debt. She was methodical. She could not sew. She read every science book she could acquire. She made a wonderful gingerbread, the recipe for which Catharine included in an 1873 cookbook (and which I tried to make, with not a hint of success). In her 1874 book, *Educational Reminiscences and Suggestions*, Catharine wrote:

> Oil and water were not more opposite than the habits of Father and Aunt Esther, and yet they flowed along together in all the antagonisms of daily life. . . . All Aunt Esther's rules and improvements were admired and commended, and, though often overridden, the contrite confession or droll excuse always brought a forgiving smile.[13]

~ঌৄ

When Isabella turned four, the family left Litchfield and moved to Boston. Once again, Lyman Beecher could not provide for his growing family on his annual salary (this time, $800), but on a broader scale Litchfield had become too small for Lyman's aspirations — and he believed the larger city was more in need of his ministrations. In his view, Boston had left Calvinism for a mushy, more liberal theology that was anathema to Beecher's fire and brimstone. In Boston, in particular, "the wealth and fashion . . . were to be found in the Unitarian churches, while the literary men and the professors at Harvard College were all committed to the new way of thinking."[14] In fact, Harvard had become so universally Unitarian that Yale University was created from Yale College as an antidote.[15]

His Boston arrival was greeted as a burst of energy to the Hanover Street Congregational Church.[16] But first, the church would have to get over its first impression of its new minister. One observer watched Lyman arrive with wife Harriet: "My first glimpse of the noted preacher, whose fame had reached our ears, was had one autumnal Sabbath morning as he rode up to the door of our new and elegant church, with his wife, in a poor country chaise covered with white cotton cloth. The horse and the minister were both alike very unattractive as well as the chaise."[17] Like Isabella, the church was just four years old, having been organized in 1822 with thirty-seven members and led by a series of itinerant ministers.[18]

The early disappointment of the congregation was not alleviated when Beecher took over the pulpit with such "unceremonious freedom that our Boston sense of propriety stood abashed!"[19] For all of Litchfield's relative sophistication, this minister was hardly refined. He was loud. He was nearly theatrical — though nothing like ministers who would follow him. But Lyman was a born orator, and the congregation could not withstand its new preacher's rhetorical fervor. Before the sun set on his first day, the old horse and chaise were forgotten. Lyman Beecher's three sermons that day kept the congregation talking for the rest of the week, and the fire burned unabated. The Bostonians found themselves drawn to their new pastor, who would delight them with statements such as "Brethren, it is my business to draw the bow, yours to see where the arrow strikes and to bring in the wounded."[20]

Later, the Reverend Artemas Bullard, a Hanover member, said "there was no minister in New England so uniformly dreaded and hated" by some Christians.[21] He and other "champions of orthodoxy thundered their challenge" so loudly that his church was said to inhabit "Brimstone Corner." Wrote one resident of the day, "We boys had been told, and seriously believed, that if we would thrust a match through the keyhole of the front door of this church it would ignite from the sulphurous fumes inside. We tried more than once to accomplish this feat, but found the theory, like many another in life, did not work."[22]

In the meantime, Isabella was enrolled in Lowell Mason's juvenile class at the Boston Academy of Music, where she learned to sing before she learned to read, as she wrote years later in a 1905 essay for *Connecticut* magazine titled "The Last of the Beechers: Memories on My Eighty-Third Birthday." Mason, perhaps the most famous native-born musician in the country in midcentury, sought to educate music teachers, and he wrote a popular instruction manual just a few years after Isabella became one of his students.[23] His collections of sacred music were classics, and he was able to accumulate a small fortune based on the sales. Lyman Beecher campaigned for his move to Hanover to shore up the choir.[24] In exchange for the use of the church facilities, where Mason was organist and choir director, Mason often gave music lessons for free.[25] It was just one more way Lyman Beecher managed to barter for the free (or inexpensive) education of his children.

While Lyman blazed against the threats of the newer, more liberal theology, his wife was growing increasingly incapacitated. Her letters to family and friends were more and more morose, and she wrote with feeling about her desire to meet her Lord. Already in retreat from her motherly and wifely duties, Harriet Porter Beecher found the demands of her husband's new job and a new home to be too burdensome, and in 1825 she suffered a stroke that further removed her from family activities. By the time of Isabella's seventh birthday, her mother was all but bedridden.[26]

The invalid woman in the bed upstairs, then, was the mother that Isabella knew, and she would have absorbed the sometimes dismissive or worse comments of her older siblings, who continually compared this timid and ill woman with the boisterous and lively Roxanna. Lyman himself appears to have conflated his first two wives, and he frequently referred to Roxanna as the mother of all his children, as if his second wife had been only a shadow. As an adult, Isabella wrote to her husband that she feared being someone like her mother, "a trial to my husband — and children — a nervous, fidgety [*sic*] old woman causing gloom in the house instead of sunshine."[27] Much of

Thought to be a portrait of Harriet Porter Beecher and daughter Isabella, circa 1830. *Courtesy of the Harriet Beecher Stowe Center, Hartford, Connecticut.*

her memories of her mother seems lifted from the pen of her older half-sister Harriet, who called Harriet Porter a "strange princess."[28] Henry Ward was more blunt. He called her "polished" but "cold."[29]

"I always felt," he said later, "when I went to prayer as though I was going into a crypt where the sun was not allowed to come, and I shrank from it."[30] She may have been a saintly woman, but she "never reached saintly status among Roxanna's children."[31]

Whatever Isabella's older siblings' impression of their stepmother, Harriet Porter would have been, for Isabella, like a distant planet — removed, unreachable, and unknowable.

3

THE EDUCATION

OF ISABELLA BEECHER

Despite his wife's frailties, in the early 1830s the ever-restless Lyman Beecher began to look west, toward Cincinnati, an outpost that had been settled mostly by New Englanders. In what was then the Far West, men like Lyman Beecher "had ample opportunity to fit shoes of virtue on the clay feet of straying mortals."[1] His work in Boston was nowhere near done, but Lyman Beecher was convinced that God in the mostly untrammeled Ohio wilderness had reached out to him to come glean the fields.

The trip would be fraught with challenges. The family could be in great peril from the diseases and uncertainties of the trail, but with a promised donation from supporters of the unearthly sum of $20,000 to Lane Theological Seminary if he took the helm, Lyman was sorely tempted.[2]

But first, he traveled with his then-thirty-year-old daughter and most trusted advisor, Catharine, to investigate the new land. While there, Catharine wrote back to sister Harriet: "I never saw a place so capable of being rendered a paradise by the improvements of taste as the environs of this city. Walnut Hills are so elevated and cool that people have to leave there to be sick, it is said."[3]

The other Beecher women had reservations about the move, but Lyman was able to rouse them.[4] Satisfied that their effort would be met with great results, in 1832 the family moved to Cincinnati, and Lyman assumed the presidency of the Lane Theological Seminary and pastorship of the town's Second Presbyterian Church. The school, which had been operating since 1829, crowned a hill about two miles northeast of Cincinnati. The seminary's ethos would have appealed to Lyman's sense of asceticism. Quarters were not opulent, and students lived simply — and often chose a vegetarian diet.[5]

Most of the family made the move in a large caravan that eschewed hotels and opted, instead, to stay with friends along the way. As they traveled, the children — most specifically, George — distributed religious tracts. As always, there was a sense of too little money. In a letter to Catharine, Harriet described their westward trip as frequent stops for her father to "beg" money from supporters.

Begging seemed to agree with him. Lyman enjoyed the trip greatly, wrote Catharine, saying he was "all in his own element — dipping into books, consulting authorities for his oration; going round here, there, everywhere, begging, borrowing, and spoiling the Egyptians; delighted with past success and confident of the future." Little mention is made of Isabella in the move, other than as a member of the traveling party. As a girl of ten, she would not have loomed large on the family landscape, but she would have been expected to mind her parents, and her manners.

When the family had to wait in Wheeling, West Virginia, for a bout of cholera to pass through Cincinnati, Lyman preached to other stranded travelers. It is not recorded whether those travelers were open to the message.

The students at Lane, who were living in fairly spacious quarters, fared better than most townsfolk during the cholera outbreak, which killed roughly 370 residents during the worst of the epidemic from April to September 1833.[6] It was one of seven outbreaks from 1832 to 1852, brought to town by Ohio River traffic, by, wrote one doctor-historian, "every boat ascending the river, and in many of the towns on the banks."[7]

The outbreak did nothing to endear her new town to Harriet Porter. Unlike the Beecher children, she did not share Lyman Beecher's enthusiasm for the move. Suffering already from a variety of maladies, she found the trip onerous, and once she was settled, her letters back home took on a decidedly melancholy turn. Even the Cincinnati presence of her cousin, Gen. Edward King, did not change her mind about her new home.[8] King, a lawyer, an author, and a member of the Ohio state legislature, may have tried to make his cousin's transition easier, but bad health continued to dog Harriet Porter.[9] In an 1833 letter to her sister, she wrote that she was always sick. A year later, she wrote that she wept night and day for her loved ones, whom she fully intended to never see again.

Though her suffering was most acute, Harriet Porter was not the only Beecher regretting the move. In a letter to her sister Mary, Harriet Beecher wrote that they were all — save for Lyman — quite homesick. That same year, the Beechers started sending one another round-robin letters, so as to include everyone and give everyone a chance to weigh in — and, perhaps, to more tightly tether those who'd moved west to their beloved New England.[10]

Epidemics notwithstanding, Cincinnati was thriving as the largest town in the West, with the exception of New Orleans. The 1830s saw the city double in size, to a little more than 46,000 by 1840. It boasted banks, a university, a museum, a theater, a bazaar, and hospitals — all of which sprang up in roughly a quarter century.[11] The family could have done worse than "Porkopolis," though the hogs roaming the streets disgusted all but four-year-old James, who once, his sister Harriet wrote, threw his leg over the back of one and rode it down the street.

About a year after they arrived, the family moved to Walnut Hills, then a small town roughly three miles from the seminary, into a comfortable home with wide hallways and open rooms suitable for church and school committee meetings. Surrounding the house was a grove of trees, and at age eighty-five, Isabella could still remember climbing those trees and hanging on for dear life when the wind blew. When her brothers Charles and Henry returned from college and entered Lane, Isabella wrote that they were a "big and happy family" until slavery began to dominate conversations in and around the school.

The abolitionist movement that started in Great Britain had jumped the ocean and was beginning to spread in the United States. In 1829, a Boston printer published a call for "the coloured citizens of the world," which condemned racism and reminded American citizens about the promise found in the Declaration of Independence.[12] Slavery was increasingly characterized by abolitionists as a sin, so the topic would inevitably arise at a seminary, though Lane's discussions were particularly heated.

Lyman Beecher was ardently antislavery but believed the answer was to send slaves back to Africa, or colonize them. Some adherents in the colonization movement were motivated more by racism than a sense of fairness, and to them, colonization was not so much a way to right a 150-year-old wrong but rather a way to rid the country of Africans. In its beginning, the Ohio Colonization Society, an offshoot of the American Colonization Society, was "guided by growing resentment that freed slaves from southern states were migrating to Ohio and contaminating the social landscape."[13] The society distributed frequent warnings that the influx of freed slaves would soon tip the racial balance in the state to a majority of blacks, and when that occurred, a revolution was just around the corner. The message gained traction in Cincinnati, where the black population was among the state's largest among urban areas.[14]

A series of debates held at Lane in February 1834 led many to conclude that slavery was a sin, and therefore needed to be abolished immediately. The debates were held against the wishes of the school faculty.[15] Organized by Lane student Theodore D. Weld, who had transferred from the Oneida Institute in New York, the discussion sought to answer the question of whether slavery should be immediately abolished and whether colonization was the Christian stance.[16] After Isabella came to the abolition movement, she might have appreciated that Weld not only preached abolition, he also unfailingly supported the rights of women to participate publicly — speaking and praying — at worship services.[17] But Isabella would long remember her father's tearful reaction to what he saw as disloyalty, and she would never quite embrace Weld's legacy.

Until the Lane debates, abolition was considered the most radical answer to the slavery question. As word began circulating, the debates helped galvanize the country beyond Lane. Lane students, who left behind the notion of colonization in favor of abolition, formed an antislavery society, raised money to support a library for area African Americans, and volunteered to teach classes for free blacks living in Cincinnati. Some Lane students, seeking to better understand their lives, moved in with free black families.[18] Fearful that association with such a radical stance would tarnish the school's reputation — and, more to the point, threaten its ability to raise funds — the school's executive committee voted to fire one of the abolitionist professors, and it vetoed further slavery discussions.[19] Ohio bordered two slave states, and Lane looked "for a large measure of its resources to that portion of American Society with which slavery was incorporated."[20]

Lyman was in Boston when the board voted, and when he returned, he could not dissuade about forty of the more outspoken students — Weld and others known as the Lane Rebels — from moving to nearby Oberlin College. Their departure left Lane struggling and Lyman with one of his few public defeats.[21] At twelve, Isabella could understand what was going on around her — including the threat the Lane Rebels' leave-taking posed to her family's livelihood.

A report published in December 1834 acknowledged that money was tight at Lane, but Easterners and Westerners agreed that "the salvation of our country and the world is intimately connected with the intellectual and moral elevation of the West; and that this school of the prophets, under God, is destined to exert a leading influence in accomplishing this important result."[22]

Meanwhile, in a July 1835 letter to his son William, then serving as first pastor of the newly formed Putnam Presbyterian Church in what would later become Zanesville, Ohio, Lyman wrote:

> As to abolition, I am still of the opinion that you ought not, and need not, and will not commit yourself as a partisan on either side. The cause is moving in Providence, and by the American Union, and by colonization, and by [Benjamin] Lundy in Texas [who supported both] which is a grand thing, and will succeed, as I believe; and I hope and believe that the Abolitionists as a body will become more calm and less denunciatory, with the exception of a few he-goat men, who think they do God service by butting every thing in the line of their march which does not fall in or get out of the way. They are the offspring of the Oneida denunciatory revivals, and are made up of vinegar, aqua fortis, and oil of vitriol, with brimstone, saltpeter, and charcoal, to explode and scatter the corrosive matter."[23]

William, however, was an abolitionist, although he may not have been as firmly committed as his wife, Katherine Edes Beecher.[24] On this and other topics, with the lone exception of Henry Ward, the Beecher women — both Beechers by birth and Beechers by marriage — tended to be more outspokenly radical than the men.[25]

Isabella would later remember her father in tears as he pleaded with the students to temper their talk, "for he loved the young men as if they were his own sons. . . . I can see him now, joining them in the little log house just opposite ours — pleading, remonstrating, with tears and almost with groans. I was but a child, but was in such sympathy with his distress that I could never forgive the young men for departing from such a loving guide and friend."[26]

There were other cracks in the life Lyman was trying to build for his family in Ohio. Despite Lyman Beecher's relatively straitlaced theology, his views were evolving from strict Calvinism, and that did not endear him to a Cincinnati body already feeling besieged by the abolition movement.[27] Lyman's official siding with the board over the Lane Rebels did not protect him from rigorous examination by his enemies, and in June 1835 he was put on trial for heresy, hypocrisy, and slander. Isabella would remember her brother Henry making jokes about their father's tormentors.[28] She wrote in her *Connecticut* magazine piece: "Well do I remember sitting in the choir gallery of the church listening to the comments of the young men and maidens led by my brother Henry. . . . It seemed a strange thing to me, even then, that ministers of the Gospel should be found fighting such a good man as my father, and I have never changed my mind."

Lyman's chief accuser, Rev. Joshua L. Wilson, of the First Presbyterian Church of Cincinnati, seemed to have had his doubts about Beecher's ability to preach the theology of the Presbyterian Church early on, based on an 1827 sermon in which Lyman Beecher denied the notion of original sin — or that humans are born sinful and cannot rise above it. Lyman Beecher's theology stated that sin is voluntary and that humans are free agents.[29] Wilson, a Kentucky native known less for his gentility and more for his pugnacity, may have been acting out of jealousy.[30] Lyman Beecher responded to the charges by arguing that he had taught precisely what Wilson taught and that he would prove his theology was scriptural. He pleaded not guilty.

What followed was eight days of what today would seem like esoteric hairsplitting, when the testimony ranged from religious orthodoxy to Lyman's motives for not publishing more sermons to whether he could be called a liberal Calvinist. At the heart of the discussion — though mostly unspoken — was the tug of modernism and whether theology could evolve and depart from the notion of original sin.[31] As hidebound as Lyman Beecher was in regard to daily application of scriptures, he was, by most Presbyterian measures, fairly liberal.

Despite Reverend Wilson's efforts, on the eighth day Lyman was acquitted. Though both accuser and accused took the trial seriously, Lyman's associate Calvin Stowe, who would eventually marry Harriet Beecher Stowe, described the proceedings as: "It is all — 'I say you did' and 'I say you didn't,' 'Joe begun at me first.'"[32]

After the trial, and perhaps in need of some familial shoring up, Lyman gathered all his children at their Ohio home. Given the age differences among the siblings, some of his offspring — including Mary and James — had never met.[33] With his children around him, Lyman could revel in his victory, even while his wife was failing.

As difficult as the trial must have been for Lyman Beecher, the transcripts and notes and news reports of the day make it appear that he relished the attention. He proved himself completely in his element as he argued his position; just defense of his faith was precisely what he encouraged from his students at Lane.

But as much as Lyman inspired his students to think — and as beloved as he was by most of his (male) students — the preacher turned a blind eye when it came to the education of his daughters beyond a certain age. Though he was willing to barter for cheap tuition for his daughters when they were young, as they grew older he assumed their education was complete. Yet on a poor minister's salary, he managed to pay college tuition for all of his sons. Years later, Isabella wrote, "At 16½, just when my brothers began their mental education, mine was finished — except as life's discipline was added with years & that we shared equally. Till twenty three, their father, poor minister as he was could send them to College & Seminary all six — cost what it might, but never a daughter cost him a hundred dollars a year, after she was sixteen."[34]

But if Lyman was not interested in his daughters pursuing degrees, his daughters were vigilant about their own and other young women's education. In 1833, having hired people to keep her Hartford school going, Catharine opened the Western Female Institute in Cincinnati, and Isabella enrolled as a student and boarded downtown at the school during the week.[35] Though as she aged Catharine became more set in her ways, and though they had their share of sisterly arguments, Catharine and her sister Harriet mostly shared the role of principal in Cincinnati. Over time, however, the younger sister found her teaching duties expanding while her role as principal diminished. She despaired in a letter to a friend that teaching took up all her time and left her no time to read or write for amusement.[36] Later, Catharine would insist that she'd been asked to open the school, and despite health issues that were plaguing her, she did. As had happened with her Hartford effort, the school soon outgrew its one room, and so Catharine rented a larger building. But, as with her father's school, funding was always an issue, and she was unable to keep the school going through the economic crash of 1837.[37]

But it wasn't just a melted-down economy that affected Catharine's school. As the Beechers became more controversial in Cincinnati — the Lane Rebels, Lyman's trial — support for the school began to wane.[38]

Dark clouds gathered, but the younger children seemed unconcerned.

They explored the large beech forest that separated the seminary from the parsonage. They hiked under the trees and practiced their singing and elocution there. The younger the Beecher, the more Walnut Hills seemed to agree with them.

But Harriet Porter Beecher was unable to regain her health. She'd tried to run the Cincinnati household, but relied increasingly on family members as she took to her bed. Even letters from diligent Mary back in Hartford did not brighten her mood.[39] Lyman would hint later that the strain of his trial had killed her, but consumption finally took her, at age forty-five, on July 7, 1835.[40] She left Isabella her dresses and books, and an entreaty that she take care of her younger brothers.[41]

This was not the magical Roxanna whose children were left bereft. A few days after Harriet's death, the Cincinnati newspapers carried a cryptic obituary that was signed simply "C." The author could have been anyone but was most likely Catharine, who was anxious to get a last dig at her stepmother, a woman she welcomed with letters but never quite warmed to. The obituary included the note that the dead Mrs. Beecher's virtues "baffled the keen scrutiny of the gossip and the tattler," and said the woman had thought of her time in the West as a "trial and privation." And this:

> When approaching the presence of a perfect and holy Being, the retrospection of the deficiencies of the past brought such anxiety and dismay that her spirit died within her, and it was not until after the most contrite acknowledgment of all she deemed her failings in duty to others . . . that her spirit found peace.[42]

Lyman mourned the death of his second wife, though "with a reservation or two."[43] He would, when speaking of his loss, sometimes confuse Harriet Porter with the much-loved Roxanna. The older children, too, talked about Roxanna as if Harriet Porter had only been a mirage. As he had earlier, Lyman waited about one year and then remarried, this time to Lydia Jackson, a Boston widow who brought children of her own into the union. According to one biographer, Lydia "displayed untiring zeal, supplying in part the lack of pastoral labors necessarily incident to Dr. Beecher's position as head of the seminary, proving, in these respects, an invaluable auxiliary."[44] In other words, Lydia was perhaps better suited to the role of Lyman's wife than was Harriet Porter. They had no children together.

Isabella continued her education at Catharine's school, where she studied geography, arithmetic, Latin, and English grammar.[45] When Isabella turned fourteen, Aunt Esther gave her the letter written for her by her mother.[46] The sensitive young woman was particularly troubled with the charge that she look out for her younger brothers, Thomas and James. Isabella confessed to Aunt Esther: "I have cried and cried again and again, over that letter of my mother's that you gave me."[47]

She remained in sister Catharine's seminary, though enrollment was lagging. The school was dealt another blow when Harriet Beecher left her role as teacher/associate principal to marry Calvin Stowe, whom she met as they both mourned the death of his first wife.[48]

Frantic for funding, Catharine wrote a scathing letter to the Cincinnati newspapers, accusing the town of being backward. The combination of the family's notoriety and Catharine's "aggressive manner, New England chauvinism, and transparent social climbing" made fundraising even more difficult.[49]

Meanwhile, Isabella proved herself to be a capable student — though from 1835 to 1837 her compositions showed an increasing dislike of sister Catharine's teaching methods. From one note made on a Monday: " . . . learned nothing new except some dry facts in Philosophy. Tired of school wish it was vacation . . . did not study any in the afternoon or evening — went to bed early. Slept soundly — dreamed of long lessons and bad marks."[50]

When the Panic of 1837 all but finished the school, Lyman suggested Isabella, age fifteen, was ready to teach and support herself. His suggestion baffled Isabella, who found the thought of teaching to be entirely confounding: "I, who had never been to school in earnest, for two years together in my whole life."[51]

Her older siblings — particularly her sisters — feared that Isabella's natural good looks and bubbly nature would get her into trouble. In a letter written in July 1837, Harriet suggested Isabella be sent to Hartford to live with Mary, as Cincinnati was "exerting a very deletirious [sic] influence."[52] "She is very much I think," wrote Harriet, "under the influence of companions with whom dress and accoutrement are the absorbing topic and who may lead her farther and farther from all serious and profitable habits." When she was approached with the idea, Isabella allowed that she could be helpful to Mary, who had four children.

Mary was married to a lawyer, Thomas Perkins, who in 1820 joined his father's Hartford law practice. Like his wife, Thomas Perkins showed a disinclination to enter public life. He did, however, serve as Hartford County's state's attorney and, in 1861, was elected a state judge of the Supreme Court by a unanimous vote of the legislature, though he declined a seat on the bench.[53] Lyman allowed his youngest daughter to leave when she promised to study hard at sister Catharine's Hartford school and help with the Perkins' four children.[54]

If the Perkins family showed no inclination for lives in the public sphere, that reticence was not passed on. Their oldest son, Frederick Beecher Perkins, a librarian and author, married a woman, also named Mary, who "personified the most 'passionately domestic of home-worshipping housewives.'"[55] Their daughter, Charlotte Perkins Gilman, author of *The Yellow Wallpaper*, was a fiery orator, author, and utopian feminist who was every bit as outspoken and troublesome as her great-aunt Isabella. Gilman, like Isabella, "suffered a neglect in American history difficult to explain."[56]

From her 1905 piece for *Connecticut* magazine:

> I was sent back to New England on account of the death of my mother and that is the last of my living at home with my father, and I knew him only through letters and his occasional visits. I date my interest in public affairs from those few years between 11 and 16 when our family circle was ever in discussion on the vital problems of human existence and the United States constitution, fugitive laws, Henry Clay and the Missouri Compromise, alternated with free will, regeneration, heaven and hell.

As much as she was nostalgic for the Cincinnati years, Isabella's move back to Hartford made sense on several levels. She could continue her education. She could help her sister. And she could avoid suffering under the tutelage of a new stepmother, where she might find herself consigned — as were her older sisters — to the role of surrogate mother to her younger siblings. Instead, she settled into a genteel, upper-middle-class home, and enrolled in Catharine's school to extend her formal education for a few years.[57]

4

ISABELLA

IN LOVE

In the mid-1830s, Hartford was on the cusp of its glory days. The town was shifting from an economy built on oceangoing commerce to banking, manufacturing, merchandising, and publishing. The railroad would come to Hartford in 1839, and the population would reach 12,793 in 1840, up from 6,901 twenty years earlier.[1]

The increasingly fashionable capital of Connecticut would yield social opportunities — introductions to potential mates chief among them — under the steady eye of Mary and Thomas Perkins, both of whom Isabella loved. If this possibility was ever broached with Isabella, the conversation is not recorded, though given her age, a good match would have been paramount in the minds of her sisters.

Within a short time after moving to Hartford, Isabella met John Hooker, a square-jawed young law student who was studying in her brother-in-law's office. The attraction was mutual, and as Lyman had in his own courtships, John Hooker set out to win Isabella through letters. He saw in Isabella — who had gained a reputation for frivolity among her high-minded family — his intellectual equal. They would be engaged before she turned seventeen, with, wrote Isabella in *Connecticut* magazine, "the understanding that if either of us found we had made a mistake we were at liberty to choose elsewhere."

She had every reason to hedge her bets. In the first blush of love, Isabella's concern about her increasingly serious relationship fit the context of her day. The notion of control over whom and when one should marry was rapidly being wrested from the fathers, who up to then did most of the choosing and blessing of their children's life-mates. Young people began to have more of a say in courtship and marriage. Young women often stalled marriage for fear that "marriage would snuff out their independence."[2] For an example of an

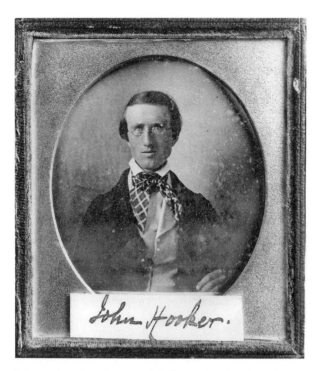

John Hooker, 1842. *Courtesy of the Harriet Beecher Stowe Center, Hartford, Connecticut.*

unmarried woman who'd managed to forge a career of her own, Isabella had to look no further than Catharine. It had to have been tempting to follow her sister into the field of education.

But even at age twenty-three, John Hooker was a rare breed. As had the much-missed Roxanna, he traced his roots back to Thomas Hooker, who'd established Connecticut's first European settlement in the 1630s and was the author of the world's first written constitution. John Hooker's ancestor had originally settled in Massachusetts, but he left to establish his own colony over a disagreement about precisely who would be allowed to vote. The elder Hooker's move may have also been predicated on a clash of personalities with the leadership of the Massachusetts colony.[3] Either way, John Hooker's family — on both mother's and father's side — boasted senators, judges, and governors. His father, Edward, graduated from Yale College in 1805 and ran a classical private school in Farmington, Connecticut, called the Old Red College. John Hooker would have a distinguished law degree and serve as reporter of the state Supreme Court.[4] Later, his name was bandied about as a potential justice on the state Supreme Court, but he declined to pursue the appointment because the timing was never right.[5]

Hooker's hometown of Farmington was a pleasant New England town through which George Washington passed several times. Whether he stopped and slept — as was so often claimed in New England in revolutionary times — is best left to one of those New England guessing games.[6]

Much of what we know about John Hooker comes from his autobiography, *Some Reminiscences of a Long Life: With a Few Articles on Moral Subjects of Present Interest*, which Hooker wrote in 1899. He was born in 1816 to Edward Hooker and Eliza Daggett, formerly of New Haven. John Hooker entered Yale at age sixteen — about the time Isabella was settling in Cincinnati — after a rigorous education by Edward in Greek and Latin. And, like the college education of his future father-in-law, his education was interrupted by illness. John Hooker was struck with typhoid during his second year, and when he recovered enough to go back to school, his attempts to catch up strained his eyes to the point that he was forced to leave school permanently. His eyesight would never recover, but John Hooker would be a lifelong student. Yale eventually gave him a degree in 1842.[7]

Unsure of a career, John Hooker did what many young men did in the early 1800s and took to the sea, an experience that was every bit as romantic as he'd imagined. He was even aboard a vessel that was overtaken by Portuguese pirates. But two years on the water was enough, and he returned to dry land and began reading for the law in the office of Thomas Perkins. At the time, law schools such as Judge Tapping Reeve's were rare, and would-be attorneys often entered the profession by serving as clerks for already-practicing lawyers.

John Hooker entered the bar in 1841. He would eventually leave Perkins's office to open his own practice and would earn a reputation for forthrightness and fairness. At the time, the law profession was mostly closed to women, but John Hooker would later break the gender barrier by taking in Mary Hall, of Marlborough, Connecticut, as his clerk in April 1878.[8] She would enter the profession as a lawyer only after a decision by the state Supreme Court allowed it, and then she would work in Hooker's office until she opened her own practice. "The decision," wrote John Hooker in his autobiography, "was a great step in the direction of the recognition of the rights of women."[9]

From his autobiography, John Hooker's understanding of women evolved over the years, though he appears to have welcomed his future wife as an equal from the beginning. Later in life, the Chicago newspaper *Union Signal*, a publication from the Woman's Christian Temperance Union, asked prominent men to give sketches of their "ideal woman." John responded that he once thought the ideal woman's "essential qualities in youth were sweetness, delicacy and modesty and in later life, a home-loving wifeliness and Madonna-like motherliness." But he'd changed his mind over fifty years, and while he still believed the ideal woman should be involved with her family, he also thought that

> . . . she is to me the noblest woman who, without mere personal ambition or self-seeking of any sort and with a great spirit of helpfulness toward all the wronged and suffering, limits the field of her work only by her ability and opportunity, making these and not any conventional rules the test of what God meant that she should do.[10]

For her part, Isabella was, by her own admission, a "spicy young girl, who hated abolitionists even more than she did slavery."[11] Perhaps the sting of her father's pain at the earlier defection of his Lane students — those he loved as his own sons — influenced her attitude. Perhaps she was more interested in social events than social issues.

If she hadn't given much thought to abolition, she had thought a great deal about marriage. Shuttling back and forth between family members, Isabella had spent time observing the marriages in her family, and if she wasn't sure what she wanted from her own union, she was at least aware of what she didn't want. She wrote John in August 1838:

> I have — for some moments in looking at the families of some even of
> my brothers and sisters — felt misgivings — many and great — but then,
> I feel that there is a radical defect in their plan — one which can be
> avoided — they did not start rightly . . . if I tho't my married life would be

such as I have seen exhibited in my own family — I never could bring myself to fulfill an engagement, other wise delightful.

Besides moving between the homes of family members, Isabella's frequent absences from Hartford would give her and her intended ample opportunity to get to know each other through letters in which no topic was taboo. While Isabella was in Ohio, her sister Mary herself wrote affectionate notes from Hartford: "I do hope and trust you will not fail to write often and long to me, we know not how long this privilege will be permitted. . . . [W]rite as soon as you get this and remember that every thing is interesting that concerns you or your friends."[12]

Mary added, a few months later, that she felt like a lover awaiting letters from Isabella as she gently chided her little sister to write more often:

I don[']t believe Mr[.] H.[ooker] is more impatient to get one, but what a naughty girl you are to have the blues so dreadfully. I think a young lady who weighs 129 lb[.] must not consider herself very much of an invalid, if you are not ethereal in your person you must be so in mind or you will lose all chance of being an angel. I don[']t believe an angel ever weighed 129 lb[.][13]

By August 1839, conversation between John and Isabella turned to marriage, but Isabella wasn't sure she wanted to marry a man who wasn't a minister. All of her brothers had followed their father into the ministry, and her family, as well, worried that the law was not of sufficient importance for a Beecher. In November 1839, Catharine weighed in with (unasked-for) advice and a bit of information about her younger half-sister that might have scared a lesser man:

. . . Belle is formed by nature to take the lead — she will every year learn more and more of her power to influence others. . . . She is growing fast in piety — in power of intellect — in power of controlling other minds. What will you find for her to do[?] . . . I do not want to see a woman of her talents and power put out of her place as a leader. She is formed to be a minister['] s wife as much as you are for a minister. If you decide to be a lawyer I shall not be very much disappointed or troubled for tho' I shall think you and Belle will in consequence be less useful and of course less happy, still I shall esteem it as the will of God that so it should be.[14]

In an October 1839 letter, Isabella wrote to John, "Every young man with the means of education and common sense is called to be a minister." And: "I have felt for some weeks past in visiting my brothers — who are ministers — that they are the only class of men, that can accomplish any considerable amount of good without turning aside from their usual business — all that a minister does, is designed in some way to save the souls of his fellow human beings. . . . Now it seems to me that it is not thus with a lawyer. . . ."

She was mostly parroting her sister Catharine's much longer letters. It would be John's first taste of his soon-to-be sister-in-law's meddling, and he was savvy enough to remain reluctant to discuss the topic with Catharine, for fear she would share his correspondence with a wider audience.

But if Isabella was pushing John toward the pulpit, she didn't seem committed to the task, and as she questioned the role of a minister, she also questioned the role of a minister's wife. In a July 1839 letter to John, she called herself a "tempest-tossed spirit" and fretted whether she would be worthy of so well educated a spouse.

She was quick to announce that she would be as dutiful a wife as was necessary, but she wouldn't enjoy the role much. In an August 1839 letter to John, she wrote that she would give him "the required obedience without being constantly reminded that such is the will of God and the exception of man." But she continued that such submission was "galling to a sensible woman."

John Hooker wrote back repeatedly that he intended them to be partners — which in any other man of that age may have been strictly a means of placating a nervous fiancée. But from John Hooker's lifelong support of his wife and his dedication to the suffrage movement, he appears to have meant it.

Meanwhile, Mary Beecher Perkins — knowing her husband's financial struggles and the hole his clerk's career move would leave in Thomas Perkins's office — was against John entering the clergy. In a November 1839 letter, she corrected her younger half-sister on her entreaties to her intended, sought to soften Lyman's weighing in on the matter, and summoned for her argument a powerful ally, Isabella's dear, departed mother:

I am surprised that father should have made the remark you ascribed to him that "every man of good common sense and piety ought to be a minister," I am sure it was uttered in the enthusiasm of the moment and that his cooler judgment would not endorse it — what would become of society if that principle should be acted upon, do we not need pious lawyers and physicians and mechanics and farmers and teachers and ought they not to be men of common sense? . . . I believe the responsibility and excitement would soon consume him. . . . It seems to me you are all running wild on this subject — pray bring common sense to bear. . . . [T]hink of your own dear mother as well qualified by education and piety as you and with a better prospect of health, after marriage her health gave way, her spirits sank, and she was ever mourning that she was so useless as she appeared to herself to be, I do not believe she would advise the change.

Mary also wrote to Isabella that from all she saw and heard from John, any career choice other than law would be "to please you and not from a conviction that he is called of God to enter the sacred offices." And she wrote, "I think it would be utter madness for you to marry a minister and I wonder at father and Catharine and Harriet that they should think of such a thing."[15]

Meanwhile, many of the rest of Isabella's siblings felt called to encourage John Hooker's career change. As boisterous and as traveled and as learned as was the family's collective approach to life, its members — save for Mary — simply could not understand a man living outside the ministry. In a November 18, 1839, letter from Charles, Isabella's older half-brother, who would later face his own apostasy charges, took a page from his father's hyperbole and wrote to a bewildered John: "You have never stood by the dark cave of Insanity — and looked with horror in at the dark door — and down the frightful chasms." Nor, Charles wrote, had John ever heard "the hideous noises — the shrieks and the laughter — feeling meanwhile your own brain boil."

Considering that threat of hellfire — or mental illness — and how tenacious she normally could be, Catharine took an uncharacteristically lighter tone. Her younger brother Henry Ward had made an inauspicious entry into the clergy but had recently moved to Indianapolis, where the members of his new congregation were pleased to have a son of Lyman Beecher in their pulpit.

Henry Ward, who would later command the attention of the country as a gifted orator, was beginning to come into his own in the Hoosier state.[16] In a letter to John dated November 27, 1839, Catharine wrote: "I think in one year my brother Henry will make his influence felt all over the state of Indiana. I have never seen persons improve as fast morally and intellectually as my brother since they commenced the duties of their mission."[17]

But there were other, more pressing topics to touch on in the lovers' letters. Isabella was in Cincinnati in December 1839 and found her family of origin much reduced. She longed, she wrote John back in Hartford, for days that were probably forever gone, when the family was gathered around the table discussing the issues of the day. And then she caught herself: "See how poetical I am growing."

Poetry had its place, of course, but plighting one's troth was a serious matter, and Isabella intended to be practical.

5

ISABELLA MARRIES,

AND FACES A CONUNDRUM

And here we pause to ponder all the women through all the years who have questioned the role of marriage in society, and wondered if the institution was quite for them.

Can you blame Isabella, really, for hesitating to take that fine Beecher brain into a legal contract — the last one she'd ever sign — that to her was little more than a type of serfdom? The laws and her religion dictated that she demurely bow her head in front of a minister, perhaps make one last wave to her friends, and disappear into the home of her husband.

Isabella reached womanhood at a time when the male sphere — the "impersonal, immoral and uncertain"— had been sharply separated from the female sphere — the "personal, pure, and circumscribed."[1] As workers moved away from farms and into more industrialized pursuits, families began to mimic the Beechers in their frequent moves in search of better opportunities. This often strained or severed ties that once bound extended families, and the resulting isolation placed the responsibility for child-rearing squarely on the shoulders of families of origin — more specifically, on the mothers. More than ever, women were encouraged to forge intense relationships with their children for the betterment of the child — but not necessarily the mother, whose well-being was to take a backseat while she created good male citizens and prepared her daughters to do the same.[2]

Middle-class women were encouraged to keep mother-diaries by cultural arbiters like John S. C. Abbott, who insisted such journals would help women stay focused, remain aware, and would encourage rigorous review.[3] Abbott was a writer and minister, and in his seminal 1835 work, *The Mother at Home*, he stressed the importance of daily asking oneself questions such as "Have I this day fulfilled all my duties toward God, my Creator, and prayed to Him with fervor and affection?"[4]

Avoiding his advice, wrote Abbott, could yield awful results. "Many an anxious mother has committed errors to the serious injury of her children, which she might have avoided had she consulted the sources of information which are within reach of all," he wrote.[5] In his proclivity for giving advice on how to achieve domestic bliss, Abbott rivaled Catharine Beecher, and Isabella paid close attention, lacking as she did a working example from her own mother.

The matter of John Hooker's livelihood remained unsettled. His decision would have a huge effect on his family's future earnings and social standing. Could he be allowed to make his own choice, or did the awesome righteousness of the Beecher clan deserve to hold sway? In a letter to her aunt Esther Beecher dated January 1, 1840, Isabella showed early signs of standing against her family's considerable sway. She wrote that she did not want to influence her husband in his choice of careers. Yet in two letters that same month, she wrote John congratulating him on his choice of the cloth and then, later, wrote that she was prepared to be a reverend's wife. It was no small thing to run counter to her family's wishes.

And then Mary Perkins again weighed in with a January 1840 letter to John Hooker, written when she heard he'd decided to attend Yale's divinity school:

> Your decision did not surprise me, and I was prepared for it — tho' I regret it, I certainly shall not suffer myself to be made unhappy by it. You and Isabella had a perfect right to decide for yourselves and I had no right to do anything but state my views and feelings on the subject, this I felt I ought to do, and have done so fully, I am perfectly satisfied you should do as duty and inclination prompt. . . . I shall hope to see you in the spring when we can talk over these matters much more calmly and rationally.

Mary Perkins may have felt comfortable defying the family because she hadn't felt much a part of it. In a December 1840 letter to Isabella, she wrote: "I never felt that Aunt H. or any of the family loved me very much & never tho't they had much reason to do so, and however much I may have regretted it I never blamed them for it — so you see there is a sort of mutual distrust. . . ."

As complicated as Beecher dynamics were, and as much as John Hooker appeared to want to stay in the good graces of his intended's family, he was born to be a lawyer, and he quit divinity school after a month to return to his first love. "My whole taste," he wrote in his autobiography, "ran toward the law."[6]

On her birthday in February of the next year, 1841, Isabella wrote John that her father was bringing the family together in the summer and that an August wedding would be as good as any. In July, she wrote to John and encouraged him not to be nervous, that only friends would be at the ceremony. She also wrote that her brother Henry Ward would be at the service, and she reassured John that she knew herself and knew that she loved him. But in a June 1841 letter to John, she wrote that "the fearfully foreboding thoughts come over me so often" and that she suffered from "sudden unaccountable changes of feeling, revulsion, and at times almost despair."

Does every bride despair before her wedding? Was it prenuptial jitters? Whatever the explanation, on August 5, 1841, Isabella married John. Standing with them were maid of honor Harriette Day and best man John Putnam, both of them friends of Isabella's from Cincinnati.[7] Isabella was nineteen, and immediately she would need to learn to settle into the upper middle class to which she'd become accustomed to living with the Perkins family, and whose status had so eluded her poor preacher father. The couple moved to John Hooker's boyhood home in Farmington, where they would stay for twelve years. If she was for the first time in her life financially comfortable, Isabella was not about to settle comfortably into her new role. From her 1905 *Connecticut* magazine article:

> My interest in the woman question began soon after my marriage when my
> husband, a patient young lawyer, waiting for business, invited me to bring
> my knitting-work to the office every day, where he would read to me from
> big law books, and in the evening I might read literature to him, as his eyes
> were so weak as to forbid his ever using them in the evening. For four years,
> we kept on this even tenor of our way, and to it I owe my interest in public
> affairs and a certain discipline of mind, since I never attended school or
> college after my 16th year.

She was stunned when she came across a passage from Sir William Blackstone's *Commentaries on the Laws of England* that explained the legal disappearing act a woman made upon her marriage. In civil law, a man and woman were separate, and could be sued separately, wrote Blackstone. But though the law recognized husbands and wives as one person, Blackstone continued:

> yet there are some instances in which she is separately considered; as inferior to him, and acting by his compulsion. And therefore all deeds executed, and acts done, by her, during her coverture, are void; except it be a fine, or the link matter of record. . . . She cannot by will devise lands to her husband, unless under special circumstances; for at the time of making it she is supposed to be under his coercion.[8]

The devil was in the footnotes, which the Hookers read aloud to one another. In this case, the footnotes said that a married woman's ability to own property was severely limited and depended mostly on the graciousness of her husband. As the daughter of a poor minister, Isabella had no property, and from where she sat in her in-laws' home in Farmington, she hadn't the means of acquiring any. The thought that the law forbade her from ever doing so angered her a great deal.

From her *Connecticut* magazine article: "I shall never forget my consternation when we came to this passage: 'By marriage the husband and wife are one person in law, that is, the very being or legal existence of the woman is suspended during the marriage, or at least is incorporated and consolidated into that of the husband under whose wings, protection and cover, she performs everything.'"[9]

A few states had what were known as "women's separate property acts," or laws that allowed women to keep control over any property they brought into a marriage. Connecticut was not one of them. Defenders of Blackstone's principles argued that "'oneness' was the core principle of happy marriage and virtuous public order."[10] Allowing women to own property would, went the argument, be the death of marriages everywhere.

Isabella's earlier concerns about how she would exist in a traditional marriage resurfaced with a vengeance. The suspension of her "very being or legal existence" had been, precisely, her fear. If she no longer "existed"—except under the wing of her beloved husband—then she no longer existed. As great as her love for John Hooker might have been, suspension of herself was something she could not countenance. The couple discussed the phenomenon exhaustively until, wrote Isabella, "the subject was dropped as a hopeless mystery."[11]

But it didn't go away. The fear only sank below the surface while Isabella, attentive to the early instructions of sister Catharine, focused on her home life.

The next year, on September 30, the Hookers welcomed their first child, a boy they named Thomas, but he died of unknown causes before his first birthday.[12] It was a bitter blow to them both. Isabella's response was to turn her attention even more slavishly to her household, and, following the advice of John S. C. Abbott, she began a series of detailed journals that recorded what can only be called the most mundane of household tidbits — the choice of curtains in the bedrooms, the china setting, the subsequent children's latest sayings — from the month the second child was born until shortly after the youngest child's birth, a span of about ten years. Her motivation may have been partly grief, and partly older sister Catharine's influence, whose writing about the "cult of domesticity" was felt particularly acutely by her younger sister.[13] The pain of losing her first son moved Isabella to focus on what she perhaps thought she could control, even while that focus removed her from the broader world, the one she had glimpsed at her father's table and during the early days of her marriage. Those hours once spent reading the law and discussing literature were now given over to running a well-to-do household and rearing children. The Hookers would have three after Thomas — Mary, born in 1845, Alice, born in 1847, and Edward (Ned), born a long — by the standards of the day — eight years later, in 1855. This span and their relatively small family of three children suggest that Isabella and John took some responsibility for controlling family size.[14]

By comparison, sister Harriet bore seven children — including twins — a family size about which Catharine, in a letter to Mary, bemoaned: "Poor thing, she bears up wonderfully well, and I hope will live through this first tug of matrimonial warfare, and then she says she will not have any more children, she knows for certain for one while."[15]

Isabella's letters to John — whose work often required him to travel — and to her family show an increasingly frustrated woman. That she loved her children is unquestioned; that she frequently feared how best to show that love and to rear them into responsible adults, equally so. Though in earlier years fathers were enjoined in sermons to rule their households and look after

Isabella with daughter Mary, 1848–49. *Courtesy of the Harriet Beecher Stowe Center, Hartford, Connecticut.*

their children, by the time the Hookers were raising a family, the duties of child-rearing had shifted to the mother.[16]

If Isabella did not feel up to the task of raising her children, she had at her disposal a variety of mothers' magazines spawned by local maternal associations intent on encouraging women to embrace their domesticity.[17] Catharine, in fact, suggested that women should be forgiven for their mistakes in mothering, as they "have never had the knowledge which they have needed"—information she, never married and never a mother, was happy to dispense.[18]

How much Isabella relied on outside resources to teach her about mothering isn't known, but without the example of an involved mother herself, Isabella

Isabella with daughter Alice, 1848–50. *Courtesy of the Harriet Beecher Stowe Center, Hartford, Connecticut.*

found herself frequently relying on the idealized version of Mother — and frequently feeling as if she fell short. Her "maternal devotion and vigilance could only have intensified her fear that the world of events, before which she and John had once stood as ostensible equals, was gradually becoming closed to her — not by the fiat of her husband, but by the all-absorbing demands of hearth and home."[19] Her frustration may have manifested itself in an increase in physical complaints throughout the 1840s. In a January 1843 letter, she wrote John that she was considering homeopathy — which in Connecticut was a relatively new form of alternative medicine — for her general malaise.[20] She apologized for her "nervous hypochondria" that was sometimes accompanied by unhappy dreams about her mother.[21]

She would eventually discover hydropathy, or the water cure, a medical regimen that involved the application of water and reformation of diet, dress, and exercise.[22] Hydropathy was especially popular in New England, and treatment involved bathing, showering, sweating, douching, and plunging one's "way back to health."[23] The regimen involved no drugs — in fact, a journal of the day described hydropathy as "every thing except poisons" and the still-evolving drug therapy as "nothing but poisons."[24] Water cures were particularly popular among women, as they were sensitive to a woman's physique in a time when doctors were ill informed as to the medical conditions of dysmenorrhea, uterine hemorrhage, and damage caused by the misuse of obstetrical devices during childbirth.[25] Hydropathy, according to one historian, existed in the space between a woman's home life and the greater world.[26] For the first time in modern history, the stages of women's lives — adolescence, childbearing, menopause — were treated as naturally occurring events and not as pathologies in need of medication.[27] Parker Pillsbury, the abolitionist and feminist who later joined Elizabeth Cady Stanton to edit the women's rights standard, *The Revolution*, argued that the water cure was "the answer to society's ills."[28] It certainly answered Isabella's concerns, and it is tempting, given her complaints after the birth (and sudden death) of her son Thomas, to wonder if she sought the treatment because of an injury during the birth of her firstborn. From her letters and journals, she was rarely physically comfortable or free of physical complaint after her first pregnancy.

Other Beechers embraced hydropathy. In the 1850s, Catharine wrote an endorsement for the *Cincinnati Gazette*:

> I have an increasing confidence in the safety of the kind of medical
> treatment when rightly applied, and of its danger when not conducted by
> a properly qualified and an attentive physician, with faithful nurses. After
> a residence of three weeks in Dr. Seelye's Hydropathic establishment,
> at Cleveland, I feel warranted in recommending it as equal, and in some
> respects superior, to any, either at the East or West, of which I have any
> knowledge.[29]

As her family grew and pressure mounted at home, Isabella began making frequent trips to Elmira, New York, to take the water cure at a facility near a church pastored by her brother Thomas, who would later preside over the marriage of Mark Twain and Olivia Langdon. The establishment's co-owner, Rachel Gleason, traveled throughout New York to give public lectures about women's health, and she wrote frequently for women's journals. Word spread throughout the East of her unique approach to health.[30] She would tell of nearly miraculous healings such as that of a twenty-six-year-old woman who arrived on a bed and hadn't walked in five years, and who was cured with a regimen of baths of a specific temperature. The woman, according to the testimony, went from being bedridden with two attendants to walking and sewing, and she returned home alone without her attendants.[31]

Hydropathy attracted the great and not-so-great alike, and between 1840 and 1900, some 213 institutions around the country were treating patients with some form of the regimen.[32] Though Elmira's hydropathy facilities are gone now, I visited a similar facility in Eureka Springs, Arkansas, in the late 1970s. I remember dressing in a gauzy gown and being sprayed with extremely cold water in places where cold water usually doesn't go. The place had multiple stainless steel baths, steam showers, and a musty smell I couldn't shake. The family that ran the facility belonged to a Christian sect that did not recognize daylight savings time. I remember that because I do recognize it, and I arrived late. By the time I visited, the medicinal purpose had all but been lost on visitors. We were mostly there to say we'd been.

But visitors to early hydropathy spas took things seriously. Sister Harriet — at times escaping one of the tensions of her marriage, husband Calvin's sexual needs — would frequently take breaks from her family and lower herself into the water cure.[33] "Wash and Be Healed," rang the motto of a popular hydropathy journal of the day.[34] It would be Isabella's perfectly respectable escape from household drudgery.

Meanwhile, if dialogue between husband and wife had shifted to more domestic matters, John Hooker did not give up his attempts to convert his wife to abolitionism. It was a tough sell. Isabella may have believed slavery was wrong, but she was unimpressed with abolitionist rhetoric, as were her sisters Mary and Catharine, who felt the arguments were entirely too base.[35] After his difficult encounter with the Lane abolitionists, Lyman Beecher continued to maintain that slaves should first be educated, then converted to Christianity and returned to Africa, where they could spread the gospel among their unchurched fellows.[36] Lyman Beecher argued that strict abolitionists were "reckless of consequences."[37] Meanwhile, a major financial backer of Lane, Arthur Tappan, sided with the abolitionists, writing that colonization societies were "a device of Satan, to rivet closer the fetters of the slaves, and to deepen the prejudice against the free colored people."[38] Lyman continued to embrace the work of the American Colonization Society, which he'd joined in 1826.[39]

John was a young adult when he came to the antislavery movement, he wrote in his autobiography. "I had attended a few public meetings of the abolitionists," but at age twenty-four, settled in Farmington, he "now looked thoroughly into the question and became convinced that they were in the right and that it was my plain duty to join them."

This was 1840, and the abolition movement was not popular, though Farmington was a stop on the Underground Railroad. John remembered attending an antislavery meeting in a Congregational church in Farmington, when, he wrote in his autobiography, "a stone was thrown with great violence through the window back of the desk" at which a speaker was orating. Fortunately, the rock narrowly missed the speaker's head.

Isabella clung to her argument that abolitionists used coarse and violent language, and so in an 1841 letter to her, John drew the comparison between the abolitionists' passion and her own father's sermons:

> Are you willing to read over carefully your own dear Father's sermon on dueling — and see why almost every argument against the severe language used by the abolitionists (and which I condemn as heartily as you) will not apply to that sermon. I never knew a slaveholder more severely attacked and abused — than the Southern Duelists are by your Father.

It wasn't long before Isabella was convinced. By the end of the next year, she wrote a letter bemoaning that her family was as tight-lipped about slavery as she once had been. In a December 1842 letter to John, she recorded her dismay regarding Thomas and Mary Perkins' indifference to the topic of slavery:

> I talked very pleasantly — but could not help, after all, feeling somewhat hurt inwardly to have the whole subject treated so lightly by so many sensible and

dear friends — for I find my sympathies more strongly enlisted in that cause, than I am aware, until opposition or ridicule calls them into action. I suppose they talk here very much as I used to — but it does not strike me either pleasantly or as becoming intelligent, reading, Christian people.

But then, the Perkinses did not have the benefit of John Hooker's patient but dogged tutelage. As a boy, John had once watched an African American man get kicked off a stage for speaking. At the time, he wrote in his autobiography, he was most concerned that the man had been treated rudely, not that the man was subject to the immoral system of slavery. He would later bemoan the "apathy of our northern states about the matter, with the universal disregard of the rights of the colored people."[40]

Isabella became a "whole-souled" abolitionist in the hours spent with her husband, and over time she became an avid reader of the abolitionist press.[41] In 1840, William Lloyd Garrison, editor of the abolitionist newspaper *The Liberator*, traveled to the World Anti-Slavery Convention in London and called the U.S. Constitution a "proslavery contract."[42] He originally had disavowed political action, but later promoted secession by free states.[43]

In 1840, while Isabella was writing agonized letters to John Hooker about her fears surrounding their upcoming marriage, Elizabeth Cady Stanton and Lucretia Mott were in London with Garrison at the convention. Stanton was not strictly an abolitionist, but her husband, Henry, was, and she'd accompanied him as part of their honeymoon.[44] The convention opened with a debate on whether to include women in the proceedings, and — citing God and social custom — the convention leaders relegated both Stanton and Mott to nonspeaking roles. This would plant the seeds for an 1848 meeting in Seneca Falls, New York, which began the arduous push for political rights for women.[45] Though women had long been organizing and pushing for legislative change, most suffragists got their first exposure to the political process through the abolition movement.[46]

The London gathering would be a pivotal jumping-off point for a variety of causes, including peace, temperance, prison reform, and labor unions.[47] But it would best be remembered as a place where the women delegates were galvanized. (In solidarity, Garrison and other abolitionists rose to sit in the gallery with them.) As Mott recorded in her diary: "I was one of the number, but on our arrival in England, our credentials were not accepted because we were women."[48] The snub moved the American women to discuss starting a movement of their own. Stanton remembered that convention as the start of her transformation as a suffragist.[49]

Isabella would come to know Garrison as an abolitionist, but that relationship, as would Isabella's with Stanton and Mott, would come later. In the beginning — much as Stanton found her life's work on her honeymoon — Isabella took up abolitionism in a way sister Catharine would have approved: privately.[50] She would argue vehemently for abolition — not colonization — in family letters, but there would be no public pronouncements.

Still, according to Marie Caskey in her 1978 *Chariots of Fire: Religion and the Beecher Family*, "John believed that Isabella's conversion to the cause had capped their union."[51] In addition to adding Isabella's considerable — though as yet unrealized — organizational and writing skills to the cause, her joining John Hooker on the side of abolition restored to the couple the opportunity for more weighty conversations, and a common goal bigger than their Connecticut lives.

Both Hookers joined the Liberty Party, which was founded in 1839 with an eye on achieving abolition through political action.[52] The party's first presidential candidate in 1840 was none other than James G. Birney, the fiery former slave owner and newspaper editor at the center of the Cincinnati riots of the late 1830s. Another of the state's frequent Liberty Party candidates was Francis Gillette, John Hooker's brother-in-law, who would eventually be the Hookers' neighbor in Hartford.[53] Gillette, too, had come to his understanding of slavery early.[54] Before moving to Hartford, the Gillette family home in Bloomfield, Connecticut, most likely served as a stop on the Underground Railroad.

Nationally, the party did relatively well. In 1842, five state legislators in Massachusetts were Liberty Party members.[55] The party enjoyed no such success in Connecticut, but that did not alter the Hookers' enthusiasm.

Nationally, women were finding their way out of their parlors and into causes and movements that allowed and even encouraged — for the first time — their presence on a national stage. Isabella would join other upper-middle-class women and embrace both the abolition and suffrage movements, as well as Spiritualism — the latter much to the delight of her detractors.

Spiritualism — the belief that the living can correspond with the dead — was intrinsically tied with reform movements. American Spiritualism started in the burned-over district of western New York state, so called because of the religious passion that accompanied the various social and religious movements — Mormonism, temperance, and Christian primitivism among them — that ignited the land in the early part of the nineteenth century. Spiritualism as it is understood today began when the Fox sisters, Kate and Margaret, began to hear raps purported to come from the spirit world. Others heard the raps too, and word spread.[56]

Isabella would have learned about Spiritualism during her frequent trips to New York to seek the water cure. In fact, in the burned-over region, the topic was nearly unavoidable, and Isabella would have grasped any opportunity to correspond with her departed mother — who, in the parlance, was "in spirit."

For most, dabbling in Spiritualism was acceptable, but Isabella was a Beecher. Dabbling was not in her nature, and as she became more of a public figure, her unwavering zeal opened her to ridicule. In an unpublished story called "Schoolhouse Hill," Mark Twain wrote disparagingly of a Spiritualist who is able to contact a spirit:

> It was Lord Byron's spirit. Byron was the most active poet on the other side
> of the grave in those days, and the hardest one for a medium to get rid of.
> He reeled off several rods of poetry now, of his usual spirit pattern — rhymy,
> jingly and all that, but not good, for his mind had decayed since he died. At
> the end of three-quarters of an hour, he went away to hunt for a word that
> would rhyme with silver — good luck and a long riddance. . . . [57]

The story is ironic because Twain was among some of Isabella's better-known neighbors who later showed more than a passing interest in Spiritualism. He was a much-traveled man, so he may have stumbled upon the beliefs on his own, but he also had an avowed Spiritualist in his home. At age sixteen, Twain's wife-to-be, Olivia, had fallen on the ice and been paralyzed for two years until a man named Dr. Newton, a Spiritualist healer, came to her home in Elmira, New York, laid hands on her, and helped her to walk again.[58] He charged $1,500 — a fortune in those days — but, as Twain wrote later, "it was easily worth a hundred thousand."[59] Her fall kept her from exerting herself for the rest of her life, but the family was always grateful to Dr. Newton. Years later, Twain asked Newton how he'd accomplished the healing of his wife, and Newton said he wasn't sure but that he "thought perhaps some subtle form of electricity proceeded from his body and wrought the cure."[60]

Interest in Spiritualism ran all the way to Lincoln's White House, where séances were occasionally held. In Hartford, Harriet, Catharine, and Isabella reported having paranormal experiences of varying intensity.[61]

Spiritualism would also appeal to Isabella because, more than any religious movement at the time, it disavowed hierarchy and the traditional (mostly male) clergy. Spiritualism, the abolition movement, and suffrage grew up together in the 1830s and 1840s. "By 1840," wrote Susan B. Martinez in her 2007 book, *The Psychic Life of Abraham Lincoln*, "the phrase 'The Sisterhood of Reforms' had been coined to cover the staggering proliferation of demands for social change, right down to the anti-cigar campaign. . . . The vituperation against abolition was as strong as against Spiritualism, and often couched in the same rhetoric and drenched with the same rancor by the same opponents."[62] Spiritualists were most frequently activists and reformers.[63]

Abolition gave many women their first taste of a social movement, but Spiritualists were able to broaden their push for reform to include suffrage. Wrote Ann Braude, in 1989's *Radical Spirits: Spiritualism and Women's Rights in Nineteenth-Century America*:

> Although Spiritualists universally condemned slavery, their organizational independence from abolition allowed them to assert that woman's rights should be the preeminent reform. Like other abolitionists, Spiritualists believed that the oppression of African Americans and of women stemmed from the same cause. A typical speaker "protested against the ownership of souls" and called for "freedom for the black man and the white woman."[64]

When the popularity of Spiritualism became a threat to more traditional religion, the pushback was swift. Mainstream religious leaders began to try to "win people back and to take away women's new voice."[65] This would affect Isabella most acutely, as she was the Beecher most involved in Spiritualism, but she never wavered.

Ironically, Spiritualism wasn't that large a leap from traditional Christianity. Christians, too, believe that the soul is forever. What differs is whether the passed-over soul can be accessed, but many traditional Christians believe in angels. A hymn from my traditional Christian upbringing included the words "All night, all day, angels watching over me, my Lord . . ." Add to that a hillbilly backdrop with grandparents for whom the veil separating the spirit and the physical worlds was fairly thin. I do not discount the notion that there's more than we see, even while I don't necessarily embrace it, either. I am an official fence-sitter when it comes to spirit communication.

And so I find myself parked on a nippy fall day in front of the National Spiritualist Church of Norwich, Connecticut, for Mediums' Day. For $20, I am allowed fifteen minutes of a medium's time to see if there are any spirit guides around me. I am an hour early. I have already talked with the Reverend Jacqueline Randall, a soft-spoken, patient woman who is accustomed to explaining both similarities and differences between traditional Christianity and Spiritualism. She explained that she came to Spiritualism later in life and has never looked back. She arrives right after I park my car and invites me into the sanctuary to wait for the mediums, who will come from around the area.

We are joined in the lobby by a young woman with bleached hair. She seems nervous. She thought Mediums' Day started at eleven. She has to be at work at 11:30, and she briefly negotiates coming back during her lunch hour. It is important she see a medium, and she asks for one by name, someone who is traveling and won't be available today. She says she's a regular, that she gets comfort from her visits. During one, she says, she was surprised to find that her great-grandmother actually liked her. All the woman did when she was living was speak harshly, and bake. In the spirit world, the woman continues to bake, but she's infinitely softer.

The inside of the church looks like the ones I frequented as a girl growing up in southwest Missouri — few religious symbols, but with lots of sunflowers, a symbol of Spiritualism. There's a sunflower tapestry draped over the pulpit, and sunflower paintings, along with the painting of Jesus knocking on the garden wall. Stained glass windows are dedicated to former members, those who've passed into spirit. There's also a print of a young woman draped in a blue shawl and a cherubic baby who may or may not be Jesus. I don't see any crosses. Reverend Randall says some Spiritualist churches are Christian-based. This one isn't. The building is a former Masons' lodge and was purchased in the early twentieth century by the president of a local bank for his wife, who was a Spiritualist.

Reverend Randall lets herself down into a nearby theater seat, leans in, and says, "I have a sporting proposition for you." Seems the medium who isn't attending today — the one the bleached blonde wanted — is interested in my interest in Isabella and Spirituality and she wants to hold an old-fashioned séance for me. Maybe we can contact Isabella, maybe not, but it's worth a try.

I'm in. I've been sending emails and leaving phone messages for Spiritualists in Connecticut for a few months, and I'm starting to feel like I'm annoying.

And here is where I get off the fence, helped in part by my father, a fierce soldier, a two-fisted drinker, an imperfect man who was perfect for me. My father died of esophageal cancer in 1992, and I have seen him twice since then — once on the day of his death, and another time during a car accident after which my son and I walked away from a totaled car. Draw from that what you will. I only know I saw what I saw. I did not make a big deal of it, did not plunge headlong into Spiritualism, but realized that for a certain breed of Christians, the idea of "angels" is not that far from "spirit guide." What little Christian hasn't heard, upon the death of a grandparent, that Grandma is now in heaven but she's watching over you? The soul is immortal, and what the Spiritualists call Infinite Intelligence is nothing more than a Christian angel.

But I'm not here to be a skeptic or a convert. I just want to talk to Isabella, and I'm told that because she's been gone so long, and because I am not related to her by blood, that may not happen.

The church folk are setting up food in the basement, and the people there all seem to know one another, either from church or from a Spiritualist summer camp in the state. Like any other church, they have AA meetings here. They have collections. I listen to the Spiritualists bustle about setting up a kettle for soup, a cheese platter, and then it's my turn to walk upstairs.

There's already a woman sitting with another medium in the corner of the church, up by the pulpit. She has lost her son. I try not to eavesdrop, but I think she's here for him. I sit knee-to-knee with a medium named Robin, a pleasant-looking man you'd never notice twice on the street. There are no crystal balls, flowing robes, or other Hollywood props. He asks my name, closes his eyes, and begins to pray very fast. It almost sounds like he's speaking in tongues, but I can make out "concise, clear messages," and then he's off and running.

Rapid-fire, with his eyes half-closed, he describes eight or nine people — a woman in a cloche hat striding confidently down a New York street, a compact man with beautiful hair, a young boy, age four to six, with curly hair, resting in a coffin.

Robin apologizes for that last one, but it doesn't ring a bell. The compact man with the beautiful hair, though, could be my Grandfather Campbell, a troubled poet, and a boxer. Robin talks about his physical strength and how he keeps stroking his throat. Spirits seem to announce themselves by touching the parts of their bodies that did them in. In my grandfather's case, it was cancer. Robin tells me my grandfather wants me to enjoy my life and that he enjoyed his life toward the end.

I am at a disadvantage because I don't know much about family members beyond my grandparents. There may well have been a fashionably dressed aunt or great-aunt walking the streets of New York. Later, I called my aunt Julie, the family historian, and she told me of a little boy in the family who'd died at roughly the age of the boy in Robin's casket. These were not necessarily comforting messages, and I'd hoped for Isabella. Back in the church, I want to ask Isabella if she regretted any of her dealings with her family. I want to ask her what she thinks of women's roles today. And — selfishly — I want to ask her if the book is to her liking, assuming Infinite Intelligence allows her to see it before it's published. To be honest, if I couldn't have Isabella, I would have preferred a visit from my father or my Grandma Marrs, my mother's mother, but neither of them showed.

Then again, what would a long-dead woman want with a biographer poking around in her journals and letters? I drive home feeling like I've asked too much.

But my research was taking me into a time in the country when a tide was turning and the national conversation was shifting — and not just in genteel parlors of the Northeast, where the economy depended on slaves every bit as much as did the economy in the South. Isabella had a front-row seat, but nagging at her was the notion that she didn't want a seat in the audience. She was a Beecher, hardwired to believe her input was vital. But she was also a woman in an age where restrictions for women were many. And Isabella, despite her lineage, suffered from a nearly crippling lack of confidence in her ability to take the stage.

The Hooker household was considered radical for its time, and it would be considered even more so after moving to the gracious home the family built in Hartford. John Hooker's firm and early stand for abolition made him an anomaly. As late as the 1830s, a series of violent attacks in Hartford left the homes of some black residents demolished. Despite the Northeast's reputation for embracing abolition, in some areas, ministers who spoke against slavery from the pulpit were threatened with expulsion — or tarring and feathering.[66]

Yet in 1845 — slightly before abolition was considered a subject for polite society — John Hooker received a request for help from a Suffield, Connecticut, minister. Descendants of an African American woman who had been kidnapped in Virginia as a free woman and then brought to Connecticut during the Revolutionary War were suing for freedom. If their ancestor was free, then, following the rule of slave law, they were free as well. Hooker expended considerable effort investigating. He interviewed some twenty descendants and sent their testimony to two Virginia lawyer-brothers, John T. and Francis T. Anderson, who argued the case all the way to the Supreme Court, which found against the plaintiffs. The case was complicated — so much so that portions of it confused even John. The family members were freed only with President Lincoln's Emancipation Proclamation, as Hooker wrote in his autobiography. He never learned their fate, though he promised himself that one day he would look up the graves of the lawyers with "tearful interest." The case was not successful, but the research sharpened his taste for the cause. If he, a well-educated lawyer, could not understand the fine points of slave law, what chance had slaves who sought their freedom?

Had her siblings embraced the cause earlier, Isabella might have felt freer to be more open about her abolitionist feelings. The ties that bind can also choke. In July 1845, her brother Thomas — the sibling closest to her in age, and another of Harriet Porter's children — wrote Isabella that she and Mary were the true Yankees of the clan, who were "too pragmatic, looking at apparent things, judging by them, making them essential to . . . happiness." He encouraged her to compare herself to her more soulful sister Harriet, which most likely would have hurt Isabella's feelings. As *Uncle Tom's Cabin* was taking off in 1852, Harriet would get a similarly chastising note from older brother Edward worrying that the attention would lead her to vanity.

Thomas's words would have exacerbated Isabella's feelings of inadequacy as she was growing increasingly aware of the intellectual divide between her better-educated husband and herself. She suffered several bouts of nervous exhaustion and chafed under the crush of domestic demands, and her letters began to reflect her frustration. In February 1847, she wrote to John expressing concern about her lack of formal education, and how an invalid schoolteacher she knew had made the most of her illness by reading subjects such as law and medicine, and that her knowledge was more impressive than that of "most professional gentlemen." At the time, the couple was still in Farmington with his mother, Elisabeth (Betsey). The elder Mr. Hooker had died in 1846.

In 1849, she wrote John that an old (male) acquaintance had flirted with her. She had rebuffed his advances, but it pleased her that he'd noticed: "The fact is, I was engaged so young — I had little time to know my power — until after my destiny was sealed." There was no hint of impropriety here. The Hookers were madly, deeply in love. But for Isabella, the attention paid by the old friend was a painful reminder that she wasn't in the larger world.

The decade closed with Isabella ruling over two daughters, ages four and two. She said that Alice was "a fancy piece to amuse and please," while Mary was "a solid article for daily use and comfort." She worried about their teeth — and paid them a penny a day to brush. She fretted over their rivalry for her affections, the efforts of which sometimes caused her to "sin with my tongue."[67]

And she was nearly paralyzed with the notion that she might make some grave error, and lead her children from the straight and narrow path. For Lyman, the devil literally stalked the earth, looking for sinners. For Isabella, the devil wasn't so actively involved as to stalk, but the potential for sin was always there. Meanwhile, she wanted so much to continue her education. In a February 1847 letter to John, she wrote of the books she'd been trying to read but continued:

If my head were stronger, physically, and my time uninterrupted, I should enjoy reading it through — but it requires close attention — and this it is almost impossible for me to give with Mary at my elbow and with my brain half asleep from want of fresh air and company and exercise. I do quite despair of ever improving much in mind or acquirements.[68]

MOTHERHOOD,

AND CONFUSION

We are standing at the carport — a later addition — of the Hooker mansion in Hartford, which is just off I-84, which runs east to west through Connecticut, effectively cutting the state in half.

You wouldn't know it from looking, but this brick home with the peeling white Gothic windows was once the center of Nook Farm, a storied neighborhood that gave Hartford its international reputation. Mark Twain came here for parties. Harriet came and left her calling card with the scribbled note "Where are you? I was here" for her little sister. The great and powerful who passed through Hartford — then something of a Venice of the Americas — dined, partied, and sometimes spent the evening here.

The Hooker House has been sold, bought, and sold again, and now sits among what Peter, the rent manager for the current owner, the Surrey Group, calls "chicken coops." And he is accurate, if chickens were prone to living in brick bomb shelters. Scattered on what was once the Hookers' spacious lawn are a series of three-story apartment buildings built in the 1960s. Across the street is the historic Hartford Public High School, founded in 1638 and second only to Boston Latin for longevity among public high schools in the country. The school has an impressive and growing archive and museum, led by a retired social studies teacher, R. J. Luke Williams, who talks about his project as a father would a child.

That sense of history has not crossed the street. Peter was unaware of the Hookers, though he said he was interested, and on a rainy fall day he gamely unlocked the door for Elizabeth Burgess, collections manager of the Harriet Beecher Stowe House, and me. She'd brought a camera. I'd brought an iron will not to be giddy.

The home the Hookers loved so much is now divided into eight apartments and, the Hartford housing market being what it is, three were available for rent. The two-bedroom apartments had wood floors and high ceilings and what looked to be original molding for $735 a month. I immediately tried to figure out what possessions I'd jettison to fit into the front apartment, the one overlooking the late-addition carport. Peter pointed out the peeling paint and apologized that the building was not better kept. He also motioned toward the steep slate roof, which had held up well, he said. Good thing. Repairs require a crane.

Peter was a willing listener, so I was off and running on the highlights of Isabella's life — delighted for a new victim for Isabella non sequiturs. He perked up at the séances. You should move here and have séances with some of the residents, he said. Some of them have been dead for years.

The front door opened to a dark entry hall that was partly covered in cherry. The Gothic staircase was carved cherry, and I told him this was the staircase that Isabella must have famously raced down at a New Year's Eve party in the 1870s. While her guests — including Mark Twain — chatted below, Isabella was upstairs in her bedroom, having a séance. She ran down the stairs — some accounts say she carried a tomahawk, though that seems weird — and frightened the guests.

We walked upstairs and Peter began to unlock apartments that weren't rented. They were clean, compact, and I had no idea what the rooms held during Isabella's day. I wanted very much to figure out which was her and John's bedroom, but the added walls and extra doors threw me. One bathroom had a claw-foot bathtub. Another had a marble sink. There was a tin roof off one bedroom, on which Isabella was supposed to have napped during hot Hartford summers.[1]

Part of me was thinking her spirit might have lingered here, though I was unclear if that is a dead Spiritualist's way. Do they "haunt?" I don't think so, but she poured so much of her self into this house, I wonder if she might have left some of her soul. At one point, I turned to look down a hall, and Beth was snapping photos in a far bedroom, backlit by the dim autumn light. I tried to imagine her in a long dress, but no. It wasn't Isabella. And if it was, would I have screamed, run to her, or kept the vision to myself?

From all indications, the Hookers had lived comfortably with John's parents in Farmington — or, at least, the outspoken Isabella left no evidence of any

Isabella in the 1850s. *Courtesy of the Harriet Beecher Stowe Center, Hartford, Connecticut.*

disharmony living at her in-laws' house. The Hartford house was their crowning achievement, a marker of how well they were doing financially. Their physical wealth made Isabella uncomfortable. She'd grown accustomed to the poverty of her father's house and worried that John Hooker's success — and, consequently, hers — would tempt them to abandon their Christian duty.

While she and John were building their Gothic mansion, sister Harriet decided to write a novel that chronicled New England from the American Revolution through Connecticut's acquisition of a state constitution. She'd thought at first to write a paean to the "moral austerity" of the previous age, as in her estimation — ever the minister's dutiful daughter — the end of the state's virtual theocracy meant "that the true heart of the region had died."[2]

But the novel was never written. In September 1850, the Fugitive Slave Act was passed, though every Connecticut legislator present in the chambers voted against it.[3] To members of the abolition movement, the law, which required that all runaway slaves be returned to their masters, embodied the worst of slavery's evils. The law particularly alarmed African Americans in the North — some of whom were runaway slaves and had every reason to fear the law, and some of whom were legally free, but worried they could be scooped up by overzealous citizens and sent south with the promise of little to no legal redress.

By the mid-1840s, abolitionists and activists had constituted a healthy network for aiding people who wanted to escape the slavery of the South. Beyond the network of the Underground Railroad, slaves who wanted to escape showed themselves incredibly reliant in gaining their own freedom. In 1848, the married couple William and Ellen Craft thrilled slaves and abolitionists alike by their ingenious escape from Georgia to Philadelphia.[4] Ellen Craft, the child of a slave owner and his light-skinned concubine, dressed as a male invalid traveling north for medical care, with her darker-skinned husband posing as her slave. They made it to Philadelphia and eventually settled in Boston.[5]

Stories like the Crafts' were anathema to slave owners, and the frequency with which these stories were repeated rendered unworkable a fugitive slave law from 1793. The earlier law allowed slave owners to recover their property in court, but that system worked only so long as free states cooperated.[6] In 1842, a U.S. Supreme Court case struck down a Pennsylvania law that was passed to protect African Americans from being kidnapped by unscrupulous slave catchers. The case, *Prigg v. Pennsylvania*, reiterated that fugitive slave laws were constitutional, though Edward Prigg, who'd earlier sought a certificate of removal as required by the state of Pennsylvania, had kidnapped a woman and her children and returned them to their state of origin, Maryland, when his request was refused.[7] He was convicted, and the Supreme Court ultimately ruled that Pennsylvania's law — repeated in other free states and often called personal liberty laws — was unconstitutional.[8] The court ruled further that state officials were responsible for enforcing fugitive slave laws, though the federal government had no authority to require them to do so. Former president John Quincy Adams, a staunch abolitionist, spent an entire day reading the decision and concluded that it was made up of "seven judges, every one of them dissenting from the reasoning of all the rest, and every one of them coming to the same conclusion — the transcendent omnipotence of slavery in these United States, riveted by a clause in the Constitution."[9] (Adams never ceased bringing the discussion of slavery to the forefront, for which he was hated by slave-owning Southerners.[10]) That case, and another, 1847's *Jones v. Van Zandt*, set the stage for a new law.[11]

Among the opponents of the Fugitive Slave Act of 1850 was the American Anti-Slavery Society, which published a book that called for the "slow-moving finger of scorn" to follow Northern legislators who'd voted to approve the measure. The tract also listed the legislators' names and included the wish that "the stings of shame, disappointment, and remorse continually visit them in secret, till they are forced to cry, 'my punishment is greater than I can bear.'"[12]

As for Southern men, the tract said, "they only appeared in their legitimate character of oppressors of the poor — whom God will repay, in his own time. The thousand-tongued voices of their brother's blood cry against them from the ground."[13]

John Hooker wrote in his autobiography that the 1850 law gave "the claimant a greater advantage over the black man, by compelling the latter to prove his right to freedom, which he might not be able to do if away from home, while the question was to be decided by a single magistrate of about the grade of a justice of the peace, and that finally and without appeal."[14]

In Hartford, the law was discussed by abolitionists who'd been in the movement for decades and by those relatively new to the movement, like Isabella. On this point, the Beecher family — individually and as a group — had evolved from its more reticent Ohio days, when Lyman Beecher was doing battle with the Lane Rebels. In Ohio, the bulk of the family stood against slavery, but against abolition as well. For the Beechers, "slavery should not be extended into the territories but should be allowed to die out gradually. . . . Abolition was too radical." The Beechers had believed abolition would create havoc in the Southern states that would only end badly.[15] Over time, however, three of the older boys — William, Edward, and George — joined abolitionist societies. William refused to be patient, as his father counseled.[16] Edward used his position as editor of *The Congregationalist* to push for abolition and to reject colonization.[17]

As the discussions grew more heated, Isabella's sister-in-law Isabella Porter Beecher — wife of half-brother Edward — wrote to Harriet, who was living in Maine with her family: "If I could use a pen like you, Hatty, I would write something that would show the entire world what an accursed thing slavery is." Harriet responded that while her baby — Charles Edward, born in 1850 — was still sleeping with her at night she couldn't do much, but as soon as he matured enough to sleep on his own, "I will do it at last. I will write that thing if I live."[18]

Isabella, too, wrote "letter after letter" to Harriet, bemoaning the injustices of the law.[19]

When Harriet did write her masterpiece, she would not go "whole-souled," as had Isabella. Instead, she would disappoint abolitionist readers when she sent her character, runaway slave George Harris, back to Africa in *Uncle Tom's Cabin*.[20] Harriet agreed with her father that colonization would work best for the former slaves. Her hesitancy to leap fully into the fray would be repeated later, in the suffrage movement, when leaders of the various factions courted her involvement but could never get her wholehearted support.

By the time the book was published, colonization "was an idea whose time had come and gone," though it would continue to be discussed for years to come.[21] At an 1853 meeting of the American and Foreign Anti-Slavery Society in New York, held a year after the book's publication, abolitionists discussed "the evil influence of the last chapter," and Dr. Leonard Bacon — a friend of the author's — informed the group that Harriet had told him she would, if she were rewriting the book, eliminate that portion of it.[22] The character Harris's desire to go to Africa made the book problematic for abolitionists such as Frederick Douglass, who in 1856 explained his opposition to colonization in a letter to a Philadelphia philanthropist by saying that colonization tended to "deaden the national conscience when it needed quickening."[23]

Harriet and Douglass also differed as to the role the church should play in abolition. In a July 1851 letter Harriet wrote Douglass asking for details of life on a Southern plantation: "After all my brother, the strength & hope of your oppressed race does lie in the church — in hearts united to Him . . . Every thing is against you — but Jesus Christ is for you — & He has not forgotten his church misguided & erring though it be . . . This movement must & will become a purely religious one.[24] Douglass was a faithful man, but he scorned orthodoxy and had a healthy mistrust of clergy.[25] Still, Douglass promoted Harriet's book in *Frederick Douglass' Paper*.[26]

If Harriet wasn't willing to go whole-souled, Isabella's fervor for eliminating slavery, once awakened, was unstoppable. She threw herself enthusiastically into Liberty Party organizing, while John wrote essay after essay for his local newspaper, and quickly gained a reputation as a soft-spoken but committed abolitionist.

That reputation led John into a most unusual position as slave owner.

Among the Northern African Americans who feared reprisal from the Fugitive Slave Act was the Reverend James W. C. Pennington, who since 1841 had been leading an African American congregation in Hartford. Pennington was, wrote Hooker in his autobiography, a respected man in the community. He had sometimes exchanged pulpits with white ministers in the area — including a congregation in Farmington where, wrote Hooker, "the people of that quiet old town had been astonished, some of them shocked, by seeing one of the blackest men in their pulpit." But shortly before the law's passage, he came to Hooker to confide that he was, in fact, a fugitive slave. He'd told no one — not even his wife. His origins were known only to some Pennsylvania Quakers who had harbored him on his way north and helped him get an education. Hooker wrote that Pennington had kept the information from his wife so as not to worry her, but now he worried constantly that his secret would be discovered and he would be returned to Maryland, where he'd been enslaved as Jim Pembroke until he escaped at age eighteen, with his harrowing trip north including capture — briefly — by slave catchers.[27] He asked Hooker for help in negotiating the purchase of his freedom from the slave owner George Frisbie Tilghman, of Hagerstown, Maryland. Hooker agreed, and suggested Pennington go to Canada while he negotiated with Tilghman. Hooker was careful to tell the slave owner that his former slave was out of the country and so out of his legal reach, and he was also careful to refer to Pennington only by his slave name, Pembroke. Tilghman responded that Pembroke had been an excellent blacksmith and that he could take no less than $500 for his freedom. Tilghman also allowed that he was glad Pembroke had made something of himself, which led Hooker to believe he knew something of the former slave's life in Connecticut. Fearing for his client's safety, Hooker suggested Pennington go to England to raise money among abolitionists there, where the movement was more firmly entrenched, and the minister left Canada to travel Europe for two years. He also took advantage of educational opportunities there, and earned his doctorate of divinity in Heidelberg. Pennington eventually settled in Scotland, where friends vowed to raise whatever sum was necessary for his safe return — as a free man — to the States. Hooker again contacted Tilghman, and heard back from a stranger, who said that though the Maryland man had died, the estate still required $150 for the sale of Pembroke/Pennington. The Maryland man needed a name to whom he could make out the bill of sale. Hooker's junior law partner — then one of Connecticut's U.S. senators, Joseph R. Hawley — went to Maryland to take the funds to the administrator and, on Hooker's advice, had the bill of sale made out to John Hooker.

"I thus became a slaveholder, and the owner of a doctor of divinity," wrote Hooker in his autobiography. When he received the bill of sale, he held it for a day "to see what the sensation would be," he wrote. Then he executed a deed of manumission — or the legal freeing of a slave, which, he wrote, "I had recorded in the town records, where it may be found in Vol. 76, page 356, under date of June 5, 1851." The act "set free my slave, Jim Pembroke, otherwise known as Rev. James W. C. Pennington, D.D. It stands on record there for the wonder of future generations." Later, Hooker would attend a celebration of Pennington's return to Hartford. The meeting was held out-doors, and Pennington spoke from a raised platform. When he saw Hooker in the crowd, he called him up, and Hooker joked to the crowd that as a slave can own nothing, and Pennington was once his slave, Hooker desired to possess Pennington's doctorate, and he asked that he be referred to as Rev. Dr. Hooker. The crowd did not know the Beecher-induced struggles John Hooker had earlier faced to avoid earning such a title.

Meanwhile, life was changing for the rest of the Beechers. Lyman retired from Lane in 1851 and moved back east to write.[28] That summer, Catharine published another book, *The True Remedy for the Wrongs of Women*, in which she — one of the foremost advocates for the education of females — wrote of women's "True Profession, Education and Domestic Economy," as well as her concerns about women who wanted to enter what she considered the realm of men — in this case, the voting booth:

> In a case like this, where a noble object is sought by wrong methods, the only way to stop the mischief is, to set about accomplishing the same thing by right methods. As in the case of some dreadful conflagration . . . we must convince them of a better way, not by sitting still and sneering at their efforts but by flying ourselves to the rescue. . . .

Also: "And in that day every woman will be so profitably and so honorably employed in the appropriate duties of her peculiar profession, that the folly of enticing her into masculine employments will be deemed . . . ridiculous."[29]

Whatever splash the book made in the general public, sister Harriet considered it required reading, if for no other reason than to help her understand her irascible sister. In a September 1851 letter to her father and brother Henry, she wrote:

> Until I read it I had no proper appreciation of her character motives of action for this eight or ten years past — I considered her strange, nervous, visionary, and to a certain extent unstable. I see now that she has been busy for eight years about one thing — a thing first conceived upon a sick bed when she was so sick and frail that most women would have felt all they could hope for was to lie still and be nursed. . . . Then she conceived this plan of educating our country by means of its women and this she has steadily pursued in weariness and painfulness.[30]

Harriet had published the first installment of *Uncle Tom's Cabin; or, Life among the Lowly* in June in the antislavery newspaper *The National Era*. The *Era* was a product of the American and Foreign Anti-Slavery Society, and its editor had worked with Birney's *The Philanthropist* in Cincinnati.[31] A year later, the serial would be published as a book to international acclaim.

Harriet said later that she was inspired to write her book while sitting in church, and that the story was God's idea, not hers. Be that as it may, Harriet supplemented God's input with stories she'd heard while living in Cincinnati. Whoever got credit of authorship, God's support would be important in the coming months. Though Harriet had tried to include kind Southern slave owners, the South was inflamed. "Never," writes Robert B. Downs in *Books That Changed the World*, "was a book more topical or better timed psychologically."[32] While legislators were split over the novel, and clergy argued both sides from their respective pulpits, Downs writes that the "surcharged moral climate awaited only a spark to set off a world-shaking explosion. *Uncle Tom's Cabin* furnished the spark."[33] The book's message spread from home to abroad — mostly with pirated copies for which Harriet received no pay. For people who couldn't read, or people who simply wanted to see the story retold in a theater, *Uncle Tom's Cabin* was recreated by countless acting troupes — again, Downs writes, without recompense to Harriet. But then, the author disapproved of theater and most likely would have refused to give permission for a dramatization anyway.

Sen. Charles Sumner said Abraham Lincoln owed his election to the book, because of the raw retelling of the evils of slavery.[34] Only the Holy Bible sold more copies in this country.

Publicly, Isabella expressed excitement for her sister's meteoric rise in the literary world, but privately, as she wrote in a June 1852 letter to John: "At first I was melancholy — in seeing the evidence of genius all around me — my own littleness fairly stared me in the face." She wrote John another letter that conveyed her annoyance that sister Harriet did not properly acknowledge her path from apathy to the literary darling of the antislavery movement: "Hatty is coming strait [sic] onto our Antislavery platform — she has been you know a father and Mr. Stowe abolitionist heretofore."

That may have been petulance, but the comparisons would become increasingly painful, as both Harriet and Catharine published multiple books throughout the 1850s at a time when Isabella found herself increasingly enmeshed in domesticity — a field that no longer held even Catharine's total attention. In 1850, Catharine published the odd book *Truth Stranger than Fiction*, with the cryptic explanation that she was "not desirous of extending the circulation of this work any farther than the evil it is designed to remedy has penetrated." The book was aimed at clergy, and Congregationalists in particular, for their handling of the case of Delia Bacon, a former Hartford student of Catharine's who promoted the notion that the plays ascribed to William Shakespeare were actually written by a group of men. Defending her former student was one thing, but Catharine's book also revisited an embarrassing episode in Bacon's life when a Yale theological student befriended Bacon but showed no interest in marrying her. Her brother, Congregational minister Leonard Bacon, brought misconduct charges against the young man. The charges were dropped, but the young man's reputation was ruined.[35]

Catharine's siblings — especially her preacher brothers — tried to convince her not to publish such a finger-wagging screed. In a March 1850 letter to Harriet, Mary wrote: "God in his mercy grant that some way may be devised to stop this meteor that threatens such evils. Henry's last advice to my girls was, 'Girls get married — don't live as old maids.'"

Catharine had not completely abandoned the cause of education for women. In 1852, she founded the American Women's Education Association to "establish endowed professional schools, in connection with literary institutions, in which woman's profession should be honored and taught as are the professions of men, and where woman should be trained for some self-support business."[36] This would further her goal of establishing teacher-training schools around the country, and raise the level of competency in classrooms.[37] While others were following her lead, and establishing female institutions of higher learning, Catharine worried that they weren't legitimate and that "those female institutions of our land which are assuming the ambitious name of colleges, have, not one of them, as yet, secured the real features which constitute the chief advantage of such institutions. They are merely high schools."[38]

But as much as Catharine was a source of amusement — and sometimes embarrassment — to the family, at least she enjoyed a national stage. Isabella watched from the sidelines and tried to content herself with providing much-needed (and often unheralded) support. As the mail from the readers of *Uncle Tom* piled up at the Stowe house, Isabella offered herself as Harriet's secretary. Earlier, Catharine had moved to Hartford to care for the Stowe children while Harriet wrote.[39]

Isabella also opened her home for Catharine's frequent visits to town. She wrote encouraging letters to Henry Ward, whose sermons at Plymouth Congregational Church in Brooklyn were growing increasingly militant on the topic of abolition. By the mid-1850s, Beecher was collecting money to buy Sharps carbines — rifles — to send to Kansas, where the antislavery settlers were beginning to fight against those who would have Kansas enter the union a slave state. Beecher hid the first shipment of twenty-five rifles beneath a stack of Bibles, and the weaponry came to be known as "Beecher's bibles." To justify the Sharps, Beecher wrote that "there are times when self-defense is a religious duty. If that duty was ever imperative, it is now, and in Kansas."[40] To the "horror" of the pacifists at Plymouth Church, he said, "Sharps rifles were a greater moral agency than the Bible."[41] Whether he was strictly seeking to make a point, Henry Ward had adopted his father's hyperbole.

He also wrote: "It is a shame that in America, amidst our free institutions, anything else should be needed but moral instrumentalities. But you do need more. You will be surrounded by men who have already committed the wickedest wrongs and most atrocious crimes."[42]

Other groups — among them the Massachusetts Emigrant Aid Co. — followed suit.

This was a far cry from Henry Ward's earlier preaching. He'd started far more tepidly, and in 1844 wrote to his brother Charles to warn him upon his ordination against preaching about abolition from the pulpit. His advice was, "Preach little doctrine, except what is of moldy orthodoxy. . . . Take hold of the most practical subjects; popularize your sermons. . . . For a time, while captious critics are lurking, adapt your mode so as to insure that you shall be rightly understood."[43]

As her siblings were achieving national prominence, Isabella told herself and her husband that she was happy with her lot in life. This may have been whistling past the graveyard, but without the distraction of an international literary career, Isabella wrote John in June 1852, she could focus on domestic issues and be a better wife and mother, "for one cannot do or be forty things at once." At the same time, Isabella added more trips to Elmira for her water cures, with side trips to Florence, Massachusetts, for retreats. In 1853, she wrote John from the Florence Water Cure with her fears that as she felt her world shrinking, his world was expanding: "I do believe that I have less self reliance, in its best sense too, than I had six or eight years ago — You have more and I seem to lose as you gain."[44]

Her complaints came at a time when the Hookers had made the move from Farmington to Hartford. John Hooker's legal practice was increasingly taking him into Hartford, a ten-mile trip from their Farmington home, and in 1851 the Hookers and the Gillettes — including Francis and his wife (and John's sister), Eliza — bought a hundred-plus-acre plot known as Nook Farm on what was then the western edge of Hartford.[45] The property was named for a crook in a river, alternately called the Hog or Park, that passed through there.

The neighborhood would become the center for literary and social movements in Hartford, with senators, judges, ministers, and Harriet and Mark Twain as residents. The land resembled an English countryside, and high-powered neighbors argued issues of the day — mostly without falling out with one another.[46]

After the purchase of land, the Hookers opened up a city street — For-

Hooker House, circa 1870. *Courtesy of the Harriet Beecher Stowe Center, Hartford, Connecticut.*

est — and built a sprawling brick Gothic mansion on the southern tip. They moved in 1853, and Isabella breathed a brief sigh of relief in her journal:

> Must chronicle moving in our new house, so called. Talked about adding on to the old house (our old parlor and halls and library) has satisfied all of us, whilest [sic] it be the good man himself of the wisdom of the decisive, and we have been for now two months enjoying even this half our possessions as much as inhabitants of dual palace ever enjoyed their . . . abode.

Having a home of her own would give her plenty of opportunity to focus on the woman's sphere. As her physical complaints increasingly centered on what she called her "nervous hypochondria," she hoped that the new house would at least give her something on which to focus her prodigious energy.[47] She described how hard she'd worked to get her daughters' room just right. She wrote about the

> . . . hasty and exciting time of putting the girls' room in order while they were gone to Middletown for Thanksgiving. If we did not fly about there! We expected them back on Saturday morning and so had only Friday to work in. Yet with "Susie's" help we made curtains (muslin and chintz, two sets) altered the old parlor carpet to fit exactly, had carpenter drive nails everywhere for pictures and then early Saturday morning Mr. Allen and Bridget put down the carpet, while papa, mamma, Patrick and Eddie and Aunt Sarah brought in the furniture from the old front chamber, hung the pictures, made the bed, swept off the carpet, dusted, hung the curtains and put everything into perfect order. It was then a lovely room to behold. I doubt if they will ever own or live in such another . . . but I pray God they may long enjoy and appreciate this. The girls did not come until Monday noon and at first I was bitterly disappointed but by dint of showing the room to Charley and Susie and others as they came in, we managed to live over Sunday and Monday noon the dear daughters came and admired to our heart's content and every day since they have seemed to appreciate their privileges and to be grateful for them in a truly Christian fashion.

Two years later, Thomas and Mary Perkins built a house nearby — which would eventually become actress Katharine Hepburn's childhood home. In 1865, the Stowes joined the growing literary society and built Oakholm. As

John wrote in his autobiography, the families "each made free of the others' houses and each keeping open house, and all of us frequently gathering for a social evening or to welcome some friendly visitor, often some person distinguished in political, literary, or philanthropic life." Isabella described the neighborhood as "a little society by ourselves."[48]

Isabella would come to be considered the "admiration and vexation" of the community, though the vexation would come later.[49] In the early years of Nook Farm, she was admired for her role as a catalyst for some of the more enjoyable gatherings, including dances and salons.

John Hooker opened a Hartford law office with Joseph Hawley, later to become not only a U.S. senator but also editor of the *Hartford Courant*, the country's oldest continuously published newspaper, which traces its roots back to 1674.

Running the household and helping her husband with his law career might have been enough to satisfy some women of her era, but privately Isabella continued to call her mind "crippled," and she wrote yearningly of the long talks she'd once enjoyed with John — now obliterated by her increasing bad health and the press of domestic duties.

Isabella was perhaps feeling the effect of a greater movement that was radically changing the American family. Whereas previously families were not much bound by emotional boundaries, by the 1850s the family "had been reduced ideologically to a sheltered social unit, whose boundaries were defined by love."[50] Popular literature of the time insisted that social reform would come only through domestic bliss. A happy home was a happy nation, and at the center of that home was the all-knowing, all-seeing, all-loving mother.

But the nation was expanding westward exponentially, and Amy Kaplan, in *The Anarchy of Empire*, writes:

> One of the major contradictions of imperialist expansion is that while the United States strove to nationalize and domesticate foreign territories and peoples, annexation threatened to incorporate non-white foreign subjects into the republic in a way that was perceived to undermine the nation as a domestic space. The discourse of domesticity was deployed to negotiate the borders of an expanding empire and divided nation.[51]

Increasingly, the same language used to describe the expansion of the empire was applied to the domestic sphere. This cult of domesticity — known as "true womanhood" by its proponents — required attention to the hearth and home. Proponents of true womanhood may have been reformers, but they differed greatly from the likes of Isabella, who was coming to believe that the differences historically assigned to genders were false.[52] By taking this stance, she was opposing one of the major forces in her life, her force-of-nature sister Catharine, who believed that "the careful subordination of women to men within the newly emerging middle-class family was necessary for the harmonious development of society."[53] In Catharine's world, men were stronger physically while women bested men at moral fortitude.

It is no coincidence that the cult of domesticity grew as a counter to the fight for suffrage for women. Consequently, the public language describing a woman's place became more positive and was tinted with the heavy brush of godliness. Women were "fitted by nature" for such self-denial — which, alternately, was supposed to bring self-fulfillment.[54] Mixing Christian duty with the push toward domesticity over public involvement made the cult of womanhood extremely difficult to avoid.

At times, John would join Isabella on her increasingly frequent trips for the water cure, but she mostly traveled alone and would stay for weeks and sometimes months. But while away, she kept in touch with her family with nearly daily letters, and her predilection for micromanaging only increased with her sisters' literary success. A September 1853 letter to Alice from Florence began "My dear little Alice" and instructed the little girl — who would have been six or so — to love her mother. Isabella also admitted to Alice that "As you know I am going to be as hungry as you are. I want to eat all the time. Everything tastes so good." That similarity of appetite would eventually be a cause for friction between mother and daughter.

By the late 1850s, ensconced back in her Hartford mansion and buried in domesticity, Isabella despaired of ever earning any money of her own.[55]

And then, in 1859, she was alternately thrilled and disheartened to read a satirical piece in the *Atlantic Monthly* magazine that asked, "Ought Women to Learn the Alphabet?" The article said precisely what she'd been thinking privately, and it saddened her that she had not been the one to say it

Isabella, 1866, silver wedding anniversary. *Courtesy of the Harriet Beecher Stowe Center, Hartford, Connecticut.*

publicly. The article's author was the minister and editor Thomas Wentworth Higginson, a well-known abolitionist and suffragist and a confidant of Emily Dickinson's. Higginson had been a soldier as well as a minister and reformer.[56] He'd distinguished himself with his public call for suffrage, including in an 1856 appearance at the Seventh National Woman's Rights Convention, when he told the crowd that he counted himself among "those who simply believed that God made man and woman, and knew what He was about when He made them — giving them rights founded on the eternal laws of nature."[57] He would later write, "I think it is a monstrous absurdity to talk of a democratic government and universal suffrage and yet exclude one-half the inhabitants without any ground of incapacity to plead."[58]

Included in Higginson's *Atlantic* piece was a passage that especially spoke to Isabella:

> Men can hardly be expected to concede either rights or privileges more rapidly than they are claimed, or to be truer to women than women are to each other. True, the worst effect of a condition of inferiority is the weakness it leaves behind it; even when we say, "Hands off!" the sufferer does not rise. In such a case, there is but one counsel worth giving. More depends on determination than even on ability. Will, not talent, governs the world.[59]

An enthralled Isabella wrote to her friend Rachel Burton in June 1859:

> There's not a vital thought there but I have had it for my own & spoken it, too, in a whisper & in my blundering way . . . I, who had never been to school in earnest, for two years together in my whole — & who had gained such physical vigor as I then had, only thro' a determined preference, for boy's games & out door sports, that added not at all to my general reputation.

She also wrote to Higginson, and, much to her delight, he wrote back. Encouraged by the attention, she sent him an essay she'd written, "Shall Women Vote? A Matrimonial Dialogue," which chronicled a conversation between a Mr. and Mrs. Smith. The article was a refutation of another article that had taken her brother Henry Ward to task for his stand for suffrage. Most specifically, the offending article had critiqued Henry Ward's speech on February 2, 1860, at the Cooper Institute in New York and found it wanting. In that speech, Henry Ward reiterated the writings of older sister Catharine as he spoke about women's natural moral superiority and their role as civilizers of men:

> Without the ameliorations which woman's nature is capable of producing upon him, man stands as trees stand in this wintry night — strong enough of root, strong enough of trunk, and strong enough of branch, but without a leaf, and without a blossom. They cast no shade, and are bleak, rugged, and cheerless. . . . No summer comes to man till leaves come and blossoms come.[60]

Both Henry Ward and Isabella clung to the notion that a woman's place was in the home, but they were also using early feminist arguments that that place had not restricted women in their development. If anything, a woman's devotion to her home and family had trained her for the bigger world, or so they said, because what was an elected political body but a larger version of a family?

In her article, Isabella/Mrs. Smith quotes Henry Ward saying that Eve led the way to sin because of her "fine susceptibilities" that, in turn, led her to "soar beyond the garden walls and reach the divine."[61] But then Isabella/Mrs. Smith takes things a step further. She suggests that women who are single by choice, and middle-aged women who'd already raised their children, are perfectly suited to serve in Congress. Middle-aged women, in particular, would have gained the skills to rule because they have "gained in this most motherly way of discriminating between her children, adapting influence and government according to the character and bringing out a harmonious whole, from so many discordant elements."[62]

In the debate, Mrs. Smith says:[63]

> . . . if absolute power were in my hands, I would not open the polls to women today — no, nor next year, nor ever, unless public opinion demanded it. I honor too highly the Divine precedent, to do such a thing as that. It has been the one thing hardest for me to learn — this "patience of

waiting." [B]ut I see more and more the strength and beauty of this gradual upbuilding — this calling on the ages to work — this doing with our might, and leaving the results with God.[64]

Had Isabella held her argument to extolling women's leavening role, Higginson might have been impressed, but this piece, her new friend responded, was too radical. In March 1860, he wrote Isabella that "it is almost impossible for any one to get compensation for anything radical, unless with a reputation previously acquired, or else under very peculiar circumstances. One may make literature a means of earning money or a means of expressing one's most progressive views — but it is very rarely that any one can unite the two."[65]

The exception, Higginson wrote, was her sister's own work, *Uncle Tom's Cabin*. Yet he forwarded her article on to his editors and encouraged her to keep writing: "For you will only have failed in an attempt ... to make a first essay, and that a radical one, palatable to editors who are rather conservative and ought to be extremely critical."[66]

He also encouraged Isabella to get to know the leaders of the suffrage movement, and he wrote:

> Nothing makes me more indignant than to be thanked by women for telling
> the truth, — thanked as a man, — when those same persons are recreant to
> the women who, at infinitely greater cost, have said the same things. It costs
> a man nothing to defend woman, — a few sneers, a few jokes, that is all; but
> for women to defend themselves, has in times past cost almost everything.[67]

And then Higginson foretold the eventual split of the nascent suffrage movement. Already, even a casual observer could see differences in approach and even life view of the various suffragists hardening into stone, so that the leaders would not be able to work together. And that was unfortunate. Higginson found more fault with the comparatively more radical group led by Elizabeth Cady Stanton and Susan B. Anthony, though he did not rebuke them by name. Later, Higginson would scold Stanton for enlisting the aid of a known racist in the suffrage cause, to which Stanton would drolly reply:

> Our "pathway" is straight to the ballot box, with no variableness nor shadow
> of running. I know we have shocked our old friends who were half asleep
> on the woman question into a new life, just waking from slumber they are

cross, can't see clearly where we are going, but time will show that Miss Anthony & myself are neither idiots nor lunatics. . . . We do care what all good men like you say, but just now the men that will do something to help us are more important.[68]

Compared to women like the Quaker social reformer Lucretia Mott and women's rights advocate Lucy Stone, Higginson wrote to Isabella:

The mass of women, especially educated women, are base: they revile their own bravest defenders: and their own aspirations become more selfishness. There is much ignorance, much sensuality and some obstinacy among men; but women are a frightened garrison, seeking a mean safety by sacrificing those who have made a heroic sortie. Let me implore you to make it otherwise with you.[69]

Isabella took this message to heart, and even though her support of the bravest defenders would cost her, Higginson once again had articulated something she could not (yet) say for herself. Later, when the suffrage movement split, Isabella would try to serve as a go-between. When an outspoken, controversial suffragist threatened the Beecher family legacy, she would fly in the face of her powerful family and defend the suffragist.

7

ABOLITION, AND

AN AWAKENING

At the dawn of the new decade, Isabella had a bloomer outfit sewn for her walks on her trips away from home. Such a wardrobe choice might seem inconsequential, but in the 1860s the bloomer (named for Amelia Bloomer, a suffragist who made the outfit notorious in the 1850s by wearing it in public) was considered scandalous. The outfit was simply a shortened skirt over full trousers, but it moved some editorial writers to see red and to pair agitation for dress reform with "Free Love, easy divorce, and the amalgamation of races."[1] Most feminists, upon seeing the distractions the outfit created in the push for votes, abandoned bloomers, though health advocates in the latter half of the nineteenth century would keep coming back to them as "rational dress."[2]

Even Isabella's more conventional sister Mary wore what was also called "gymnastic dress," or bloomers. She'd had one made "to practice in at a gymnasium."[3] Back in 1853, when Amelia Bloomer gave a Fourth of July speech in Hartford, she wore her namesake trousers and was greeted with no incident.[4] Still, there were news stories of bloomer-clad women being pelted with eggs or stones.[5] Amelia Bloomer may somehow have been allowed to wear trousers, but everyday women stood a much greater chance of being ostracized for such an outfit in 1860s Hartford — and it was barely acceptable in upstate New York.[6] Her adopting the new and newly controversial bloomer is an indication that Isabella was at least current and a little bit willing to risk public censure.

Her public life was just on the horizon, but Isabella was still struggling within the confines of the woman's sphere. She squirmed under compliments about her mothering; in January 1860, she wrote John: "I think you praise me too much. I am going to be a better mama after this." John had mentioned her upcoming birthday, a matter of some distress for Isabella, who was again feeling her own smallness. She responded: "As to the birthday, you touch a tender point. Oh my soul if you would only teach me how to earn money. But there's no use in hoping. I can't write a book or draw pictures or do any other productive work. I have myself told you that you overestimate your wife. I hope you are satisfied of it now."

She visited her brother Henry Ward in Brooklyn, where she received the unhappy news that her father, Lyman, who'd moved in with his son a few years previously, was slowly slipping into dementia. She heard the news from Henry Ward's wife, Eunice, whom she didn't much like, she wrote John. During her visit, Isabella could witness debates about her brother's leadership of the American Board for Foreign Missions. Henry Ward was under attack from Theodore Tilton, who previously had looked to Henry Ward as a mentor. Though Tilton attacked Henry Ward for what he saw as the pastor's inconsistencies in regard to censuring slave owners, he was still invited to dinner at Henry Ward's house, and they all, Isabella wrote John, had a "jolly time."

Henry Ward lent his considerable influence to the cause of suffrage, as he had for the emancipation of African slaves. Later in the decade, despite the tug on his time by his duties at the growing Brooklyn Plymouth Church, Henry Ward would be elected president of the American Woman Suffrage Association. He, like his older sister Catharine, believed a woman's refined nature brought her closer to God and that only with her involvement on the national stage could the country be saved.[7] As he said in a February 1860 speech in New York: "Woman is appointed for the refinement of the race. She is God's secular ordinance for purity and goodness. Shall we understand her power, and employ it directly, or shall we ignorantly and by accident take her indirect usefulness?"[8]

As great as was his perceived influence in the emancipation efforts, women's suffrage may have given him his much-desired political launching, starting with an 1864 collection taken up at his church that netted $200 for the cause — much to the distress of both sister Catharine and wife Eunice, who clung to the notion that female suffrage activity and female suffragists were unseemly.[9] Catharine held such a view despite her agreement with Henry Ward about a woman's role in society.

Isabella took a break from April to August for an extended stay in Elmira for hydropathy, during which she wrote John that she had finished Charles Dickens's *A Tale of Two Cities*. She used the time for reflection and devotion — and to wonder again why she hadn't been granted a larger public podium. Catharine and Harriet had stayed within the women's sphere and had still managed to forge self-supporting careers with no more education than she'd enjoyed.

In a June 24, 1860, letter to John, Isabella warned that as her menopause approached, her mood swings might be more erratic, and that "there was quite the possibility of flowing to death then — or if not that — an almost certainty of from five to ten years — of invalidism, severe and painful — and no certainty of any good health afterward thro' life." However, in the same letter, she reassured him demurely that if he were to join her, Mrs. Gleason, co-owner of the Elmira water cure, thought Isabella could make him "most heartily welcome and could do so, without detriment to health."

She also wrote him in May to say that the freedom from care and housework alleviated some of her homesickness. She again suggested that John join her, as he probably needed a break from his own cares and work. On other occasions, John would acquiesce and join her, though it appears he understood and respected his wife's need to get away. Perhaps his not joining her this visit annoyed her. In June, she wrote that she was lonely, "hungry for my husband, half-starved," and then she chided him for his upbeat letters back:

> . . . the fact is you have all — from the best of motives — rather overdone the cheerfulness at home. I have been conscious of it more than once. I have had to struggle against the inevitable depression occasioned by it. "Of course, I want them to be happy." (I have said) & to get along nicely without me. I should be worried if they did not. But then if they can get along . . . without me what's the use of gubbing about here to get well. I can't care about the pain of being sick & feeble — nor of dying, even. It's only because I want to do something for somebody & be of use in the world that I am willing to stay in this dismal place.

In June, she wrote: "It is funny, how, everywhere I go — I have to run on the credit of my relations — no where, but at home can I lay claim to a particle of individuality — to any distinction of goodness, smartness or anything else whatever."

By August, she appeared ready to return. She wrote John, "It seems almost a selfish thing to be grateful for happiness."

In 1861, Anna Dickinson, then just nineteen years old, came to Hartford to speak against slavery at a meeting of the Republican Party. Dickinson was the daughter of Quakers and she had burst upon the national scene — and helped break the barrier for women public speakers — after William Lloyd Garrison's abolitionist paper, *The Liberator*, published her response to anti-abolitionist activity in Kentucky.[10] She was fourteen at that time and spent her teen years giving speeches to adoring audiences who considered her "a second Joan of Arc."[11] Her speaking style was unadorned, though — when necessary — she was skilled at sarcasm. Isabella and John went to hear her, and Isabella was enthralled. Dickinson spent the night at the Hookers' home, and she told her hosts about Stanton and Anthony, and the fine work they were doing securing the vote for women. Isabella was polite, but she had read her sisters' work, and she feared that they were right, that suffragists were immoral. Still, she became fast friends with Dickinson, so much so that Dickinson began calling Isabella "Mamma." As John Hooker had before her, Dickinson began suggesting books and articles to enhance Isabella's education. One of the first on her list was *The Enfranchisement of Women*. Though the tract was published anonymously, subsequent research would point to Harriet Taylor Mill as the primary author.[12]

In the essay, Mill argued that rendering inferior people who are physically weak made sense during the time of the law of the sword, but the way of the future would be democratic revolutions — with both genders bearing equal weight, responsibility, and rights.[13] Isabella loved the message, and she and Dickinson grew so close that Isabella invited her to her daughter Mary Hooker's wedding in October 1866, though Dickinson had to decline because of previously scheduled speaking engagements.

Mary Hooker's marriage to Harry Eugene Burton was not a happy union, and her parents may have suspected it wouldn't be. In recording the marriage in her journal, Isabella wrote that the family had "added a new son to our household, a man in years, but a child in heart." And she added cryptically: "The history of Eugene and Mary cannot be written here but is so engrained on hearts, it needs no recitation. There is ample correspondence to which contains nearly the whole."

Isabella and Edward (Ned) Hooker, 1863. *Courtesy of the*
Harriet Beecher Stowe Center, Hartford, Connecticut.

The latter was one of her few more veiled entries. Isabella found two platforms in which she could be blunt. She did not censor herself in her journals or in her letters. If there was no time to sit and discuss world events with John, she could at least visit them as she wrote seated in her big chair in the parlor. From an 1862 entry, Isabella said that her thoughts "are often as vivid to me as if spoken in public or in earnest debate, but many of which escape me, almost immediately, though they do seem at the time worthy of *some* attention."

And she considered where her journals would eventually land:

> Now that it is understood . . . that my daughters are to have these books, when they come to years of maturity and of need, that they have always been and always will be written in great haste in moments fairly snatched from other duties and there fore must be utterly destitute of carefulness in style and they may not be judged critically on that account. I feel more sensitive on this point than most persons would suppose possible — possibly because my good husband is so critical and would be so pleased to have me reach the high standard of which he thinks me capable of reaching and quite as much, because my own state has become fastidious, when it is too late for me to change, sensibly, in style of writing.

Just thirty-nine days after President Abraham Lincoln took office, the first shots of the Civil War rang over Fort Sumter. Earlier, suffragists had reluctantly agreed to focus on the abolition of slavery, with the idea that the woman question would be settled once that victory was achieved.[14] All eyes turned to the war. The *Hartford Courant* carried a June 17, 1861, article that warned against traitors nesting in the rival *Hartford Times* building, "fast becoming a formidable enemy to the Union. And before this war is ended, we shall, unless we crush them now, suffer very serious trouble from them."

Early in April 1862, Isabella wrote that she'd been confined to her bed with a "severe attack of quinsey," an abscess in her throat. Just as she was recovering, Bridget, the family maid, brought Ned into her bedroom. He would have been about seven at the time. He was, wrote Isabella, "all pale and shivering." The women placed him in a chair by the fire. Wrote Isabella, with characteristic self-criticism:

I was in dismay. He looked so ill and I had been almost nothing to him during my sickness. I told her to undress him and put him into his little bed in his room, not to mind but he looked so piteously toward my big bed and said he was so cold, I could not resist and so took him in there. I often despaired for his life. And more often perhaps prayed for his death from the fear of what life would be to him after such an illness for he soon grew very deaf in both ears and it seemed hardly possible that he could ever recover strength or hearing again.

She began writing down things the feverish Ned was saying, including "Thy will be done" and "Teach me how to pray."

"What a light to this house he is," his father said.

Ned recovered and grew up to be a homeopathic doctor, and he cared for his parents and aunts and uncles as they aged.

With everyone in the family in good health, Isabella traveled with sister Harriet to Boston for a New Year's concert. Seated in the balcony at the Boston Music Hall, Harriet was called to the railing when it was announced that President Lincoln had signed the Emancipation Proclamation. As the audience cheered, Harriet wiped tears from her eyes.[15]

Early in 1863, she and Harriet visited their father, Lyman, in New York. Lyman's characteristic forgetfulness had blossomed into serious senility. Isabella wrote of her father — whom she was seeing for the last time:

He looked perfectly lovely — with his long soft grey hair floating over his shoulder his face white and smooth and plump as a baby. He did not exactly recognize us — but our presence seemed very soothing and pleasant to him and when we sat one on each side and sang hymns — in a humming tone — and when we stopped brightened up and said distinctly and with much animation, "Well that is good."

Isabella wanted to bring him home to Hartford, but she was told he was too ill to be moved. Lyman Beecher died January 10, 1863, and was buried in New Haven's Grove Street Cemetery. Harriet joined an Episcopal church soon after, a move that was "meant not as a violent repudiation of her past but a respectful setting aside of a whole approach to religion, and especially formal theology, which she had simply moved beyond."[16]

After the proclamation was signed, a suffragist Isabella would come to know and love, Elizabeth Cady Stanton, was galvanized to action. She and Susan B. Anthony were not inclined to involve themselves in bandage rolling and other war-support activities adapted by women of the North, but after the emancipation they figured out a way to make women a part of the political discussion. The women had met in 1851 at an antislavery meeting in Seneca Falls, New York, and Stanton convinced Anthony of the importance of women's suffrage.[17] In May 1863, they brought women to New York to form the Woman's Loyal National League, which was dedicated to the notion that the war should free the slaves and establish women as equal citizens.[18]

In August 1863, Isabella wrote her friend Elisabeth P. Philleo that women should be more involved in politics, but she was still on the sidelines, living vicariously through her friend Anna Dickinson. Meanwhile, Harriet, husband Calvin, and their children moved into a spacious Nook Farm mansion they'd built and named Oakholm in 1864. They would not stay long. Despite the money coming in from Harriet's book sales, and Calvin's biblical treatises as well, the house proved to be too much and the family moved to a smaller and more manageable home on Forest Street near the Hookers.[19]

That same year, as she wrote in her *Connecticut* magazine article, Isabella traveled to South Carolina, where Bostonian Caroline M. Seymour Severance was living while her husband worked for the government. Isabella had found a new friend and a patient tutor in Severance, whose mother, Caroline Clarke, had also advocated women's rights.[20] Severance was a gifted public speaker and had been a teacher at a Massachusetts girls' school.[21] Just two years Isabella's senior, Severance had been in the movement her entire adult life and was one of the founders of the New England Woman's Club of Boston, known as the Mother of Clubs.[22]

The women stayed in touch, but it would be four years — two years after the marriage of her daughter Mary and two years before the marriage of her daughter Alice — before Isabella would take a public step for suffrage.[23]

Despite the turmoil of the rest of the nation, then three years into the Civil War, Isabella remained resolutely focused on her family. In February, she traveled to Brooklyn to spend time with Henry Ward and his family. There, she again listened to her friend Anna Dickinson, who was passing through town on a speaking tour. In May, Isabella wrote in her journal of her son complaining of being teased. His parents tried to help him think of possible answers, but Ned was disinclined to take their advice. "The little darling — so pure — and honest and lovely as he is, so generous, high minded and obliging," wrote Isabella. "I just mother him with kisses and told him it would take all the good in . . . common boys to make one so dear and lovely as he."

There was some fleeting time for discussions with John. She wrote in her journal of an evening when she and John had taken up the Constitution with their children, and Isabella was reminded again that she enjoyed exploring such topics:

> . . . that wonderful instrument of our fathers and made some headway in it, clause by clause, to the great instruction and edification of the girls who had never looked at it before. Alice was poring over it alone (she being the literary gourmand of the family) just now because her teacher had reproached the class the day before for their neglect of such a glorious document. . . . The old love of expounding was upon me and often took the words out of his mouth but one thing pleased me not a little . . . tho' I had no recollection of ever having read the venerable paper though its core seemed familiar and I understood the piece.

She credited her gut feel for the document to her antislavery education early in her marriage. Abolitionists know their Constitution, she wrote, as well as the relation of the federal government to the states.

Meantime, the people of Hartford threw themselves into the war effort. In 1862, when a call went out for lint by the statewide organizer Hartford Soldiers' Aid Society, residents donated enough lint and bandages "for any emergency," said the local *Hartford Daily Courant*.[24] Isabella joined the Sanitary Commission, one of a multitude of mostly female organizations formed to provide aid in the way of sheets, pillows, blankets, towels, clothing, dried fruit and jellies, games, books — anything to make a soldier's life a little more bearable. Sometimes the donations were meant to lift the soldier's spirits, and sometimes the gifts were rather macabre. The *Litchfield Enquirer* reported that one donation had included a pair of ragged socks meant for "Jeff Davis," with a note that the socks could be worn by the Confederate leader as he hung from a tree.[25]

Isabella also traveled to Washington to meet President Abraham Lincoln with her sister Harriet.[26] At a reception there, President Lincoln was supposed to have said, "So you're the little woman who wrote the book that started this great war." That retelling is most likely apocryphal, as none of the witnesses to the meeting recorded the exchange. Whatever occurred, the visit at least allowed Harriet the opportunity to talk to the president, and it allowed Isabella a chance to meet the president, with whom she was less than impressed. She wrote home describing Lincoln:

> . . . a rough scrubby — black — brown withered — dull eyed object as
> advanced to meet us — on entering — I can give you no idea of the
> shock — sister Hattie immediately became so engaged in silent observation
> of the unexpected apparition — there was no conversation to be expected
> from that quarter — so I put in vigorously on behalf of the charming
> open wood fire — & started various topics — till at last Mr. Lincoln — was
> "reminded of a man out west"— & then I collapsed & enjoyed myself
> vigorously — tho' quite internally — so we all did.[27]

She wrote further that President Lincoln appeared to have no idea whom he was meeting.[28]

When the war finally ended, suffragists waited in vain for their compatriots in the abolition movement to throw their energies into pushing for votes for women. The day before her birthday in 1867, Isabella wrote daughter Alice that "I do not find it easy to give up thinking, wherever I am and however occupied and of late this question is taking such practical shape I can hardly keep out of the fray — though it is twenty years since I shut my teeth with a snap & resolutely vowed I would not talk with any man who was not already of my own mind in the matter."

Meanwhile, in March 1867, the Kansas legislature let voters decide the fate of suffrage. It was suffrage's first popular test, and organizers took the vote seriously.[29] The suffragist Lucy Stone traveled down every Kansas road campaigning, sometimes twenty-five to forty-five miles a day to talk to anyone who would listen.[30] When her voice gave out, others took over. The suffragists adopted the sunflower — Kansas's state flower — as their symbol and distributed yellow ribbons that said "When Freedom's banner is unfurled, no star among its folds of blue shines forth to nations far and wide with luster brighter, with beams more true, though oft mid clouds 'tis hidden quite, it rises ever for the right."[31]

The fields were considered particularly ripe because abolitionists in Kansas were veterans of the battle.[32] Abolitionists and suffragists argued that linking the two causes would strengthen their case.[33] That did not prove to be true. Kansas was, as Carolyn Summers Vacca wrote in her 2004 book, *A Reform against Nature: Woman Suffrage and the Rethinking of American Citizenship, 1840–1920*, a "microcosm of all the forces that threatened to splinter reform movements into shards." Their campaign was met with a virulent and active — and, ultimately, successful — countercampaign from Kansas Republicans, who played votes for newly freed slaves and votes for women against each other, to the detriment of both.[34] Hoped-for support from opinion makers such as Horace Greeley was lukewarm or late.[35]

The referendum was defeated, but along the way Elizabeth Cady Stanton met George Francis Train, an avowed racist who pledged to fund the suffrage newspaper she'd founded with Susan B. Anthony, *The Revolution*.[36] The newspaper promised to be "the mouthpiece of millions, hoping to be emancipated."[37] However, the newspaper's circulation rarely went higher than three thousand, and revenues were hampered because Stanton would not accept advertisements for patent medicines, which she considered dangerous and bogus.[38]

Train's involvement helped further split the suffrage movement. "He may be of use in drawing an audience," said William Lloyd Garrison, "but so would a kangaroo, a gorilla, or a hippopotamus."[39] For their part, Stanton and Anthony elected to hold their noses and take Train's money.[40] Later, in 1873, Train spent five months in jail for publishing an excerpt from the Holy Bible that was considered obscene. A judge eventually declared Train not guilty by reason of insanity.[41] Train, a flamboyant and successful businessman and financier, was erratic and uncontrollable, and his funding for *The Revolution* soon evaporated, but the damage to the movement was done.

From her home in Hartford, Isabella was shocked that a racist like Train — who, said one historian, "occupied a space somewhere between brilliance and insanity"— would be brought into the movement. She considered him too coarse, and his presence made her question whether Stanton was the proper person to lead a movement.[42]

The tug-of-war continued between the Boston and New York factions of the suffrage movement over Isabella's allegiance. She'd been introduced to suffrage by Caroline Severance, of the Boston contingent, yet she held out hope that the two wings could join together. As she wrote to Severance in August 1869: "[W]e are bound for the same port and must virtually take passage on the same ship — at least there is but one line of vessels and we must not think of such a thing as running athwart each other — the overriding vessel is just as likely to go down as the other and deserves to be a great deal more."[43]

In May of that year, a new organization — the American Equal Rights Association — had formed to push for suffrage of women and African Americans.[44] The organization lobbied that the vote be granted to "all without distinctions of color, sex, or race."[45]

Isabella did not suspect it, but her private life was coming to an end. Stanton's alliance with the controversial Train may have exposed the longtime activist's weariness with the politics of the movement. She'd moved to New Jersey, while her husband, Henry, stayed in New York. Most of her children were in college, and her marriage was struggling.[46] She and the movement needed new energy.

In January 1868, Mark Twain visited Henry Ward's Plymouth Church. An avowed agnostic, Twain nevertheless owned copies of Beecher's sermons. There, the minister advised him to drive a hard bargain with his publisher for his next book, *The Innocents Abroad*. From a letter Twain wrote to his mother, Jane:

> This great American Publishing Company kept on trying to bargain with me for a book till I thought I could cut the matter short by coming up for a talk. I met Rev. HWB in Brooklyn, and with his usual whole-souled way of dropping his own work to give other people a lift when he gets a chance, he said, "Now, here, you are one of the talented men of the age — nobody is going to deny that — but in matters of business, I don't suppose you know more than enough to come in when it rains. I'll tell you what to do, and how to do it." And he did.

Twain followed Henry Ward's advice and received a percentage higher than any other American author of the day, save for Horace Greeley. Based on letters Twain wrote later, he seemed to have enjoyed his time at the Beechers' home in Brooklyn, even while he wished for an alcoholic beverage and found the strain of genteel folk a little wearying. Again, Twain wrote his mother, Jane: "I expect I told more lies than I have told before in a month. We had a tip-top dinner, but nothing to drink but cider. I told Mr. Beecher that no dinner could be perfect without champaign [*sic*], or at least some kind of Burgundy, and he said that privately he was a good deal of the same opinion, but it wouldn't do to say it out loud."

He pronounced Henry Ward "a brick." Twain then went from New York to Elmira, his wife's hometown, and then he stayed a few days at the Hooker house, in Hartford. In another letter, he wrote again of the strain of bringing his rough-hewn manners to bear in stodgy old Hartford: "I tell you I have to walk mighty straight." He continued, "Puritans are mighty straight-laced and they won't let me smoke in the parlor, but the Almighty don't make any better people."

And:

I desire to have the respect of this sterling old Puritan community, for their respect is well worth having — and so I don't dare to smoke after I go to bed, and in fact I don't dare to do anything that's comfortable and natural. It comes a little hard to lead a sinless life, but then you know it won't be for long — I can let myself out when I get to Washington. I have promised to be Mrs. Hooker's special Washington correspondent, and so I shall have to be particular again.

In April, Isabella wrote to a family friend about her daughter Alice, who was showing herself to be less than serious and entirely too willing to poke fun at her mother's passion:

You know she has a passion for theatricals — has always thought to act in parlor plays & now, just at the moment that I thought I had her judgment & Mary's in favor of equal suffrage (I have read them my manuscript and they like it) . . . she is persuaded into taking part in a play entitled *The Coming Woman* which is a burlesque upon woman's rights technically so called & a mere piece of buffoonery at best.

Isabella insisted she didn't mind Alice's activities, though she was puzzled that her daughter would be so cavalier about such an important topic. She wrote to a family friend: "My pride of womanhood was always so great & so vividly uppermost. But young folks generally care only for fun and what is fun. . . . Alice is driving herself pretty hard these last months, determined to get pleasure out of her studies and her young friends."

Alice herself was going off to take the water cure in Elmira, and Isabella asked that there be no return letter, in part because she didn't want her daughter to know she'd taken the family friend into her confidence.

In 1867, Frances Ellen Burr, sister of Alfred Burr, the publisher of the progressive *Hartford Times* newspaper, introduced a bill in the Connecticut legislature that would have allowed women the vote. Burr, who would later serve as recording secretary of the Connecticut Woman Suffrage Association for forty-one years, was known as the "greatest and littlest of the Burrs."[47] She'd been a suffragist since she'd attended a women's rights convention in Cleveland in 1853.[48]

The bill was defeated, but the vote was 111–93, a hopeful sign to Burr, who later wrote to Susan B. Anthony that she was "pretty much alone in those days, on the woman suffrage question."[49] Both the vote and the discussion around it piqued Isabella's interest, and the next year she wrote "A Mother's Letters to a Daughter on Woman Suffrage"—first published anonymously in *Putnam's* magazine and later with her byline, courtesy of the Connecticut Woman Suffrage Association. Taking on the style prevalent at the time—and reflecting her earlier matrimonial conversation—she wrote the essay as a conversation between a mother and a daughter. The essay's form was similar to the Beecher tradition of round-robin letters. With the essay, Isabella showed that she had been seriously thinking about suffrage.[50] Echoing Harriet Taylor Mill, she wrote that any government that did not include women "has not yet fully emerged from the barbarism of ancient times."[51] She also—clinging to the woman's sphere—encouraged the fictional daughter to "welcome, then, blessed privilege of motherhood, with all thy anguish, care and sorrow; in thee, at last, lies the purification of our race, and abundant compensation for ages of suffering and subjection, and as unwritten history"; and she wrote: "Let no men fear, then, to trust to woman the guidance of her own life in all the ages to come."[52]

She was forty-six, the mother of three, and facing what she called a "half-forsaken nest." Daughter Mary had wed two years earlier. Daughter Alice would marry the following summer. That left only her son, Ned, at home, and she could see the day when her house would be empty, save for herself and John.[53]

In early 1869, Isabella began writing Stanton and Anthony fairly regularly. She sent Anthony some arguments about why working women needed suffrage. She wrote Stanton criticizing *The Revolution*, of which Stanton was the chief writer.[54] Stanton wrote back in April 1869: "We can throw Train overboard the moment we can find friends enough who will give their money to support a paper that is bound to unveil the abominations in high and low places."

In May 1869, Anthony and Stanton attended a meeting of the American Equal Rights Association in New York, in which discussion about suffrage for former slaves and suffrage for women grew heated, and their liaison with Train was questioned. The anticipated showdown between the two factions of the suffrage movement caused an unseemly fight for tickets, according to the *Brooklyn Daily Union*, which bemoaned the "lawless scrabble."[55] At one point, in a debate with Stephen S. Foster, an abolitionist, Anthony snapped: "The old anti-slavery school says women must stand back and wait until the negroes shall be recognized. But we say . . . if intelligence, justice, and morality are to have precedence in the Government, let the question of woman be brought up first and that of the negro last."[56]

Anthony would put forth "hierarchical racial concepts" in the pages of *The Revolution*.[57] Stanton's rhetoric as well became less about universal suffrage and far more about women's suffrage, at the expense, if necessary, of the black man. In a June 1869 editorial, she wrote: "I have seen and felt . . . the far-reaching consequences of this degradation of one-half the citizens of the republic, on the government, the Saxon race, and woman herself. . . . As you go down and down in the scale of manhood the idea strengthens . . . at every step, that woman was created for no higher purpose than to gratify the lust of man."[58]

Whether this kind of writing was presented as an appeasement to the full-on racist Train or whether it was considered politically expedient is not known. The rhetoric, however, lent a reputation to the women's movement — which it has yet to shake — that the "enfranchisement of women" meant most specifically the granting of rights strictly to white women of certain means. Though the referendum was defeated, the hated Train helped gain support for women's suffrage among the white men of Kansas by encouraging them not to place women "still lower in the scale of citizenship and humanity" than African American men.[59]

Such talk would have been anathema to Isabella, and to John, who insisted on universal suffrage, but the racist rhetoric did not interrupt the correspondence flying between Hartford and New York. Isabella began asking Stanton for advice on a women's property bill she was writing with John. They sent each other their essays (Isabella) and speeches (Stanton) and asked for critique.

Isabella also wrote a letter to *The Nation* to defend that publication's criticism of Anna Dickinson's book, *What Answer?*[60] In a November 1868 letter, she wrote, "I am deep in reform matters just now and am urged to write for periodicals and much wish to do it — but time is wanting."

Isabella also wrote and distributed a public announcement for a suffrage convention planned for November in Boston that year. In Boston, her old friend Thomas Higginson pronounced this "the woman's hour," while Frederick Douglass begged reformers to focus their attention on suffrage for black men.[61] The cry became "The Negro once safe, the woman comes next" to close discussions among influential abolitionists.[62] The sentiment was boiled down to "the Negro's hour." The women would come later. Politically, this made sense to some — such a drastic upheaval of American culture, both the emancipation of slaves and of women, would never fly. The enfranchisement of both groups would stand a better chance if taken separately. Some suffragists — such as Julia Ward Howe, who is probably best known for writing "The Battle Hymn of the Republic"— agreed. Howe had said at a speech in Boston in 1868, "I am willing that the Negro shall get the ballot before me."[63] Howe was rewarded for her acquiescence with a top leadership position in the American Woman Suffrage Association.[64]

Some — like Lucy Stone — proposed the Republican Party "drop its watchword of 'Manhood Suffrage'" and give the vote to all men and women as a right of citizenship.[65] At the same time, the interested formed the New England Woman Suffrage Association and launched a newspaper, *Woman's*

Advocate, as an obvious rival to Stanton and Anthony's more radical *The Revolution*. Despite the former's name, the organization proposed that "black enfranchisement should take strategic priority over woman suffrage."[66]

It became clear that women's suffrage would be Isabella's cause. She would not work in the shadow of John Hooker. This would be hers alone. Excited, she spoke often with sister Harriet about her new friends, the suffragists. As she had among abolitionists, Harriet tended to hover in a middle ground.[67] She could not commit to throwing her considerable cultural weight into women's suffrage, though both Stanton and Anthony courted the Beecher sisters for their name — and the potential funding that might follow.[68]

Even more than they did with abolition, the Beechers' views on women's suffrage varied widely. As dedicated as Catharine was to women's education, she could not support women's right to vote because "women's roles were the conservation of the home, guarding and developing the human body in infancy, and education of the children."[69] If given the right to vote, women, wrote Catharine, would abandon their home duties and the country would fail. In 1871, the popular monthly *Godey's Lady's Book and Magazine* — the bible of true womanhood — published an antisuffrage petition that used the Bible, the welfare of children, and women's innate frailty as its foundation for opposing suffrage.[70] The petition, promoted by nineteen women noted mostly for their marriages to prominent men, warned that suffrage must be opposed:[71]

> Because we hold that an extension of suffrage would be adverse to the interests of the working women of the country, with whom we heartily sympathize. Because these changes must introduce a fruitful element of discord in the existing marriage relation, which would tend to the infinite detriment of children, and increase the already alarming prevalence of divorced throughout the land.[72]

Catharine's public antisuffrage stand may have fueled Isabella's ire, so that in May 1869 the younger sister wrote the older an uncharacteristically harsh letter after Catharine came to Hartford and overstayed her welcome. Isabella suggested to Catharine that the family would not be able to continue to support her — and she wrote that Catharine meddled too much. She suggested

Catharine find a boarding house for her next visit — something unheard of in their close-knit family — and Isabella added the extra dig that she was probably speaking for all of Catharine's siblings.

Catharine fired back with a sermon that included the remonstration that Isabella remember her Bible classes of old:

> A true Christian home is not complete without aged or infirm members — who are preserved in life that the young may be trained to reverence gray hairs and tenderly care for the feeble and infirm — In no other way can they follow Christ's command, "Bear ye one another's burdens." . . . I love you and trust you as one anxious to do right in all things.[73]

Isabella, for her part, began calling the suffrage movement "woman's church."[74] As sister Harriet had believed working for abolition was the work of the church, Isabella believed that God had ordained that women would lead, and Christian churches should lead the way in supporting them.[75]

Despite the equanimity the suffragists had shown in Hartford to various speakers and programs, by the middle of 1869 the movement was struggling with a significant difference in philosophy. The Equal Rights group, which originally vowed to seek universal suffrage, had focused entirely on gaining the vote for African American men. The Fifteenth Amendment, which granted African American men the right to vote, was law by the time of the national convention in Washington, D.C., in May; Stanton asked that the movement support a Sixteenth Amendment that would grant the vote regardless of color, race, or gender. Her suggestion was roundly ignored.[76] By the time of their meeting, dissension was at a fever pitch. The association ended up endorsing the Fifteenth Amendment, and Stanton and Anthony wondered if the movement had too many men in it. Nationally, the movement was splitting, starting with Stanton's resolution at the Tenth National Woman's Rights Convention that called for support of divorce in certain cases. Stanton maintained that a marriage license was a civil contract, and thus subject to nullification, but any discussion of divorce was anathema to the New England set, who considered divorce too big a dip in the pool of free love.

Free love was associated mostly during the antebellum period with people such as Mary Wollstonecraft, a "towering figure in the development of rights-based feminism."[77] The British feminist, according to a biographer, "loved a woman and at least three men, bore an illegitimate child during the French Revolution and was vilified by the nation as a whore and an 'unsex'd Female.' Yet, despite being sexual and passionate, she was profoundly, even irritatingly, moral and puritanical."[78] Free love and women's rights shared the idea that the best relationships occurred between equals.[79] While on paper suffragists may have agreed that traditional marriage was not conducive to equal rights, most were horrified at the impropriety of successive sexual partners.

Free love proponents insisted that traditional marriage was little more than state-sanctioned slavery and that women suffered most because of it. Proponents sought to ground their beliefs in the Bible. Free lovers also believed that women's rights were paramount. All free lovers were suffragists — though hardly all suffragists were free lovers. In fact, most of the outspoken suffragists were appalled to be associated with such utopian ideas. To avoid being tainted, some suffragists even refused to discuss divorce laws, which were notoriously sexist at the time. At a New York meeting in 1869, Lucy Stone decried that free love was even a topic of conversation:

> "If any one says to me," she said dramatically, "Oh, I know what you mean, you mean Free Love by this agitation," let the lie stick in his throat. You may talk about Free Love, if you please, but we are here to have the right to vote. To-day we are fined, imprisoned, and hanged, without a jury of our peers. You shall not cheat us by getting us off to talk about something else. When we get the suffrage, then you may taunt us with anything you please, and we will then talk about it as long as you please.[80]

Opponents soon found that the quickest way to dismiss suffragists was to claim they embraced free love — just as earlier accusations of infidelity could silence an antislavery speaker.[81]

Frustrated by some of their colleagues' comparatively limp approach to gaining the vote for women, Stanton and Anthony formed the National Woman Suffrage Association and banned men from membership, a rule they later amended to insisting on an all-woman leadership. The organization would focus on a constitutional amendment — like the Fifteenth — to gain women's enfranchisement.[82] In retaliation, Lucy Stone and others formed the American Woman Suffrage Association and installed Henry Ward Beecher as president. The AWSA focused on suffrage, leaving the issue of free love untouched, and worked to get the vote in state-by-state campaigns. The AERA was no more.

Paulina Wright Davis, who had studied medicine in New York, began focusing her energies on the women's movement. She introduced herself to Isabella and suggested that women not turn on one another. Stanton and Anthony both wanted a Beecher within their ranks, and they managed to impress Isabella into joining with them. In Isabella's estimation, the Boston group tended to be more mean-spirited, while the New York group, led by Stanton and Anthony, spoke well of its northern brothers and sisters in letters to Isabella. Isabella also said the Boston group was "sick until death with propriety."[83]

At a Newport, Rhode Island, suffrage convention run by Davis, Isabella stood and spoke. She brought her biblical argument for women's rights. She based her speech on the second chapter of the book of Genesis, where man and woman are portrayed as "simultaneous creations," and she argued further and "presented a number of scientific facts to prove that the highest types of vitality take the female form."[84]

The experience exhausted her nerves, but she'd taken an important step to being a public and vocal advocate for suffrage. Stanton asked her to contribute to *The Revolution* with the words "When will you be ready to give your first sermon?"[85]

As for Harriet, she wrote Anthony that she was "not quite ready to join the Woman's Rights Church."[86] Anthony wrote to Isabella, "[W]hen she does enter it — I can tell you there will be rejoicing in our heaven not less than that we read about." Stanton hoped that Isabella would be president of the national organization and Harriet would edit *The Revolution*. The Beecher name would lend much-needed aplomb and gravity to the movement.

The August 1869 meetings were an unqualified success. Isabella wrote her friend Caroline Severance in giddy excitement about Stanton:

I have now spent three days in her company and in the most intense heart-searching debate I ever undertook in my life. I have handled what seemed to me her errors, without gloves and the result is that I love her also, just as I do you — I have handed in my allegiance to you three women [the third was Paulina Wright Davis], as worthy leaders and representatives of the cause dearer to me than any other in the world. . . . And now as to Susan [B. Anthony] herself — the one really hoofed and horned demon of this movement to all minds — mine among them — I have studied her day & night for near a week in all. . . . She is a woman of incorruptible integrity & the thought of guile is not in her heart.

In fact, Stanton and Anthony supported the reform of divorce laws. Though laws varied widely from state to state, divorce laws had been liberalized somewhat around the country.[87] In Connecticut, for example, divorces could be granted for "misconduct" that "permanently destroys the happiness of the petitioner and defeats the purposes of the marriage relation."[88] (A report by the Ohio secretary of state said that the result of similar legislation was a rise in divorces, from one in thirteen in 1860 to one in ten by 1867.[89]) This matter was yet another breaking point with the Boston group, which wanted to focus specifically on suffrage and leave the other issues — temperance, divorce reform, and such — for a later day.

Meanwhile, Harriet had, as her brother Henry wrote in August 1869, "stirred up the annual family row — sometimes it is one, sometimes another of those Beechers, that keep people in hot water." In the 1850s, Harriet met Lady Anne Isabella Milbanke Byron, who alleged that her late husband, the poet Lord George Gordon Byron, had carried on an incestuous affair with his half-sister, Augusta Leigh. Harriet had met Lady Byron on one of her trips to England as the darling of the abolition movement. Lady Byron, a staunch Christian, had shared her tale with Harriet, who was suitably outraged at her friend's treatment. When Harriet published an account in The Atlantic magazine, the newspapers jumped into attack mode. Isabella had moved to New York City to help edit her sister's book, and while she was there, John Hooker wrote her letters advising her to get wealthy female backers and become a preacher. He encouraged Isabella to bring her sisters into the suffragist fold — and into producing The Revolution, in particular. Perhaps, he said, Harriet could write an Uncle Tom's Cabin for women.

But Lady Byron Vindicated was not that work, and public outrage over the details of the alleged scandal would not go away. Stowe's reputation as the standard-bearer for equal rights began to slip, though the book's content was not the entire cause of her decrease in popularity. As Joan Hedrick wrote in her 1995 book, *Harriet Beecher Stowe: A Life*, Harriet saw her public stock drop in part because of the "polarization of literature along gender lines that was such a striking feature of the post–Civil War period. The masculinization of literature, rather than the Byron affair, brought down not only Stowe but a whole generation of women writers who used literature to advance political issues." Even with the support of influential friends such as Mark Twain — and an unexpected editorial by Stanton defending Harriet in the newspaper Harriet shunned, *The Revolution* — book sales dropped, and Harriet and her family abandoned Hartford to retreat for a few years to Florida. She wanted to involve herself in bettering the lives of the former slaves there. She wrote to her brother Charles to suggest he buy property next to hers in Mandarin, just south of Jacksonville.[90]

As for Stanton's tribute in *The Revolution*, she wrote: "Mrs. Stowe's fearful picture of the abominations of our social life, coming out simultaneously with J. S. Mill's philosophy of the degradation of women, will do much to rouse wise men to new thought on the social wrongs of the race."

Harriet went into seclusion in Florida, but she would return. A scandal that would strike at the core of her family would call her back — and set her at odds with sister Isabella. But for now she would enjoy the climate down south and encourage her son Frederick, who had been battling alcoholism since he was a teenager, in a career as a cotton grower.

Around the same time, Horace Bushnell, a Hartford Congregational minister with a national reputation, wrote *Women's Suffrage: The Reform against Nature*, in which he acknowledged that his book would not settle the discussion and that he did "not propose to continue this discussion, but to abide the criticisms laid upon me with what of patience I am able."[91] In the book, the minister took up Catharine's argument and said that voting rights are not inalienable, and that women would better serve Christian America by remaining in their own sphere, the home.[92]

On page 21 of his book, Bushnell writes that a woman is not qualified, say, to be a judge in court, and he extols the "finer equity of her womanly disposition," saying that she "is not wicked enough to sift, expose, and vigorously score the lying tricks of evidence. Besides, women lack authority, and never bear it well when they assume it."[93]

Reverend Bushnell gave an inscribed copy to Isabella, and her notes in the margins include, on page 21: "We have more Christian women than Christian men; their piety ranges higher, and they have many of them higher gifts of experience, and practically speaking, a more instructed insight of the Christian truth and life."

On page 44, Bushnell writes that voting is a right, that neither men nor women have a title to it, and that women should gain the vote as men did: through history, with preparation and causes.[94]

Isabella's note: "What if they should be allowed the privilege of giving now and then. It is more blessed to give than to receive in every sense."

Her notes were no more barbed than any of her journal entries. Perhaps this, then, was the beginning of Isabella's public life, and she would not go about her transition quietly. Isabella began planning an independent suffrage convention in Hartford. In preparation, she wrote Stanton in September 1869: "I am just leaving town and have only time to laugh a little at your anxiety — that we should all put our best foot forward in Hartford. . . . Our dress, manners, and speech shall be worthy of a place in the opera house of Hartford."[95]

Isabella described what she would wear and how she would fix her hair with "an extra curl and wreath my face in its sweetest smile." Stanton wrote back and said she would simply be herself.

The convention assembled on October 28, 1869, at the Roberts' Opera House in downtown Hartford. The day before, suffrage movement luminaries — among them Susan B. Anthony, William Lloyd Garrison, Henry Ward Beecher, and Elizabeth Cady Stanton — met at Isabella's home for breakfast. As they placed their orders for drinks, Henry Ward told Susan B. Anthony: "Now, Miss Anthony, you know you have to make a big speech today. When I want to be very effective and make people cry, I drink a cup of tea before speaking; when I want to be very clever and make them laugh, I drink coffee; but when I want them to cry half the time and laugh the other half, I take a cup of each."[96]

The group moved downtown for the meeting, and at promptly 10 a.m., the Honorable John Hooker called the meeting to order and the Reverend

Henry Ward Beecher opened with prayer.[97] The Reverend Nathaniel Judson Burton, pastor of Hartford's Park Church, was elected president.[98] In his autobiography, John Hooker called Burton a "liberal congregationalist."

Harriet Beecher Stowe, who may have been the most conservative suffragist there, was named vice president.

Isabella Beecher Hooker was placed on the committee for resolutions. Resolutions included, from recording secretary Frances Burr's notes, opening up membership to people from other states, as well as acknowledging the ballot would "bring to women a higher education . . . a wider field of thought and action; a sense of responsibility in her relationship to public welfare"— and, "in place of mere complaisance" from men, the higher and truer respect of men.

By the second day, the hall was overflowing. Reverend Burton praised Isabella for organizing the meeting, and she was appointed to prepare a circular that would emphasize the importance of suffrage for those who didn't attend. There was some discussion as to how to draw newspaper coverage, but no agreement was reached on whether to include *The Revolution* — though there was "animated discussion" on the latter topic, according to the secretary.

At the meeting, Isabella presided over the founding of the Connecticut Woman Suffrage Association, which would focus on suffrage activities in the Nutmeg State. She also brought the New York and Boston factions together at the same venue.[99] Stanton wrote Anthony later that she gave the "most inoffensive speech I could produce," and the people of Hartford seemed at least willing to listen.[100]

Isabella was disappointed that the gathering did not reunite the movement's factions, though she found herself increasingly drawn to Stanton and Anthony. The Boston group continued to accuse the New York group of supporting free love, an accusation that gained traction over time. The tug between the New York and the Boston wings would continue after the meeting. Garrison would warn Isabella against the "immoralities" of her chosen group. Isabella would insist that the New York agitators — Stanton and Anthony chief among them — were good, Christian women.

But when Harriet Beecher Stowe professed concern over the name of Stanton and Anthony's newspaper, *The Revolution*, Isabella agreed. The two sisters tried to convince the women to change the name, but despite the potential financial windfall the Beecher family might have brought, Anthony declined.[101]

Though the suffrage factions did not rejoin, the leaders at least behaved themselves — including Stanton, Severance, and Henry Ward — as well as the wild card, the suffragist most likely to speak her mind, Anthony. Isabella wrote to Mary Livermore, a former Civil War nurse and a popular speaker for women's rights, in November:[102] "It was an entire surprise to me . . . to find the one woman I had brought forward with fear & trembling as the monster who might drag us all into disgrace . . . was the one most commended by both gentlemen & ladies as gentle — wise — logical & convincing."

Isabella was not alone in her desire to see the Boston and New York groups joined to battle together. That same month, a man who would figure prominently in Isabella's life in the next few years, Theodore Tilton, editor of *The Independent* — one of the premier Christian antislavery newspapers — suggested another peace plan in Cleveland, to no avail.[103] In November 1869, Severance told Isabella that a union was impossible. The factions had drifted too far apart. The egos were too big, and no amount of Isabella's appealing to everyone's Christian sensibilities helped. That same month, the old abolition firebrand William Lloyd Garrison wrote to Isabella that "nothing in regard to controversial matters had ever been settled by the Bible." This claim would not have sat well with Isabella, the preacher's daughter and devout believer. Mostly, however, Garrison was reacting to his aversion to Stanton, whom he considered an egomaniac and unsuitable to lead.[104]

Isabella could not give up on the notion that the two groups could come together peacefully. She even suggested to her brother — then leader of the American Woman Suffrage Association — that he could preside over the new, reunified group. Despite appeals from some of the better-known suffragists of the day to join one of the groups, Isabella finally decided she was needed more in the National Woman Suffrage Association, where she would put her considerable energies behind a constitutional amendment that would grant women the right to vote.

The same personality traits that drove others from Stanton and Anthony drew Isabella to them. She wanted firm leaders — though she was still subject to her outspoken siblings' influence.

Now approaching her seventies, in December 1869, Catharine showed

John Hooker an essay she'd written against suffrage, "An Address on Female Suffrage," in which she called the ballot "the gift of oppression." John wrote to Isabella that the piece was "as weak a thing as I ever did read." He reiterated his desire to write a book with his wife.

Meanwhile, letters continued to fly between Stanton and Isabella. Even if Isabella didn't get the newspaper's name changed, would she consider critiquing — right down to the spelling — *The Revolution*? asked Stanton. Isabella would.

In fact, in December 1869, Isabella published her first contribution to *The Revolution*, a defense of her brother Henry Ward against charges that he supported free love. Earlier that month, Henry Ward had given a lecture in Hartford in which he said, "Men must overcome the causes of unhappiness within the household, or else endure them. To open an easy and wide door out of wedlock is to take the misery off from two and put it upon society at large. The remedy must be applied at the door of entrance into wedlock and not at the point of exit." He said that marriage was God's schoolmaster, where "two hearts are to be shut up, and forbidden to go out until they have adjusted all their differences — and then they will not wish to go out."

After Train withdrew his support for *The Revolution*, Isabella stepped in and offered to edit and fund the newspaper if Stanton and Anthony would change the name to something less inflammatory, such as *True Republic*. Isabella also suggested Tilton and his wife, Elizabeth, be involved. "Our parlor," she wrote, "needs her demure, motherly, angelic sweetness, as much as our platform needs him [Theodore]. These little, quiet domestic women are our trump cards, nowadays. I wish we had a whole pack of them."

But the name change wasn't acceptable to Stanton, who wrote Anthony that "A journal called the *Rose-bud* might answer for those who come with kid gloves and perfumes to lay immortelle [*sic*] wreaths on the monuments which in sweat and tears we have hewn and built; but for us, and that great blacksmith of ours who forges such red-hot thunderbolts for the Pharisees, hypocrites and sinners, there is no name but *The Revolution*."[105]

In the end, Isabella decided against writing for the newspaper, and Susan B. Anthony turned over editorial control and sold the paper in 1870.[106] As she recorded in her diary, "[I]t was like signing my own death warrant."[107] Ironically, in the end the newspaper was propped up by Laura Curtis Bullard, whose family had made its fortune in patent medicine.[108] An accomplished author, Bullard had edited her own paper, *The Ladies Visitor, and Drawing Room Companion*.[109] *The Revolution* continued for about a year and a half, and then it folded.

At home, Isabella said good-bye to daughter Alice, now married to the lawyer John C. Day. She wrote that she and John missed her more than they had expected.

"We are all as weak as when you left," she wrote. "The truth is I never had a conception of what it would be to me, to live without my daughters in the house."

A WOMAN'S WORTH,

A BROTHER'S SHAME

In January 1870, Isabella revealed in *The Revolution* that she intended to "preach Christ and his dear gospel to 5,000 people every week."[1] This was a decidedly new tack for *The Revolution*, and may have been an indication of how much Stanton, in particular, wanted the Beecher name attached to the movement. Stanton took loud and public issue with many of the Christian suffrage leaders because they shared with Isabella the belief that religion should play a role in the movement. In Stanton's mind, a fundamental interpretation of the Bible left women enslaved in second-class citizenry. In the 1890s, she presided over the publication of *The Woman's Bible*. In that work's introduction, she wrote:

> Come, come, my conservative friend, wipe the dew off your spectacles,
> and see that the world is moving. Whatever your view may be as to the . . .
> proposed work, your political and social degradation are but an outgrowth
> of your status in the Bible. . . . [H]ow can woman's position be changed from
> that of a subordinate to an equal, without opposition, without the broadest
> discussion of all the questions involved in her present degradation? For so
> far-reaching and momentous a reform as her complete independence, an
> entire revolution in all existing institutions is inevitable.[2]

Their radically different approaches to theology were fodder for much discussion. In 1873, Isabella wrote Stanton about her concern that the leader did not mention the afterlife in her speeches, to which Stanton answered, in a letter to another friend, "To suppose this short life to be all of this world's experiences never did seem wholly satisfactory, but at the same time I see no proof of all these vague ideas floating in Mrs. Hooker's head."[3]

Isabella believed the Holy Scriptures supported the suffrage movement, and she did not entirely abandon the tenets of true womanhood. The idea that a woman's place was in the home dovetailed nicely with orthodox Christianity. In early 1870, Isabella wrote to a friend, Susan Howard, that she felt a woman's ability to lead was conditional upon her devotion to her family. Howard had asked whether Isabella's new friends supported free love. Isabella explained further that Stanton "has come to look upon easy divorce as a blessing and a necessity. But to say that she ever advocated this as a means of personal gratification to woman or man is simply to insult her."[4]

If Isabella and Stanton could reach a truce on their different approaches, Isabella's uniquely hybrid suffrage notions — that it was God's intention that women vote, and that women could do so and remain faithful wives and mothers — ran counter to those of her sisters. As her friendship with Anthony and Stanton deepened, Isabella continued to read and educate herself, and her theology shifted into something not found in father Lyman's pews. As she began to embrace Spiritualism and call herself a Christian Spiritualist, Isabella was hardly bound by the interpretation of the Bible she'd learned as a girl.[5]

Motherhood was the source of her moral superiority. What women lacked in physicality they more than compensated for in moral strength — or so Isabella and many of her siblings believed, or so said Isabella.[6] And though that echoed Catharine and Harriet's beliefs, it did little to soften their concern that she'd wandered too far afield.

To convince her sisters that the women in the New York suffrage movement were decent and God-fearing, Isabella reminded them that Stanton was devoted to her husband and seven children. The never-married Anthony, however, remained a worry of the older Beecher women — ironic, considering that Catharine, too, remained unmarried and childless.

John Hooker, however, was not convinced. Writing to Isabella from New York City on January 5, 1870, he lamented Stanton's lack of refinement. He said that he believed, as a man with a sensitive nature, he could judge such matters.

Meanwhile, Henry Ward took over the publication of *Christian Union*, which grew to be the most-read Christian newspaper in the country. Under his editorial lead, the periodical was a vehicle for ecumenicalism — a radical idea for some of his parishioners. "Not only shall we not labor for an external

Isabella, 1873. *Courtesy of the Harriet Beecher Stowe Center, Hartford, Connecticut.*

and ecclesiastical unity, but we should regard it as a step backward," wrote Henry Ward.[7] As Isabella saw *The Revolution* as her opportunity to preach, Harriet considered the *Union* her pulpit. In a letter to Henry Ward, Harriet wrote, "I have all my life but especially lately gone with a gospel burning in my bosom which I longed to preach but could not because I was a woman . . . but if we can make the *Union* so distinctively a gospel that seekers and enquirers shall come to it as their natural food . . . then my idea of the C. *Union* will be filled up."[8]

She wrote in the same letter: "Keep strong and Beecherism and the paper will be all right."[9]

Harriet, her husband, and other Beecher members — though not Isabella — began contributing, and *The Revolution* praised *Union's* first edition.

But Henry Ward Beecher would enrage suffragists later by his lukewarm support of Daniel McFarland, an elocution teacher who in November 1869 shot and killed *New York Tribune* editor Albert Richardson, who planned to marry McFarland's ex-wife, Abby, with whom Richardson was living. The subsequent trial did not seek to prove McFarland's innocence, but instead looked at whether the behavior of Abby Sage McFarland, an actress, had moved her ex-husband to act insanely. Richardson died just days after he was shot, but not before the Reverend Henry Ward Beecher performed a deathbed wedding between Richardson and his beloved. This bit of theater enraged more than suffragists. As one writer said, "Does Mr. Beecher know what is meant by the words, 'Thou shalt not commit adultery.' 'Thou shalt not covet thy neighbor's wife,' and similar expressions? If he does understand it, as we presume he does, how can he reconcile his conduct in this matter? . . . Mr. Beecher has compromised himself as a Christian man, has made himself odious to the whole Christian church."[10] In May 1870, McFarland was acquitted by reason of insanity — yet he was awarded custody of the child he'd had with his ex-wife. A protest meeting was held at Apollo Hall a few days later, with Stanton. She used the opportunity to talk about how divorce laws were heavily weighted against women. She also reminded the crowd that she'd been married and living with the same man for thirty years, and that accusations that she supported free love could be countered by her own marriage.

Writing to Isabella, Stanton said her own opinions on suffrage would have offended Isabella twenty years ago, and in twenty years her views on divorce would seem reasonable.[11]

But the accusation that the New York contingent supported free love would not go away. In an 1870 letter to Susan Howard, Isabella wrote that the National Woman Suffrage Association's goal is "pure suffrage," and she enclosed a copy of the association's constitution as proof — even while she checked off the names of women on the list who might be considered potential adherents to the free love doctrine. Isabella continued:

I only wish my dear brother could be persuaded to hear some of these things and not because I wish to wean him from his new alliance or friendships but because he could be much more useful to them and to the whole cause by understanding the countercurrents . . . if he does not allow himself to be warped and set against other workers. . . . Oh Susie, few men know what this battle means — but many women, wives and mothers, know and feel it all, feel it for their sisters if not for themselves. I am one of these and I stagger under the weight of my load.[12]

Meanwhile, the Fifteenth Amendment, which prohibited states from denying the right to vote on the grounds of race, color, or previous condition of servitude, was ratified on February 3, 1870, making the Constitution "truly color blind for the first time in U.S. History," even while it, according to the Stanton-Anthony camp (which now included Isabella), established "the most odious form of aristocracy the world has ever seen: an aristocracy of sex."[13]

That same month, Susan B. Anthony celebrated her fiftieth birthday, and a New York reception drew Henry Ward Beecher, the Tiltons, and Isabella, who helped plan the party. At his wife's request, John Hooker, who stayed in Hartford to work, wrote a poem and sent son Ned running to the post office so that it would reach the party in time.

Ah, fearless Susan, even then
Thou saw'st in dreams us horrid men —
Our laws made only for aggression,
Thy gentle sex in sad repression,
The boys unlovely, girls unloved;
No wonder thy young heart was moved,
And that thou vow'dst an infant vow,
Which thou has kept from then till now,
To keep us savage men indicted
Until that dreadful wrong was righted.
Susan, thou well that vow hast kept;
No nun in lonelier cell e'er slept;
On lonely ways thy walk thou'st taken;
All common earthly joys forsaken;

— Sweet home, to none more dear than thee,

The charm of prattling infancy,

All that thy loving heart could bless,

Thy heart of rarest tenderness.[14]

That same month, John wrote an essay favorable to women's suffrage for the *Hartford Courant*, in which he said how women would vote didn't concern him, only that they did vote. He also called Stanton an advocate for easy divorce, a description with which she took issue, and she wrote Hooker correcting his assumption, saying she hated and repudiated the phrase and "the promiscuous relations it seems to indicate." She also wrote: "What I have always insisted on is, that the laws of marriage and divorce, whatever they are, shall bear equally on man and woman, which never will be the case until woman has an equal voice in their enactment and administration."[15]

Meanwhile, Isabella began a grueling speaking tour, planned right down to how many tracts she needed to carry for distribution along the way.[16] As the Beecher family had proselytized on their way to Ohio so many years ago, Isabella began to spread the word about the suffrage movement. The energy she'd previously spent writing copious letters to family members, she now devoted to writing speeches.

The tour took Isabella to Illinois, Iowa, and Kansas to address suffrage groups and set up local organizations to push for enfranchisement. She began planning another suffrage meeting in Connecticut and asked Stanton to speak, but said she wanted Stanton to focus on suffrage and not divorce or free love. She wrote Stanton that if these conditions were not favorable, Isabella would speak in her stead. If the offer surprised Anthony and Stanton, they appreciated Isabella taking the lead.[17]

From minutes recorded by Frances Burr, the Connecticut Woman Suffrage Association met in September 1870, at Hartford's Allyn Hall. John Hooker was named treasurer. Isabella contented herself with serving on the executive committee, which voted to meet monthly. The members discussed having meetings around the state in places like New Haven, Stratford, and Willimantic. The following month, Isabella spoke at a meeting in Bridgeport, and Burr, the recording secretary, wrote that her speech was a "decided success."[18]

In November, Isabella wrote her daughter Alice that Isabella's brother Charles had visited and they'd discussed Spiritualism. Charles was concerned it was of the devil, though he would later incorporate Spiritualism into his Christian theology. They also discussed rumors of infidelity regarding their older brother Henry Ward, who was enjoying great success at Plymouth.

"And when he told me he was sure there was a conspiracy against Henry — he being utterly innocent, which was of the devil surely, my confidence in his judgment of Spiritualism was weakened — especially as he acknowledged the phenomenon to be largely true," she wrote.

With the Hartford meetings attracting more attention, Isabella began to cast her eye toward a larger stage, and other suffragists noticed. In December of 1870, Martha C. Wright, sister of Lucretia Mott, wrote to Stanton that the "Beecher conceit surpasses all understanding."[19] However, that conceit allowed Isabella to take on more work, which was much appreciated by warhorses of the movement. Stanton wrote to forty-eight-year-old Isabella in January 1871: "You are younger & have more leisure. . . . I am too burthened with cares already."[20]

Isabella's midlife entry into public life would at least have made sense to other Beechers. As her nephew Lyman Beecher Stowe wrote in 1934: "Like her eldest sister, Catharine, and, in lesser degree, the other members of the family, she believed that anything was her business, all the way from rearranging her daughter-in-law's furniture to changing the legal and civic status of women, which gave her opportunity to help either an individual, a group of individuals, or humanity at large."[21]

In preparation for the third annual National Woman Suffrage Association meeting in 1871 in D.C., Isabella offered to take over for the more experienced workers, which amused them greatly. Stanton said, "[L]et us exalt Mrs. Hooker, who thinks she could manage the cause more discreetly, more genteelly than we do. . . . I am ready to rest and see the salvation of the Lord."[22] Anthony responded that Isabella was like every new convert to every new reform, and added, "I have no doubt but each of these Apostles in turn, as he came into the ranks, believed he could improve upon Christ's methods."[23] In fact, Isabella wanted to turn the larger suffrage movement toward a more sedate, publicly acceptable crowd — not as a means of public relations, but more in keeping with Isabella's own attitude about reform.

Stanton decided to skip the Washington meeting and continue with her lecture circuit. She sent Isabella $100 for expenses, but Anthony insisted Stanton come. Acting as a go-between, Isabella wrote Stanton a tactless letter that said, "I don't know what to say. You will talk more forcibly than any one else and in committee you are invaluable. Still, I want your money, and I could do without you on the platform."[24]

Meanwhile, Catharine continued her assaults on the movement. In December, she debated Mary Livermore, a member of the American Woman Suffrage Association, in Boston. Catharine presented no new information: Men had the power, and women had the power to influence them. Most women did not want the vote, she said, and men would not relinquish it until women demanded it.[25]

For her trouble, Catharine saw her performance critiqued and found wanting in the January edition of *Woodhull & Claflin's Weekly*. The newspaper, founded by sisters Victoria Woodhull and Tennessee (Tennie) Claflin, decried "the Catharine Beechers who now clog the wheels of progress, and stand forth as the enemies of their sex . . . doing their utmost to cement the chains of their degradation, giving to man the same power over them that he possesses over his horses and dogs."[26] Catharine was undeterred. In her 1872 book, *Woman's Profession as Mother and Educator* (subtitled *With Views in Opposition to Woman's Suffrage*), Catharine wrote about her mother, Roxanna, and the local women of Litchfield — including the wife of Judge Tapping Reeve, her aunt Esther Beecher, and Miss Sarah Pierce, her first teacher — and how, though none had the education of their male peers, "I used to hear my mother and aunts discussing a variety of literary and scientific topics, and especially remember their enthusiastic interest in the new discoveries of chemistry by Lavoisier, and their practical test experiments in the kitchen and study."[27]

Surely these unlettered women were an example for modern women similarly deprived of formal education. The point, wrote Catharine, was that women unfettered by the cares of the (male) world were free to educate themselves more fully. She added:

A variety of intellectual training which is pursued in connection with such interesting practical results as woman's employment involve, tends to produce a vigorous and well-balanced mind, far more than devotion to one or two professional pursuits such as the business of most men requires. And even in science and literature, we not infrequently find some of the most learned men entirely deficient in intellectual balance and executive power; while their less learned mothers or wives are respected as wise and practical counselors.[28]

Isabella discovered that her sister's detractor, Victoria Woodhull, a suffragist, Spiritualist, and one of the few female stockbrokers in New York, would be in Washington at the same time that she would be at the third annual National Woman Suffrage Association meeting. Woodhull would testify before the House Judiciary Committee that the Fourteenth and Fifteenth Amendments already gave women the vote, and she would be the first woman to so testify.

The *New York Herald* reported that "there is no disguising the fact that the woman suffrage advocates are making headway in Washington."[29] Isabella and others met for three hours to decide how to respond to the testimony of Woodhull, who was appearing without the sponsorship of a suffrage group. Already weary of tussling with the American Woman Suffrage Association, the group was hesitant to stir up more opposition. While in D.C., Isabella was staying with Sen. Samuel C. Pomeroy, a Kansas Republican. She was unenthusiastic about attending Woodhull's testimony, given the woman's reputation for advocating free love (and not under the guise of divorce reform, either), but Pomeroy convinced her that, considering Woodhull's growing notoriety, Isabella needed to attend. Perhaps Isabella was drawn to the woman for her criticism of Catharine, who was becoming more intransigent. Perhaps the final straw was Anthony, too, encouraged her to meet Woodhull.[30] Whatever her motivation, Isabella met with Woodhull, chatted with her for two hours, and thus was born a friendship that confounded Isabella's friends and family. Isabella wrote that she was immediately impressed

> . . . profoundly, and in a manner I could never describe, with the conviction that she was heaven sent for the rescue of woman from her pit of subjection.

She has ever since appealed to me as then — a womanly woman, yet less a woman than an embodiment of pure thought, soul and reason — a prophetess, full of visions and messages to the people which it would be woe unto her to refrain from proclaiming, even though martyrdom were sure to follow. She is an idealist — a visionary perhaps — but she is without consciousness of self and absolutely without selfishness. Her standard of benevolence is unapproachable to most of us — and she has lived up to it.[31]

After Woodhull gave her speech before the House committee, the other suffragists in attendance invited her to the national convention to repeat her message. The more squeamish of them were won over by Woodhull's keen mind, and newspapers of the day immediately trumpeted Woodhull's arrival on the national stage.[32] A *New York Herald* story focused on Woodhull and her sister's brokerage firm, followed rather quickly by a laudatory story in the *New York Sunday News*, in which the writer congratulated Woodhull and her sister for their success in opening to "female minds a great outlet for their present pent-up energy."[33]

The tone of the coverage would change shortly.

Woodhull was a rare woman. She ran for president. She was a Spiritualist medium. She possessed inordinate personal magnetism and impressive speaking skills. Her weekly newspaper, which had criticized Catharine Beecher, made *The Revolution* look tame, yet if granted a face-to-face meeting, she usually was able to win people over.[34] In 1870, Cornelius Vanderbilt, also a Spiritualist, helped set up Woodhull's brokerage near Wall Street, and she'd been financially successful, though accumulation of wealth appeared to be only part of her goal. That same year, she started publishing, and the paper adopted the slogan "Progress! Free Thought! Untrammeled Lives! Breaking the Way for Future Generations!" Later, the newspaper would become a source of muckraking journalism. Woodhull advocated women's vote, as well as Spiritualism, birth control, and free love. Yet despite that last cause, the buttoned-up Isabella found in her a soul mate and was calling her "my darling queen" by February 1871.[35] Isabella maintained her devotion even a month later, when Woodhull was advocating licensed prostitution.

If Isabella was supposed to bring a sense of decorum to the New York wing of the suffrage movement, in Woodhull she brought, instead, a hammer. One suffragist wrote to Isabella: "If Mrs. Woodhull was a real lady, she would refuse to hold office. A repentant Magdalene I can accept — even in office and before the world — but a woman who 'glories in her shame' — never!"[36]

Her sisters were apoplectic. Harriet, especially, was baffled by her sister's new friend.[37] She described Woodhull as "a snake who should be given a good swat with a shovel."[38] Isabella, however, was firm in her belief that Woodhull was special, and she asked that her sisters meet her — so that, she told them, they could convert her to Christianity. She arranged for a meeting between Catharine and Woodhull, which occurred in February 1871 in Central Park. It did not go well. Woodhull told the imposing older woman that her brother had strayed outside his marital vows. Catharine denied it and even threatened to strike Woodhull, but instead she walked away.

Isabella was hardly bothered by her oldest sister's response. In fact, she appeared to take pride in her new friend's ability to put Catharine in her place. She wrote later that month: "Catharine returned last night. She saw Victoria and, attacking her on the marriage question, got such a black eye as filled her with horror and amazement. I had to laugh inwardly at her relation of the interview and am now waiting for her to cool down!"[39]

Perhaps Isabella saw in Woodhull a forthrightness she thought she lacked. Then, too, Woodhull was a vocal suffragist. She'd been a Spiritualist for years. And she possessed a unique ability to sway opinion. Any one of these attributes would have been incredibly appealing to Isabella.

When Isabella wouldn't listen to their pleas, her sisters begged Isabella to come "back to God and away from that harlot."[40] John Hooker, who rarely spoke against his wife's actions, was concerned as well, and he sent letters seeking more information about this woman who held his wife in such thrall. Isabella sent letters also, including one to Anthony in which she wrote that she was perplexed that her family so vehemently refused to acknowledge her friend's righteousness. "I could make pages of commendations of her manners," she wrote, and insisted that criticism of her new friend never came from people who'd met Woodhull, but only from those who drew their conclusions from negative press reports.[41] In a March 11, 1871, letter to Anthony, she wrote, "I can't guess who is really behind her nor what will become of herself and paper and party if she has any. You will send this I hope to Mrs. Stanton and . . . she will be able to make some examination of this mysterious family. Of Tennie C. I hear the most dreadful stories — yet she has the face of a sweet innocent child."[42]

A few days later, on March 16, 1871, Isabella wrote to Mary and Harriet: "Do you believe I could have taken her to my heart as I have done, if I did not believe her true and pure?"

About the same time, Stanton wrote Martha C. Wright that she intended to research Woodhull — particularly in regard to her relationships with a series of well-known men. Already the subject of accusations of loose morals, the high-wattage Woodhull, in Stanton's view, may have been seen as bringing the wrong kind of attention to the movement. She wrote to Wright:

> We shall begin with the men. Now I have heard gossip of undue familiarity with persons of the opposite sex — relative to Beecher, Higginson, Butler, Carpenter, Pomeroy — and before I shall consent to an arraignment of Woodhull or any other earnest woman worker . . . I shall insist upon the closest investigation into all the scandals afloat about those men — not one of whom have I heard Mrs. Hooker or any other woman express any fears of accepting whatever they may say or do for us.[43]

Meanwhile, Anthony wrote Isabella:

> When we begin to search records, past or present — of those who bring brains or cash to our work for enfranchising women — it shall be with those of the men — not the women, and not a woman — not Mrs. Woodhull — until every insinuation of gossip of Beecher, Pomeroy, Butler, Carpenter shall be fully investigated — and each of them shall have proven to your and our satisfaction — that he never flirted or trifled with or desecrated any specimen of Womanhood. No! No!! Mrs. Hooker — it won't do to begin that — are we more accused — Christ repeats to you and to me and to all women — "Let her who never sinned in spirit or in act cast the first stone"— not until we chastise and refuse men will I consent to question women — all of an enslaved class — that we ever dream of such a thing. . . . You see the theory you propose for the Woodhull Scandal applied to men, living or dead is simply ridiculous."[44]

Meanwhile, the work continued state by state. An April 1871 Connecticut suffrage meeting was held at Isabella's house and lasted six hours, from 3 to 9 p.m. There, Isabella spoke about Woodhull, and the treasurer announced the group was $1,600 in arrears — no small sum considering American workers at the time were earning less than $1 a day.

In May 1871, Woodhull spoke — over the objections of some — at a National Woman Suffrage Association anniversary in New York's Apollo Hall. Horace Greeley's powerful *New York Tribune* was now fully engaged in its battle against suffrage, in part because Greeley felt that embracing someone like Woodhull meant embracing free love. Earlier, the newspaper had given the suffrage movement cautious support, but it now labeled the suffragists' efforts as "interference."[45] Greeley peppered his publication with headlines such as "Free Love Is Free Lust." Woodhull fired back in print and called Greeley's home life "a sort of domestic hell."[46] (Greeley was spending little time at home with his wife, the former Mary Young Cheney, who had been a Connecticut schoolteacher. He preferred to spend time in New York boarding rooms.)

And then things moved into an even stranger realm for Woodhull. A few days after she shot back at Greeley, Woodhull's mother, Roxana Claflin, brought charges against Col. James Harvey Blood, Woodhull's second husband, for alienating the affections of Woodhull and her sister from her parents — ostensibly because Blood had "drawn them into the realm of social radicalism."[47] If newspaper editors needed any further ammunition against Woodhull, this was of sizable caliber. The tide of ink began to turn with a vengeance.

Isabella, however, stood firm. In a May 23, 1871, letter to Sara Burger Stearns, the first president of the Minnesota Woman Suffrage Association, she wrote:

> I do not understand all her views — and I have had no time to ask her concerning them — nor to study these new social theories . . . but they know as well that if they can frighten us into disavowing any sympathy with such a powerful woman as Mrs. W. is proving, both because of her own brain and heart and because of her command of money . . . then they have dealt a severe blow at the whole suffrage movement and set it back years.

Her concerns aside, Stanton at first also defended Woodhull, though more as a matter of principle than any personal fondness for her. Such attacks on suffragists were not unusual, and Stanton would not stand for them. Anthony had long since become skeptical of Woodhull's motivations. Stanton, too, eventually dropped her support of Woodhull, but their early difference over the woman created a rift that lasted for years.[48]

In June, the Connecticut Woman Suffrage Association voted to send a copy of the 1871 tract *Legal Disabilities of Married Women* to every state legislator. The tract was the product of George A. Hickox, of Litchfield, and included essays by Sir William Blackstone, Oliver Wendell Holmes Jr., and John Marshall, among others.

Back home, if Isabella ever considered wavering in her newfound enthusiasm for women's suffrage, she had only to reread the personal letters that began streaming into her Hartford home, including one from a Mrs. S. H. Graves dated October 24, 1871. Mrs. Graves had lived in Norfolk, Connecticut, for seventeen years and was the second wife, she wrote, of an "old-fashioned farmer" who did not want children, which left her with "only the dreary routine of household cares to occupy my mind." Her husband, she wrote, went to town to spend his money while "I *amuse* myself by mending his old pants."

Mrs. Graves continued:

> I write to you as a friend, for you are a friend to us. . . . Of course, such a man is bitterly opposed to "woman's rights." I have no money and but a few clothes. He forbids my giving anything away, so anything is *his* and nothing mine. In short I am nothing but a housekeeper without wages doing *all* the work of the family. I have no fondness for this kind of life, but on the contrary have as keen a relish for amusement, concerts . . . as any woman in the city of Hartford.
>
> Now Mrs. Hooker, please give me a little advice. Is it my duty to spend my life in this way? Would it be wrong for me to go to Hartford this winter for a few weeks or to some other place where people *live*? Have you any friend who would give me a pleasant home, and an opportunity to attend an occasional entertainment in exchange for my services? If you ask what

I can do I reply I can do what women in the country usually do. I can sew, or do anything necessary to be done can take care of children and teach them...

My husband's father buried his *fourth wife* a few days since. She laid down the burden of life willingly at sixty-two years of age. He will doubtless marry again soon, as it *costs too* much to hire a housekeeper.

She wrote that Isabella was her only confidante and added that her husband has "bonds, stocks and notes and to these he is wedded."

In October 1871, in preparation for a November visit to Hartford by Woodhull, Isabella wrote an article for her local *Courant*, which she eventually followed up with a letter to her Nook Farm neighbor Charles Dudley Warner, novelist and then-editor of the newspaper. If he couldn't print an article she'd written without negative comment, she wrote, then he should return it. Of her friend Woodhull, Isabella wrote she had "heard this great souled and pure hearted woman . . . enough and do not care to provoke further unfavorable comment. She must bide her time and I can wait as well as she."

On October 15, 1871, Stanton wrote to Isabella: "I am glad you have burned all your bridges and feel ready to work with all the daughters of Eve." However, the daughters of Eve remained split over Woodhull. Isabella's involvement with Woodhull moved one New Haven church to withdraw its invitation for Isabella to preach. It was a disappointing postponement for Isabella, who aimed to bring suffrage into law through faith groups.

In advance of the Hartford visit by Woodhull — now called "The Woodhull" in the press — Catharine wrote to the governor's office requesting that he ban the speech, but he refused.[49] She also wrote the *Courant* decrying free love and calling on Christians of Hartford not to allow it to be discussed in public. She signed her letter "A Lady of Hartford." To this, Isabella wrote to Anna Savery, with whom she stayed when she traveled to Iowa:

. . . the feeling on this Woodhull matter has nearly killed me. You at the West have no conception of Connecticut phariseeism & bigotry nor of what I have suffered in consequence. . . . I am driven to death — & just now my sister Catharine is attacking Mrs. W's private character infamously so as to keep people from going to hear her — the result is she will have a jam next week & last week had a good house in a stormy night. But it is dreadful this having foes in your own household — if you can escape that you can live.[50]

Isabella correctly predicted the turnout. Some seven hundred people came to Hartford's opera house to hear Woodhull, who drolly read Catharine's letter from the stage and said she hoped to exceed her detractor in Christian living.[51]

Woodhull, meanwhile, was dropping hints in her newspaper of a huge, unspoken scandal — that Henry Ward had strayed outside his marriage — and Theodore Tilton, the preacher's protégé and husband of his rumored paramour, arranged for accuser and accused to meet.[52] Woodhull later wrote about the meeting and shared the scandalous news that the respected minister kept a spirit table at Plymouth Church and thought current laws on marriage were obsolete. When Woodhull asked why Henry Ward didn't preach this latter thought from the pulpit, Henry Ward reportedly said he would preach to empty seats — "milk for babies, meat for strong men."[53] Woodhull's report of the meeting included Henry Ward dropping to his knees, taking her face in his hands, crying and begging her not to publish the rumor of his infidelity.[54]

In January 1872, Isabella, Stanton, and Anthony argued before the Senate Judiciary Committee that the word *sex* should be included in the Fifteenth Amendment.[55] They'd originally asked to speak before the entire Senate but had been referred to the committee, since protocol, the women were told, prevented them from addressing that august body as a whole. Isabella was the chief speaker.[56] Drawing from Acts 22:28, she told the committee, "For my own part I will never willingly consent to vote under a special enactment conferring rights of citizenship upon me as an alien. Like Paul, I was free born. 'With great Sum obtained I this freedom.'"[57]

While they were lobbying, Woodhull proposed an Equal Rights Party, with herself as the presidential candidate. She named abolition stalwart Frederick Douglass — without his knowledge — as her running mate.[58] Douglass, who earlier had split with Stanton and Anthony over the passage of the Fifteenth Amendment, let it be known that he was unable to run.[59] Anthony thought the ticket was insanity.[60] Isabella, however, was entranced.[61]

A May meeting of the National Woman Suffrage Association ended with Anthony having a janitor shut off the lights to keep Woodhull from taking over.[62] What a successful takeover by Woodhull would have looked like is anybody's guess, and Anthony, for one, was unwilling to speculate. "A sad day for me," Anthony wrote in her diary. "All came near being lost. Our ship was so nearly stranded by leaving the helm to others, that we rescued it only by a hair's breadth."[63]

That same month, Isabella wrote Anthony: "Did you suppose that I was cutting loose from Victoria and her strange and heady followers for all time, and going on a sailing voyage of my own, never to cruise with them again?" She added: "My dear husband is well over the Ocean, where he can't be troubled by my radicalism, I shall join . . . if I think best, when the time comes."

When it came to Woodhull, Isabella would not be moved, and Stanton worried that Woodhull would take over. In a March 13, 1872, letter to Isabella, she wrote:

I tell you I feel utterly disheartened — not that our cause is going to die or be defeated, but as to my place and work. Mrs. Woodhull has the advantage of us because she has the newspaper, and she persistently means to run our craft into her port and none other. If she were influenced by women spirits, either in the body or out of it, in the direction she steers, I might consent to be a mere sail-hoister for her; but as it is, she is wholly owned and dominated by men spirits and I spurn the control of the whole lot of them, just precisely the same when reflected through her woman's tongue and pen as if they spoke directly for themselves.[64]

But to Isabella, Woodhull was a sweet victim of vicious people. Public censure certainly did not dissuade her. She'd seen her older sister Catharine — an admittedly difficult woman to like — being hounded for her public stances, and she'd seen Harriet's social stock drop precipitously after the publication of her Byron book. Isabella understood that public women might make unpopular public choices. (For her part, Catharine wrote decrying Isabella's "ignorance and mistaken zeal" and her inability to see "how much moral power is gained by taking a subordinate place — as the Bible and Nature both teach is her true position."[65])

In fact, few things energized a Beecher more than public disdain, but Isabella's enthusiasm started to annoy even longtime friends. Mary Abigail Dodge, a Beecher family friend, wrote to another friend that "Mrs. Isabella Beecher Hooker is here fashing [sic] herself with the suffrage, and doing all that a bright, good and beautiful woman can to make herself a bore."[66]

Away from public attention, Isabella wanted to make sure Woodhull knew she did not subscribe to the younger woman's more radical ideas on marriage. She wrote Woodhull in July 1872: "Lest you should misunderstand my position on the question of Social Freedom let me state it briefly here. Human law should not attempt to regulate marriage — this is a sacrament of Souls owing allegiance to God and their own consciences only. But the ideal marriage is between two only."[67]

As fierce as had been her family discussions growing up, Isabella wasn't prepared for Harriet's hasty retreat from the suffrage movement in the wake of public criticism. Harriet had stood by a friend like Lady Byron, but perhaps the negative reaction to that gesture had dampened her taste for public brawls. To cement her retreat, Harriet wrote *My Wife and I; or, Harry Henderson's History*, a satirical look at the suffrage movement as a whole, and Woodhull and her sister in particular. In that book, serialized in Henry Ward's *Christian Union* newspaper, Isabella's character, a Mrs. Stella Cerulean, is a naïve woman enthralled with Woodhull's character, known as Audacia Dang-yereyes.[68] Harriet even managed a few shots at Anthony and Stanton, who'd so recently wooed her to the cause. "I trust," the narrator, a sympathetic journalist, writes on page 3, "that Miss Anthony and Mrs. Stanton, and all the prophetesses of our day, will remark the humility and propriety of my title. It is not I and My Wife — oh no! It is My Wife and I. What am I, and what is my father's house, that I should go before my wife in anything?" It was a sentimental novel that landed squarely on the side of disenfranchisement.[69] Audacia lives up to her name, and Mrs. Cerulean and her colleagues, says one character, "have long since risen above anything like common sense; all their sense is of the most uncommon kind, and relates to a region somewhere up in the clouds, where everything is made to match. They live in an imaginary world, and reason with imaginary reason, and see people through imaginary spectacles, and have glorious good times all the while."

When another character allows that Audacia is a "tramp," and Mrs. Cerulean is a respectable woman, he is told that Mrs. Cerulean, when confronted with this claim, said, "Do you men ever inquire into the character of people that you unite with to carry your purposes? You join with anybody that will help you, without regard to antecedents!"[70]

Explaining herself to Henry Ward for *My Wife*, Harriet sought to defend men: "This is my plan and being to some extent a woman's rights woman, as I am to some extent, something of almost everything that goes — I shall have a right to say a word or two on the other side."[71]

But Catharine did not ostracize her youngest sister Isabella. For her, family loyalty trumped other concerns, even if she vehemently disagreed with her sister's public stances.[72]

However, the other Beechers had not exhausted all their weapons. As Isabella became further enmeshed in the suffrage movement and in her passionate friendship with Woodhull, some Beechers — Henry Ward and Harriet among them — began questioning her sanity. Their concerns may have started as family supposition but escalated into a public denouncement. Which Beecher floated the original rumors questioning Isabella's sanity isn't clear. John Hooker suspected it was Harriet, but she denied involvement when he confronted her.[73]

For Isabella's part, the enfranchisement of women was important enough to risk public ridicule — though she had no idea what that would cost her later.

Nor would her opponents let up on their public stance against her push for the vote. In early 1871, Isabella and Francis Gillette argued about suffrage in a series of front-page articles in their local newspaper, the *Courant*, and Catharine could not resist joining in with a letter on February 1, in which she argued that suffrage for women was in no way a universal goal: "This is not true either of myself or of a large majority of my family and personal friends, most of whom would regard such a measure as an *act of injustice and oppression*, forcing conscientious women to assume the responsibilities of the civil state, when they can so imperfectly meet the many and more important duties of the family state, and the connected ministries of instruction and benevolence."[74] It was not her only letter decrying her younger sister's passion.

But Isabella would not back down. She felt that women should enjoy freedom of speech, regardless of their backgrounds — and this may have

cal. As Laura Hanft Korobkin described the trial in her 1998 book, *Criminal Conversations: Sentimentality and Nineteenth-Century Legal Stories of Adultery*: "Transformed from a titillating, gossipy set of newspaper stories into a formal trial that became an increasingly undecidable interrogation of hypocrisy, the trial touched one of the country's rawest nerves. Following each day's testimony in their newspapers, Americans saw not just a beloved figure and longstanding role model on trial, but also the reliability of their own methods of judgment."[83]

Woodhull's timing was impeccable. As much as he was beloved at Plymouth, Henry Ward had acquired more than a few Spiritualists among his enemies, as well as a good number of slaveholders and men and women who opposed suffrage. Spiritualists had expressed concerns that a religious leader such as Henry Ward could garner such devotion from his followers.[84] The zeal with which the parishioners exalted their leader was disturbing to Spiritualists, who shunned hierarchy and considered Henry Ward's role abuse of hierarchy at its most blatant.

Earlier, Theodore Tilton had argued publicly with Henry Ward over how to treat slave-owning Christians. Tilton thought his minister should take a harder line condemning those who professed to belong to the faith yet still clung to human chattel. He had aligned himself with the more radical New York wing of the suffrage movement, while Henry Ward led the Boston branch. Tilton agreed with Woodhull about free love, and this was a public stand Henry Ward could not countenance. (Later in the trial, Elizabeth Tilton would say that her husband's characterization of himself as a victim was a "lamentable satire upon the household where he himself, years before, laid the corner stone of Free Love, and desecrated its altars up to the time of my departure; so that the atmosphere was not only godless, but impure for my children."[85]) Tilton was replaced as editor of *The Independent*, but only after Henry Ward gave him $5,000 — a considerable sum — to start his own newspaper. When Tilton accused Henry Ward of making improper advances toward his wife in the course of the scandal, he did so in the context of a simmering rivalry and the acute feelings of a young man who was heartily disappointed by his mentor.

Both John and Isabella knew of the rumors of Henry Ward's infidelity long before Woodhull's revelations, though they hadn't confronted the minister because Isabella preferred to think her brother innocent.[86] In January 1870, Joseph Howard, editor of the *New York Sun* and son of family friend Susan Howard, wrote John Hooker that allegations of Henry Ward's affair were well known — and mostly accepted as true — in Brooklyn. The editor's list of those in the know included Stanton, about whom Hooker wrote, "From what little I have seen of her I do not fancy her at all. She is a bold and strong thinker but she has not a refined nature. She is however a pure woman, and seeking to promote purity in others. There is not a particle of sensuality that we generally regard as incident to 'free-lovism' about her."[87] Various suffragists besides Stanton knew as well, but they'd dismissed the information as so much rumor.[88]

If Isabella wanted to believe the best of her brother, John Hooker operated under no such belief. He suspected early on that Henry Ward had breeched his faith, and in October 1872, while traveling, he wrote a dramatic plea to Isabella, whom he feared would choose family over fidelity:

> And if I never see you again, do I beg of you, heed my earnest request
> that you will in no circumstances defend, or excuse, or palliate, the awful
> sin of our brother H. . . . If the ship was going down & I could send two
> outcries that would reach you — one would be of undying love & the other a
> supplication that you will never, by one word, defend the action of H. Take
> these as my last words.

He said his brother-in-law had sinned "deep & black." Isabella finally could only agree with her husband, and she sought Henry Ward's confession in letters and in private meetings. Her stance confounded the rest of her family, which was so accustomed to a unified front on personal matters. In the beginning, Harriet attributed Isabella's insistence that their brother had sinned to the evil influence of Woodhull. Harriet wrote a family friend in December 1872, certain that it wasn't Isabella seeking a confession, but Woodhull, whom she called a witch: "No one could understand the secret of her influence over my poor sister — incredible infatuation continuing even now. I trust that God will in some way deliver her for she was and is a lovely good woman & before this witch took possession of her we were all so happy together."

On November 8, 1872, Henry Ward wrote to Isabella:

My dear Sister Belle, Your great heart is a refuge to those who need sympathy. But you take too serious a view. At present you will help me most as will all my family, friends by a calm silence. These miscreants have shamelessly distorted and defiled the specks of truth there were, and they do not know about the root or stem of things on which the reality stands. God knows, God Comforts. God will defend and deliver. . . . I have no philosophy to unfold and no new theory of society. The matter has already sunk out of sight in NY. My own people are calm and noble. The infernal machine will have exploded in vain I think and hope. For your love, confidence and sympathy I more than thank you. You are nearer to me as a sister and companion than ever, or than ever could have been without this great need.

Lovingly yours, HWB

From one retelling, Isabella could not accept that her brother was innocent after he wouldn't discuss the charges with her and after he refused to join her in a reunified women's movement, according to a letter written by a G. H. Beecher in the *Brooklyn Eagle*.[89] Later that month, Mark Twain returned to Hartford after a three-month absence and told his wife, Olivia, that she should not speak to Mrs. Hooker and that, if he saw her, he would tell his neighbor why.[90]

Undeterred, Isabella, with typical Beecher surety, offered to come to Brooklyn to read a confession from Henry Ward and to take over Plymouth Church while he righted himself. Her offer was rebuffed, and for a time Harriet was installed at the church to make sure Isabella didn't try to take the pulpit without Henry Ward's approval.[91]

Isabella and Henry Ward continued to correspond, though, and in December, Isabella wrote John from New York that she'd met with Henry Ward, that she couldn't go into the details of their meeting, but that she'd spent hours talking to both the minister and to Theodore Tilton. Afterward, she remained confused but had "some hope of persuading to truthfulness all round." She even walked to church with Elizabeth Tilton, and they "met in a long kiss of love and trust."[92] She wrote that Henry Ward told her he'd always felt closest to her of all the siblings, but that closeness "can't be even now."[93]

It wasn't until the following year that Henry Ward broke his public silence to pronounce his innocence — too late for most suffragists — while Woodhull was defending herself in court for publishing her charges.

In the middle of the furor, Isabella published a book, *Womanhood: Its Sanctities and Fidelities*, in which she argued two points that might have been inspired by her brother's predicament. One, she insisted men cool their passion and show sexual restraint. Two, she suggested that women of a higher calling show compassion to their more degraded sisters (read: prostitutes). The book "treated of the marriage relation and of the education of children to lives of purity, in a courageous, yet delicate way."[94] That same year, Mark Twain wrote *The Temperance Crusade and Woman's Rights*, in which he said: "I wish we might have a woman's party now, and see how that would work. I feel persuaded that in extending the suffrage to women this country could lose absolutely nothing and might gain a great deal."[95]

Unfortunately, the essay was not published until after his death in 1910, with the vote still a decade away.

The nation could not get enough of Beecher-Tilton. The *New York Times* carried at least 105 stories and thirty-seven editorials about the scandal during the summer and fall of 1874 — including seventeen page 1 references.[96] Isabella soon joined John in Europe, where she found the story on the front page of Europe's papers as well. When she arrived back in England after a tour of the continent, a stack of clippings awaited her.[97] Along with the ever-present news stories, there was no escaping the condemnation raining down for her support of Woodhull from her fellow suffragists and her family.[98]

She also couldn't escape her family's suppositions about her sanity. Some of her siblings had started consulting doctors on her behalf.[99] And the Beechers weren't Isabella's only accusers. Others floated rumors that included speculations about the inordinately close relationship enjoyed by Isabella and Woodhull. A meeting with Theodore Tilton resulted in (said Tilton) Isabella bursting into tears as the man threatened to accuse her of "adultery and criminal insanity."[100] (Later, her descendants would limit access to Isabella's diary, so great was the fear that the pages would reveal her as being less than sane.[101]) The public carping moved Stanton to write to a bewildered Isabella on November 3, 1873, that "there is too much money locked up in Beecher's success for him to be sacrificed. The public especially those who have a financial interest in this matter would rather see every woman in the nation sacrificed than one of their idols of gold. They think if they can separate us from one from another, prevent us writing or meeting, sowing seeds of discourse all around they can manage the public."

She continued:

> We are in the midst of a great social battle that will end in the absolute freedom of woman. . . . I have been sacrificed in this matter as much as you — have lost friends in the family, and . . . I am faced every day with some phase of "the Woodhull" come up by word and letter until it turns, I feel like shirking everything disagreeable. But through it all I see one thing, we must stand by each other. Women must be as true to women as men are to men.

On November 19, 1875, Isabella wrote about the lives of male reformers, "from Abraham down to present time." She elaborated: "They had marked peculiarities to say the least — individualities . . . which history calls faith, genius, magnetism, eloquence and so on. Women reformers cannot escape the first misjudgments of their world if they would win the later verdict."

On November 27, 1873, Charles Beecher wrote to Isabella that though the family appreciated her moral stand, they "could not approve your course toward Henry, even supposing the charge were true, a supposition we never for a moment admit as possible."

In response to the attention, in June 1874, Henry Ward appointed a committee to explore the allegations, though the members were generally friends and not inclined to give a rigorous investigation. Mark Twain wrote to his friend the Reverend Joseph H. Twichell, "If Mr. B. had done this in the first place no doubt it would have been better."[102]

John Hooker met with Harriet and Mary in Hartford, where both sisters argued that Isabella cease her public denouncing of her brother. If she didn't, Mary declared that she wouldn't be welcome until she'd stopped "all discourse with Mrs. Stanton and Miss Anthony and all that set."[103]

In a September 23, 1874, letter to Isabella, John said a statement by his brother-in-law only further convinced him of the man's guilt and he didn't understand Isabella's privately voiced hope that Henry Ward might be innocent. "Your belief in his innocence sounds strange in view of the last disclosures," he wrote. "His case has never looked so bad." He maintained, however, that she'd chosen foolishly to align herself with Woodhull, who had brought nothing but trouble to the family. Isabella seemed at least aware that her continued patronage of Woodhull would only mean trouble for her. In a November 5, 1874, letter to Mary Porter Chamberlin, a Nook Farm neighbor who was serving as an intermediary between the siblings, Isabella wrote that she had avoided, for the sake of her brother, any contact with Woodhull while in Europe — "but I do assure you that I had no sense of irritation against her because of her being the mouth-piece of the charges against my brother."[104]

If most of her family was questioning Isabella, her local suffragist friends supported her. At the end of 1874, Isabella was elected president of the Connecticut Woman Suffrage Association.

The inquiry within Plymouth Church cleared Henry Ward of the charges but excommunicated Theodore Tilton. He sued, and a trial began in January 1875 that lasted six months and ended in a hung jury.[105] It was far less than an exoneration for Henry Ward, and it would be years before the family would repair the wound — and, for Mary, the wound would never quite heal. She wanted Isabella to apologize and admit that Henry Ward had remained true to his marital vows, but Isabella could do neither.[106]

Imagine Isabella as the trial was going on. Her husband — generally the one person on whom she could count for support — was angry that she'd aligned herself with such a dangerous woman as Woodhull. Many of her siblings were not talking to her. The suffrage work was stalled. At this low point, Isabella experienced a profound Spiritualist event. In a Paris hotel room, she was visited by her long-dead mother, Harriet Porter Beecher — only this Harriet Porter was healthy and was able to offer her daughter support she sorely needed. Harriet Porter reassured Isabella that she was taking the right moral stand, and that one day her half-brother would kneel before Isabella and ask forgiveness. She also told her daughter that she would one day lead a matriarchal government, and — mindful of a woman's place even beyond the grave — Harriet Porter shared some household tips.[107]

Isabella told no one of the visit, though she ruminated on it extensively in her journal, and she began devoting much of her time to meeting with mediums and Spiritualists who could explain to her the phenomenon.

Spiritualism was considered fairly avant-garde during the middle of the nineteenth century. The pain of losing so many young men during the Civil War — plus a high infant mortality rate — made the thought of sustaining contact with a loved one most appealing. Traditional Christians had the hope of seeing their loved ones in heaven. Spiritualists didn't have to wait nearly so long for such a glorious reunion. Spiritualism was wholeheartedly embraced by a fervent minority — and dabbled in by a majority. Dabbling was acceptable — President Lincoln dabbled. But throwing oneself into the belief system was considered social suicide.

Isabella rarely dabbled, and her full-on acceptance of Spiritualism did nothing to repair her reputation. Given her public stance against her popular brother, and her belief that she could talk to the dead, the public tide could only turn against her, and the animosity continued. For months, neither Samuel Clemens, as the Beechers undoubtedly called the great author, nor sister Harriet would allow Isabella in their homes. The Beechers closed ranks, and Isabella was outside.

Some historians have never quite forgiven Isabella her visions. From a 1941 biography of Harriet, Forrest Wilson wrote that Isabella was

> . . . hugging to her heart a great secret, a secret so vast and awful that she could not yet impart it to her own husband and children. . . . It was this: the Millennium was close at hand. The whole world would soon become a single matriarchy . . . and she, Isabella Beecher Hooker, of Hartford, Conn., was to rule it as vice-regent of Christ — "with Him to usher in the millennial day." Bellea kept whispering to herself her title — "the inspired one." Thomas wrote her telling her to hold her tongue. She wrote Henry Ward Beecher: "I can endure no longer. I must see you and persuade you to write a paper which I will read, going alone to your pulpit and taking sole charge of the services."[108]

Isabella's suffrage work faltered, and she wrote in her diary in 1876 that she had "not been able to get into public suffrage work yet scarcely know why — the hindrance has been entirely from within."[109] Meanwhile, her sons-in-law, John Calvin Day and Henry Eugene Burton, cut their in-laws off from contact with their grandchildren because of the Hookers' radical political views, Isabella's liaison with people they deemed of questionable character during the Beecher-Tilton scandal, Isabella's meddlesome tendencies, and her Spiritualism. Even rock-steady John Hooker was starting to explore communication with the dead.[110] The last straw for Burton was his mother-in-law's insistence that spirits had warned her of the death of her granddaughter Katharine Seymour Burton. She'd also insisted the police protect the Burton home from kidnappers to forestall her granddaughter's abduction, which was also heralded by the spirits. When neither of those events occurred, Burton made it clear that his mother-in-law was no longer welcome in his house or around his family.[111]

Despite those false prophecies — and the personal blow of her family's estrangement — Isabella delved deeper into Spiritualism as she sought answers and, perhaps, some control. During an August 1876 séance at her house, she visited with her father, Lyman, whom she scarcely had known growing up and who "came in prayer."[112] The British actress and novelist Florence Marryat wrote in her book *There Is No Death* of accompanying Isabella to a séance held by a Dr. Carter or Carteret, in which the dead wife of a friend of Marryat's appeared, with the help of the doctor's control, or intermediary, an African American woman named Rosa. The dead woman appeared draped in white and was soon replaced in rapid succession by, among others, three departed friends and her dead stepson. "You must please to remember that I was not alone, but that this sight was beheld by Mrs. Hooker as well as myself (to whom it was unexpected as to her) and that I know she would testify to it to-day."[113]

On New Year's Eve 1876, guests at a Hooker party — including Mark Twain and his wife — gathered on the first floor of her home while Isabella assembled Hartford's best-known mediums in her upstairs bedroom.[114] Here, again, Isabella awaited spirits to tell her that she was to rule a new world order.[115] The year ended, Isabella had not ascended to her new ruling role, and her faith in Spiritualism remained unchanged.[116]

In the spring of 1877, the Connecticut Senate passed a resolution that allowed Isabella to testify on behalf of the married woman's property tax bill that she and John had drafted, a bill that had been introduced every year since 1870. The bill went to the core of the suffrage movement, the right of women — married or not — to claim independence from others. As Julia

Ward Howe said in an 1870 speech before the American Woman Suffrage Association, the culture — under the rule of law — relied on marriage as one of its cornerstones. Therefore, it was incumbent upon the law to make sure the marriage contract treated both parties fairly.[117] When the Hookers' good friend Richard D. Hubbard was elected governor in 1877, his first message to the General Assembly "stated in very strong terms the injustice done to married women in respect to their property by the law as it stood."[118] John carefully crafted the Hookers' property bill — and removed, upon the governor's suggestion, a section that might have allowed fraud — and with Hubbard's heavy support the bill became law.[119] On March 26, 1877, Isabella wrote her friend Samuel Bowles, former editor of the *Springfield Republican*, that she spoke "face to face with every man of them." Her retelling was positively triumphant: "Now friend — how do you account for it, that this privilege, which has never before been extended to any 'white male,' should have been thus thrust upon me, the friend of Mrs. Woodhull & all other sinners?"[120] Bowles responded that the success of the bill could be attributed to its own rightness, to the agitation of the question, to the governor, and to Isabella and John. "With such things going forward in national politics and such a sign in the heavens as this in Connecticut," he wrote, "we ought to be very happy and I believe I am. . . . I salute you both with honor and with affection."[121]

Connecticut women were no longer under what law books at the time called the "common law disability," and the law's effect was profound. Prior to its passage, married women could not own property of their own and could not enter into a valid contract other than marriage. Common law was considered to be "sufficient to protect herself against herself."[122] The new law granted wives their own legal identity, "which had formerly merged in that of her husband."[123]

Governor Hubbard sent Isabella a note that said, in part, "Thank yourself and such as you for what there is of progress in respect to woman's rights among us."[124] The bill took effect April 20, 1877.

It should have been a transcendent moment, but the Hookers were arguing over what John called Isabella's "monomania." Responding to a letter in which he condemned her behavior, Isabella wrote that she was considered important to the suffrage movement and was still writing articles in newspapers. "I think this is the pot calling the kettle black," she wrote.[125]

In an 1878 journal entry, Isabella was angry that John had told her a photo she sent to admirers requesting one made her look like "one of these dancing girls." The argument expanded into her concern that he did not trust her judgment — even to the point of dictating what photo she should send to admirers. The argument became heated, according to her notes. John told her he'd had to lie to their sons-in-law in order to present an adequate defense of her, and she answered heatedly that John had ridden Isabella as Balaam rode the ass, from the biblical parable set during Moses' time. In the story, Balaam was a priest who was called by Balak, king of Moab, to curse the Israelites. Balaam, having consulted God, refused. Balak pressured him with gifts, and Balaam eventually rode a donkey to do what he was asked, but as he headed toward Moab, an angel — seen only by the donkey — stood in the way, with a sword drawn. Three times the donkey refused to move forward, and three times Balaam beat him until the donkey asked, "What have I done to you, that you're beating me?" When Balaam — apparently comfortable with a talking ass — explained, the donkey reprimanded him, and then Balaam was able to see the angel, and God, too, reprimanded him for beating his donkey.[126]

Isabella reminded John that it was the ass who saw the angel, not Balaam.[127]

It was a remarkable exchange, which Isabella immediately regretted — so much so that she claimed she was only channeling the sharp-tongued Catharine, who'd died just a few weeks earlier after a stroke. By blaming Catharine, Isabella was able to "deflect responsibility for her negative feelings towards her normally supportive husband. Transforming herself once again into a mediator, she functioned not only as a 'passive' intermediary between her husband and the spirits . . . but also as a modifier of their outspoken and somewhat harsh 'messages.'"[128]

Isabella's journals could sometimes be a roller coaster when it came to her moods. She would also shift to third person, and her handwriting shifted too. In one entry from the same year, the handwriting became more angular, and she encouraged John not to yield to his more masculine nature (obstinacy) but rather to be more spiritual. But — again — this was not Isabella speaking. She noted that that remonstration came from their great friend, the newspaper editor Samuel Bowles, who'd died January 16, 1878.

John Hooker, 1878. *Courtesy of the Harriet Beecher Stowe Center, Hartford, Connecticut.*

The spirits could say things Isabella could not. The spirits could be her go-between and perhaps handle some of the inordinate pressure she felt during her brother's trial. But if Isabella thought to avoid more public condemnation, the spirits would not serve.

In January 1878, at the tenth annual Sixteenth Amendment Convention of the National Woman Suffrage Association, suffragists put forth the resolution that "it is the duty of Congress to submit a Sixteenth Amendment to the Federal Constitution prohibiting the several states from disenfranchising United States citizens on account of sex." This was known as the Susan B. Anthony Amendment.[129] The organization needed fifty votes in the Senate and two hundred in the House. Isabella Beecher Hooker was listed among six correspondence secretaries. Other officers of the NWSA included Julia and Abby Smith, of Glastonbury, Connecticut, and Elizabeth Cady Stanton, of Tenafly, New Jersey.

Earlier, sisters Julia and Abby Smith — then eighty and seventy-five, respectively — had refused to pay Glastonbury town taxes in protest against not being able to vote.[130] The Smith sisters were the daughters of Hannah Hickok and the Reverend Zephaniah Smith. Reverend Smith preached in a Congregational church until he came to the belief that no one should accept money for preaching, and then he left to study law and, later, to serve in the Connecticut state legislature.

The Smith sisters were rigorously educated at home, and they'd been fierce abolitionists. Julia taught French, Latin, and arithmetic at the Emma Willard School in Troy, New York, and she translated the King James Bible into Greek, Hebrew, and Latin.[131] In 1869, the Smiths, who had transferred their abolitionist efforts to the suffrage movement, attended Isabella's suffrage association meeting in Hartford and returned home "to develop their skepticism."[132] They'd been arguing about the placement of roads in Glastonbury and were angry that, though they were required to pay taxes, they had no say in how those taxes were spent. Particularly galling was an $18 highway tax they'd refused to pay.[133] In short order, their tax assessment had increased to $100, with no explanation. The next year, the Smith sisters attended the American Woman Suffrage Association meeting in New York, listened to the speakers, and came home inspired to continue not paying taxes. On New

Year's Day 1874, the local tax collector came to claim seven of the sisters' eight cows. Neighbors conspired to buy and return the animals to the sisters, but the town tax collector hounded the women to pay, and they continued to refuse. At one point, contrary to state law, the collector seized their land. The women fought their tax bills with suits and appeals, and Isabella sent them $5 for their defense fund.[134] In 1876, the sisters' land was returned, but they still owed taxes and still lacked the right to vote.

Despite the public support shown nationwide for the Smith sisters, the Sixteenth Amendment failed and the national organization's brochure the next year began, "Whereas, in the recent elections for the popular branch of the National Legislature, the question of woman suffrage was wholly ignored by each of the great political parties, even our more zealous friends not risking a vote in behalf of his principle."

The disappointment was acute. Stanton wrote to her son Theodore:

Whereas, in President Hayes' last message, he makes a truly paternal review of the interests of this Republic, both great and small, from the army, the Navy and our foreign relations, to the ten little Indians in Hampton, Va., our timber on the western mountains, and the switches of the Washington railroads; from the Paris Exposition, the postal service and the abundant harvests, to the possible bulldozing of some colored men in various southern districts, cruelty to live animals and the crowded condition of the mummies, dead ducks and fishes in the Smithsonian Institution; yet forgets to mention twenty million women citizens robbed of their social, civil, and political rights.[135]

By now, the suffrage movement was "moving out of the middle-class drawing room" and into the town halls.[136] Suffragists would try to educate the public through publications and speeches and vigorous lobbying on the state and national level. Later, strategy would shift to ratifying a separate women's suffrage amendment — but for now?[137] The ladies would maintain decorum. Only in the last decade before ratification would picketing and protests become part of the movement.[138] Sadly, other than a few state victories such as Connecticut's property law, the 1870s would end with little to show for the efforts of suffragists. The movement had lost momentum as abolition took center stage, and then it had split over tactics for gaining the vote.[139] In the political arena, Republican leaders became more conservative, while Democrats were rebuilding their party after the Civil War. If Republicans were the party of Lincoln, the suffragists were rapidly losing faith in them, and they would soon form new alliances.[140]

A SPIRITUAL

DIGRESSION

If you watch Steven Spielberg's movie *Lincoln* closely, you'll see Daniel Day-Lewis, playing the president, lose his cool with his wife, Mary Todd Lincoln, played by Sally Field. She has chastised him for allowing their son Robert to enlist in the Union's cause — something they've both resisted — and he tosses his hand skyward and begins to berate her for her overwhelming grief after the 1862 death of son Willie. Another son, Eddie, died at age four in 1850, and Mrs. Lincoln was prone to depression — debilitating and dark depression. In a rare show of anger, Lincoln mentions his wife talking to "ghosts" and, in that one word, sums up his wife's reliance on people who've passed. Though she did not call herself a Spiritualist — she even emphatically said she wasn't one — by seeking to communicate with her dead sons, Mary Todd, a well-educated and complicated woman, at least succeeded in reuniting the family that was so important to her.[1]

Just as was Isabella, Mrs. Lincoln was accused of suffering from mental illness, including, depending on your source, bipolar disorder and depression, and later in life she was institutionalized by her only surviving son, Robert. That part didn't make the movie. Mary Todd, too, has mostly been cast aside by history as a crazy woman, though latter-day research paints a much more nuanced picture of the president's wife, and Sally Field's portrayal of her is one of the most nuanced ever. If you think about the losses suffered by Mrs. Lincoln — she, too, lost her mother at a young age — you can certainly see where she might find the way a bit bumpy.

I have visited mediums before, mostly on a lark, and I generally leave thinking, "That was interesting," but the visits haven't been life-changing. And I'm not even sure they're supposed to be.

But I'm intrigued. Spiritualism, to me, is a throwback, an anachronism — until, that is, I examine my own theology, which allows for the possibility of a life after this one, and if I can accept that, then communicating with people who've passed on doesn't seem nearly so weird. And so I dig in. A Spiritualist in Connecticut offers to have an old-fashioned séance — table and everything — but that doesn't happen. Instead, I opt for a séance via a telephone call to Marianne Michaels, a Pennsylvania medium.

Michaels's backstory is worth a Lifetime movie. According to her *A Second Chance to Say Goodbye: Building a Bridge to the Other Side*, Michaels was always able to talk to spirits, even as a child. Because that ability wasn't treated as strange by her Italian Catholic family, she continued to do so. The accidental death of her twenty-three-year-old brother changed her life, but she took a detour into being the girlfriend of a mobster. I know. Awesome, right? But that wasn't the life for her, and she eventually came back to talking to the spirits, and now she does it for a living, $75 for an hour-long session over the phone, $78 if you want a cassette of the event to listen to later. She specializes in reconnecting family members with brothers, sisters, children who died too soon. Hence, the "second chance" in her book title. I call her and she explains that spirits are everywhere, but we lose the ability to talk to them by atrophy. Children often see them, but the adults in their lives encourage them away from the visions, and over time the children give up. The spirits keep speaking, but no one's listening, except people like Michaels.

I make an appointment that lands right in the middle of a hurricane, and both Michaels and I lose power and don't connect until a week later. I am sitting in my living room with my laptop in my lap, preparing to take notes. I decide not to at the last minute, because I want to concentrate and I don't want to put notes between me and the experience. Michaels makes no small talk, but almost immediately asks if my father is in spirit. Yes, and he has been since 1992. She tells me he's proud of me and that he wishes he'd told me that more often. Through Michaels — who speaks slowly, as if she's translating from another language — my father's shade tells me that he still watches over my mother, which surprises me because their divorce couldn't have been more acrimonious without the introduction of weaponry. I am trying not to give Michaels too many cues with my answers. I am not testing her, but I am interested in how much she can tell me.

For fifteen minutes, she talks about my father and his feeling of failure as a husband and a father (this is not news to me; I know he felt like he failed, though I don't think he did), and then she says, "There's an older woman with him." I find myself sitting forward in the chair. The older woman is in her seventies, maybe eighties, and she's wearing garb from an earlier time and she's holding her head. Isabella died of a cerebral hemorrhage. Maybe it's she. The more Michaels talks, the more I wonder if it isn't, indeed, she. She talks about trying to be a mother and not enjoying the role that much. "She says she grew her children up fast," says Michaels, and I laugh. Isabella says, through Michaels, that she was given credit for being a good mother, but she never felt she earned that credit.

That sounds right.

And then she says she likes "your first lady," and I have to ask, "Michelle Obama?" Yes. Isabella likes Michelle Obama — but she's saddened that there's been no female president yet. Yes. That sounds right too. Everything John Hooker did, Isabella was behind him — including taking in Mary Hall as an apprentice lawyer. In the same way, Isabella says through Michaels, Barack Obama is doing things with the support of Michelle — but, sadly, she says, as it was in her day, "He gets a country, and she gets a cause."

I laugh at that too.

And then Isabella says that she felt guilty about the wealth she enjoyed as John Hooker's wife, and she made a point to give money away. The current state of Hartford's poor saddens her, Michaels says. And then the sound of a heartbeat on the tape nearly drowns out what she's saying, but Michaels is talking about Lyman and how he taught his daughter — all his children, really — to work hard for whatever they wanted. Growing up poor only sharpened Isabella's teeth.

I am fascinated. I had told Michaels earlier that I wanted to contact this woman, whom I was writing about, and she could have gotten some of this information online, but not the detail, not the frustration, not the resolve. It is one thing to tell a daughter that her dead father is proud of her, but Michelle Obama?

And then Michaels says that our time is ending. She has another session, and is there anything more that I want to know? I can't think of what to ask. I figure spirits come a long way to chat with the living, and it's better to just let them do the talking. Michaels is signing off, but first she says that Isabella has enjoyed the chat, and if I need to talk to her again, I should just ask. I mumble something, and Michaels says, "Not through me. If you want to talk to her, she's right there with you. You only have to ask."

Uh. Okay. Except even with a portion of Michaels's book that is supposed to tell me how, I have no idea how to call her. And I don't know if I even want to.

10

IN THE

THICK OF IT

The new decade had to come as something of a relief to Isabella. The 1870s saw her emerge from the private, constricted, and culturally approved female sphere, though at great cost. After the Beecher-Tilton scandal, two of her sisters were not speaking to her. Her brother Henry Ward was still in contact, but only through polite correspondence. Her reputation in Hartford had suffered immeasurably, though she could take comfort that her married woman's property bill had passed after seven years of trying, and votes for women seemed just around the corner.

Within a relatively short period of time, Isabella had moved to the forefront of the suffrage movement. She counted among her friends Elizabeth Cady Stanton, Susan B. Anthony, and Frederick Douglass. She'd gone from being a genteel housewife dedicated to the advancement of her husband's law career to something bigger and, to her, something more in keeping with her destiny.

Still, the scandal moved her to curtail her public activism somewhat. A *Hartford Courant* notice from March 15, 1880, reported that the *Brooklyn Eagle* said that, while in New York, Isabella made new friends and "yesterday she was flattered with an invitation to occupy a seat in the director's box in the Philharmonic rehearsal on Monday afternoon and has accepted the invitation." That was an acceptable kind of news coverage of an active, social woman that carried not a hint of the scandal that attended her previous activities.

While she was pushed back from her public activities, Isabella found herself concentrating more on her notebooks and journals filled with snippets of verse and glued-in newspaper clippings. As time went by, her scrapbooks began filling with the obituaries of the people she loved. She pressed flowers. She wrote recipes.

But Isabella could not content herself with long discourses about which curtains to hang in the parlor, and her friends in the movement wanted her back in the fray. In a December 18, 1880, letter, Stanton wrote her: "The work is missing Isabella. So put on your boxing gloves." Earlier that year, Stanton's New York legislature had sought to give women the right to vote in school meetings, but "the law was ineffective," according to a history of women's suffrage edited by Stanton.[1] In Wisconsin, the Woman's Christian Temperance Union — a valuable ally in the appeal for women's rights — had split on whether to petition the Republican Party for women's votes, and the powerful union was starting to commit its resources to getting the vote.[2] Anthony testified before the U.S. Senate Judiciary Committee, and Sen. George F. Edmunds, of Vermont, said her testimony was "well-suited to a committee of men trained in the law."[3] The suffrage movement had moved into a new, more politically savvy phase and needed more organizers like Isabella.

Still, it must have been tempting for Isabella, after a bruising decade, to stay home. There was certainly plenty at home to amuse her. Hartford in the 1880s was a model of innovation and modernity. Albert A. Pope, a Boston industrialist, had turned the city into the bicycle capital of the world.[4] The American Publishing Company — which motivated Mark Twain to move to Hartford — was churning out the author's latest, and was one of a dozen or so publishing houses in the capital city.[5] The local Colt Firearms was expanding.[6] The immigrant population was exploding, and the rest of the state's population was leaving the farmlands for the city and demanding of its cities the finest in entertainment. Their influx into the cities — ill prepared for the growth — gave rise to social ills that would, in the next decade, draw the attention of men and women intent on reform.[7] The country's largest privately owned department store, G. Fox & Co., anchored itself downtown and competed for customers with Brown, Thomson & Co., a similarly well-appointed establishment. Blue-suited street crews (known as bluebirds) hand-swept the main roads. Downtown shoppers could choose from seventy boot and shoemakers, thirty blacksmiths, and 150 saloons.[8]

Meanwhile, the family was growing, and the Hookers welcomed a granddaughter named Isabel in 1881, the first child of their son, Ned, and his wife, Martha.[9] Unlike his sisters, Ned, now a homeopathic doctor, enjoyed a warm and congenial relationship with his parents.

Isabella, 1888. *Courtesy of the Harriet Beecher Stowe Center,
Hartford, Connecticut.*

Later, Isabella would write to her namesake, "Isabel, I don't ask you to keep the Ten Commandments — you probably will anyway — but if I ever catch you being bored I'll disown you."[10]

Despite the estrangement from their daughters' families, Isabella and John could no longer ignore the inability of Mary Hooker Burton's husband, an alcoholic, to live up to his responsibilities, and though it was scandalous at the time, by 1883 Isabella's ailing eldest daughter moved back to Hartford, where her mother could nurse her. The Hookers sold their Nook Farm home in 1885 and moved with Mary into the home of their son, Edward.

"This mother love is such a tremendous thing I doubt if there is anything like it, and I do hope some day it may find its own and be satisfied," she later wrote to her daughter Alice.

But even Isabella's ministrations could not help Mary, who died of consumption — then a broad term for a number of wasting diseases, including tuberculosis — on January 20, 1886.[11] She was just forty-one.

Hers was a keenly felt loss. Though none of the Hooker children followed their mother into politics, Mary Burton was at least aware of the toll a public life took on Isabella. When a Washington correspondent for a consortium of New York papers wrote a satirical article about Isabella in the 1880s, Mary responded that the correspondent obviously didn't know her mother. She wrote:

> If you were poor and in trouble you would turn to her as surely as the magnet to the pole. The question of woman suffrage is little discussed in our family. My mother is content to have each one hold her own opinions. I have never attended a suffrage meeting. I have never heard my mother speak in public. But knowing the woman, I know you have misrepresented both her manner and her speech. Whatever she does she does with her whole heart. But that she would appear other than an earnest, womanly, modest woman absorbed in (to her) a great cause, is impossible. . . . I felt the stab of your pen the more keenly; therefore I appeal to you to guard your sparkling wit, lest it scorch where it should only illuminate.[12]

If Isabella had been interested in Spiritualism before, she became even more convinced after Mary's death. In an October 4, 1889, letter to Alice, she wrote that she'd recently seen Mary, dressed in her bridal arrangement, standing and smiling at her. These visits — which Isabella would describe in great detail in her journals — were both welcome and bittersweet. Two days after her letter to Mary, Isabella wrote that she'd gone back to read from her journals of forty years so that she could relish a time when her family was all together.

John joined her in attempts to contact their beloved child, and her suffrage work sometimes took a backseat as Isabella immersed herself in the spirit world. While Isabella struggled to leave the woman's sphere of home and hearth, Spiritualism offered a solace beyond the obvious portal through which to correspond with loved ones who'd died. Unlike the Christian faith of her youth, with a male hierarchy and a locus outside the home, Spiritualism placed religion directly in the home, in the parlor séances. Charles Beecher, who with Isabella was the most dedicated Spiritualist practitioner among the Beechers, said, "It is not in its published literature, its periodicals, its lectures and its public mediums that the strength of the movement lies. It is in its family or home circles."[13]

By 1888, John was lecturing about Spiritualism alongside Isabella. In December of that year, he spoke in front of the clergy of Hartford at their weekly conference. He so impressed a lawyer who'd attended — Edward W. Seymour, later a state Supreme Court judge — that the man asked John to speak in Bridgeport, Connecticut. At both venues, John Hooker explained what a Spiritualist is — someone who believes spirits may communicate with the living — and why he believed.[14] He based his faith on personal observation, he told audiences. He'd seen too many situations where only the intervention of a spirit could explain the physical phenomenon he'd witnessed. He described the return of his great friend Samuel Bowles. Bowles had died recently, and in a variety of settings with a variety of mediums, he addressed Hooker as he had while living, and at one point the spirit introduced another spirit, a Dr. Smith of Springfield, Massachusetts, who spoke to John Hooker with a stammer, as he'd done in life. John also told of his brother-in-law, Francis Gillette, giving him business advice from beyond the grave.

For the naysayers, Hooker insisted that Spiritualism went beyond the "sanctions of 'Orthodox Christianity,' as a deterrent from vice and an encouragement of all that is good."[15] Hearing from souls that had sinned early on and were now in a place of darkness and desolation was a powerful deterrent, he said.

For Isabella, Spiritualism also allowed a retreat from her public persona. As she'd once disappeared to Elmira, New York, for a stay at Mrs. Gleason's spa, now she could disappear into the world of spirits. When she was most bereft, she could cling even more tightly to Spiritualism and the spirit guides — including her mother — that would help her through. If her traditional God was not answering her prayers, the spirits stood ready.

But the tug of suffrage work ultimately proved greater. In March 1883, Isabella spoke to the Washington, D.C., gathering of the International Council of Women, the first time women had reached across international boundaries to push for equal rights. Great Britain was the "storm center" of international suffrage, and the conference was the result of decades of correspondence and ideas shooting back and forth between U.S. and British activists, starting with the 1840 World Anti-Slavery Convention held in London, when Stanton and others weren't allowed to sit with the delegates, or speak.[16] The D.C. gathering was a program of the National Woman Suffrage Association, as Stanton's brainchild, though the bulk of the work fell to Anthony and others, as Stanton was again traveling in Europe.[17]

Isabella gave the convocation and spoke about constitutional rights for women. In her speech, Isabella equated discussions about legislation with discussions about morality. Neither true manhood nor true womanhood was attainable so long as women didn't have the right to vote.[18] She also tried to explain why she thought women should vote and men should support them:

> Because questions of legislation to-day are largely questions of morals, and men alone are incompetent to deal with the morals of a community, however wise and just they may be, and however honest in their desire to promote the general welfare. Education, secular and religious, temperance, chastity, police regulations, penal institutions and reformatories — who has more interest than women citizens in all these questions, or more wisdom to bring to their solution?[19]

The woman question was becoming increasingly difficult to ignore as the United States expanded westward. Debates over statehood — and who would be enfranchised, and who would be ignored — had to include women. While Congress sought to define the political status of groups like Native Americans and Mormons, women kept pushing for recognition. As suffrage was "broadly understood in the Civil War era as a key to political identity," incoming states were the crucial locus of whether women would at last be allowed to vote.[20] In Utah, for example, which would not achieve statehood until 1896, women were given the vote by a Mormon legislature in 1870. For some, the law was another reason to mistrust the Mormon sect, and in 1882, Vermont's Senator Edmunds wrote the Edmunds Act, which declared polygamy a felony. But the law did little to diminish Mormon power, and anti-Mormon forces began to campaign against suffrage as a means of cutting Mormon political power in half.[21] Anti-polygamists framed their argument in slogans such as "woman suffrage in Utah means only woman suffering."[22] Many conservative and moderate Americans looked to Utah as a test case for women's suffrage, which put an extreme burden on Utah women.

As support for suffrage in Utah was waning, some suffragists focused on the issue of uneducated voters, and at times the rhetoric turned ugly.[23] In a December 1877 letter to Massachusetts congressman Benjamin F. Butler, Susan B. Anthony bemoaned the state-by-state pursuit of the vote as "worse than insult." She encouraged him to travel out west "to persuade the Irish Miners & Mountain Men, the Mexican Greasers and Negroes — as I did last September — & then come down through Nebraska, Iowa, Wisconsin, Minnesota — among the Bohemians, Swedes, Norwegians, Germans — Begging them to vote to let you vote — you'd feel the insult as keenly as I do."[24] She also used the word *greasers* as a derogatory descriptive in a September 1877 letter to Isabella.

The frustration of the 1870s had carried over into the 1880s, but the western expansion was keeping the suffrage conversation alive. From the efforts of women like Isabella, women's suffrage associations had been formed in almost every state.[25]

In 1887, in the fortieth year of his ministry at Plymouth Church, Henry Ward suffered a stroke — or apoplexy, as it was called.[26] As he lay dying in his Brooklyn home, Isabella had a visitation from spirits — it isn't clear which ones — that said her brother wanted to ask her forgiveness.[27] She rushed to Brooklyn. As it turned out, Henry Ward had forgiven his sister her lack of

Isabella with Martha K. Hooker and Isabel Hooker Merritt, 1892.
Courtesy of the Harriet Beecher Stowe Center, Hartford, Connecticut.

loyalty during the Tilton scandal, but his wife, Eunice, had not. She refused to let Isabella see her brother, and so Isabella paced the sidewalk in front of his Brooklyn Heights home and gave what one biographer called "appalling" interviews to reporters gathered outside. Henry Ward died on March 8, 1887. His reputation — tarnished though it was by the Tilton affair — was still such that no fewer than four funerals were held to accommodate the overflow from the services at his Plymouth Church.[28]

But even an expanded funeral did not make room for Isabella. Eunice made sure she was not allowed inside the church, forcing Henry Ward's half-sister to line up with the other 50,000 to walk past his bier.[29] She went home to refocus her attention on suffrage.

In a March 23, 1889, letter to an Ednah Dow Cheney in Hartford, she said that the American government was "a weak oligarchy [that] has called itself a republic for a hundred years." Ever the minister's daughter, the question of the day, she said, was "What must I do to be saved?"

In a May 17, 1889, letter to Alice, Isabella wrote that she'd traveled the state and formed clubs dedicated to the study of political science — "then in parlor meetings women will be reading and talking about the same things and getting ready to manage town affairs as they should be managed." She also wrote that her neighbor Samuel Clemens was deeply interested in suffrage and had promised a $100 donation to the cause — though she was still waiting for the money. She said she and John had already contributed $150, as well as "all my time and strength, as much as your father."

Alice and her family had followed her husband, Calvin, to live in Europe for several years, and though Calvin kept their children from their eccentric grandmother, Alice and her mother maintained a conversation through letters — many of which, from Isabella, contained apologies for her busy schedule. She started a January 30, 1889, letter to Alice: "My dear precious daughter: I have had no time to think of you since I came here a week ago last Saturday." She added that a speech she'd written recently would be going into the Congressional Record, and she underlined Congressional Record. A May 17, 1889, letter to Alice included: "Much as I love you and enjoy your letters I can hardly bring myself to writing you in this last day for mailing, because I am so absorbed in our work."

She also wrote that she'd spoken at a hearing before state legislators in which she lobbied to strike the word *male* from the Constitution. Her performance was so impressive concerning constitutional amendments that one legislator said that "Mrs. Hooker was fit to be President of the U.S." though he'd insisted she was not typical of her sex.[30]

Meanwhile, her dreams of a reunited women's movement were about to be realized. Organizers knew they could no longer afford divisions, including the historic one between the American Woman Suffrage Association — Henry Ward's old organization — and Isabella's National Woman Suffrage Association. Slowly, the suffrage movement was expanding to include working-class women, who embraced enfranchisement enthusiastically and weren't so concerned about the personalities of the movement's leadership.[31]

Isabella found herself particularly drawn to younger women, who may have served as substitute daughters. A May 27, 1889, letter to Alice extolled the virtues of Mary Seymour Howell, an Albany suffragist: "I have just parted with Mrs. Howell after four weeks of earnest work for 'the daughters of Connecticut' and we may say the sons as well, and your father feels as I do that it is like parting with a dear daughter."

11

THE ELUSIVE

BALLOT

After years of animosity, in February 1890 the two factions of the women's suffrage movement reunited as the National American Woman Suffrage Association. Anthony helped with the merger, and Stanton served as the first president of the group until 1892, when Anthony succeeded her until 1900.[1] Stanton worried that the new organization would limit its focus to suffrage only and ignore what she saw were equally important issues around marriage, divorce, and women's health. Still, upon her election as president, she left for Europe and left the organization in Anthony's hands.[2]

The group immediately began pushing for school suffrage and for a national suffrage amendment.[3] In the spirit of broadening the cause's base, Isabella befriended Susan B. Anthony's old friend Frances Willard, a suffragist who'd risen to lead the Woman's Christian Temperance Union. In 1890, the WCTU had one hundred times the membership of the reconstituted NAWSA, and Isabella began sitting on the platform at the temperance meetings — the Beecher name was still a draw — though she was mostly there as window dressing. She did not speak. She wasn't a teetotaler and thought the union's stand was "narrow" and even "bigoted." Instead of prohibition, she advocated moderation in alcohol consumption.[4]

Isabella was soon back in D.C., and she wanted Alice, who was still in Europe, to join her, but Alice declined. From the capital, Isabella wrote Alice that she was impressed "by the participants' patriotism and statesmanship. In spite of their lack of formal education, women had 'gathered our wisdom and knowledge while caring for our children in the family or teaching other people[']s children in the schools.'"[5] She added wryly: "I am so glad men have had to have mothers as well as fathers. Though you wouldn't suspect it from history or current literature."[6]

Upon her return to Hartford in February 1890, she wrote to Alice that she was so exhausted, she slept on the train and caught a cold — though son Ned nursed her back to health. She was so tired that she gave an uncharacteristically short speech one evening with no preparation, but the speech was a success because — or so suspected Isabella — Henry Ward had taken over the speaking from beyond the grave.

This was not the first time her dead brother used her as a conduit. Of the night of the speech, Isabella wrote to her daughter: "One gesture I remember especially and the house was convulsed with laughter and moved to tears alternately. He has entreated me many times to give myself up to his control — but I have not been quite ready to trust him to speak for a woman's soul — possibly he saw his opportunity and used it so well I shall never be afraid of him again."

She was also impressed with the other women who spoke — presumably without the benefit of help from the spirit of a gifted orator. "I am more than ever impressed with the superior mental and moral power of womankind. In all those four days there was not a weak word uttered from young or old," she wrote.[7]

In May 1890, the descendants of Thomas Hooker held a reunion in Hartford. One by one, the speakers extolled their male ancestors until Isabella stood and said:

> It seems to me that we have talked about the forefathers long enough; we want some foremothers, and we want to begin the new regime here and now, where there are so many women who are full of this grand blood of Thomas Hooker and his wife. There is not one of you who has Hooker blood in you who is not just as much indebted to Thomas Hooker's wife as you are to him. Don't forget that! Don't give Thomas Hooker all the credit![8]

In a January 27, 1891, letter responding to a question from Alice about Isabella and John's finances, Isabella wrote that her husband was a proud man who paid his debts before they were due and that she shouldn't worry about their financial standing. In June 1891, sensing she'd seemed almost "mean," Isabella wrote that she "only feared you were circumscribed where doing anything for your parents moneywise as you have been all your married life. I was sorry I had bothered you."

"You are generosity itself — like your mother," Isabella continued. "I know just how you feel. The one blissful thing in life is to do things and give things that give happiness to some one who is in trouble or needy in some way — I have come to that place that this is my chief source of happiness — doing little things to make a smile on someone young or old. Everything else has taken wings some how and I have to live on little bits of sunshine that I create for myself."

She also — ever eager to lend advice — encouraged Alice to "take time to answer my letters immediately and fully. That is all you can do for me and it is a great deal."

Over time, Isabella had created a system for letter writing, and she urged Alice to do the same. She read letters and made notes of what and how to answer in a small notebook that she kept "for the purpose, with the date of mailing. Thus I can review my last letter to you and know just where we stand. I wish you would do this hereafter and really it does not take so very long and it keeps one's soul at peace. The truth is I have tried to put my soul, my very self into my letters not only for your sake but for my dear grand-daughters." She bemoaned that the estrangement meant her granddaughters did not know her.

Isabella again traveled to Washington, D.C., in February for a meeting of the National Council of Women of the United States, where she was introduced by her new friend Frances Willard as "Queen Isabella." Isabella told the crowd that earlier, she'd traveled to Chicago in preparation for serving on the Board of Lady Managers for the Columbian Exposition in Chicago, the Chicago World's Fair — and as vice president of the Queen Isabella Association, named after the Catholic monarch who'd funded Christopher Columbus's trips. She said she'd had her expenses paid, "just as if I were a man." The crowd laughed at that. She also dismissed concern over Queen Isabella's Catholicism.

"If Protestantism is afraid for itself, and cannot survive except by maligning a noble woman whom five centuries have pronounced a model wife, mother, daughter and ruler of empires, then Protestantism had better go under and let Romanism come up," she said. "I believe in survival of the fittest." The crowd applauded.[9]

She said that she and other women bristled at being called ladies: "We are so thankful that Congress for once has recognized that we are ladies, although we hate the term 'ladies' . . . we know the Congress has been the Lords of Creation so long that perhaps it is time there were some ladies, and we accept that against our faith."[10]

By 1891, Hartford — including most of the Beechers — had forgiven Isabella's earlier behavior around Henry Ward's scandal, and the couple's fiftieth anniversary was the height of the social season.[11] In the weeks leading up to the celebration, Alice hadn't been forthcoming about whether she'd attend, and so Isabella wrote her that her daughter's absence would be "noticeable in the end and we must know what to say when asked — and although our invitation says 'no presents' of course near friends will not forget us and our children surely must not. But I can't bear to have you made uncomfortable even and I can send you $50 out of my allowance without any trouble. I would do so at once if I thought you would like it."

She wrote and underlined, "I so want to . . . see you and the girls."

According to a *New York Times* article from August 5, 1891, nearly two thousand invitations were sent to friends and family around the world. The article described John's family and included his legal work and his popular poems "of a humorous, pathetic, or sacred nature" published in various periodicals. "For years," the article said, "he was the only anti-slavery lawyer in the State." Isabella, the article said, had devoted her life to "what she terms 'the amelioration of her sex.'" The bride, according to the newspaper, would be wearing the same gray silk gown she wore for her twenty-fifth wedding anniversary.

The event was held at the City Mission Room in Hartford, and longtime friend (and John's former law partner) Sen. Joseph Hawley was master of ceremonies.[12]

John Hooker was settling into genteel old age. In a round-robin letter dated December 29, 1891, Isabella wrote that she was looking forward to reading to her husband, but now, alas, he could only keep awake to hear the *Hartford Times*, because he arose so early every morning — "and in the morning I can only hear bits of the *Courant* which he reads while I am dressing."

In February 1892, Stanton was again in Washington to speak at the U.S. Senate Committee on Woman Suffrage, where she delivered what might have been the most important speech of her career, "The Solitude of Self."

In the speech, she ingeniously explored the estrangement she felt from her own movement. And she said:

> No matter how much women prefer to lean, to be protected, and supported, nor how much men desire to have them do so, they must make the voyage of life alone, and for safety in an emergency, they must know something of the laws of navigation. To guide our own craft, we must be captain, pilot, engineer; with chart and compass to stand at the wheel; to watch the wind and waves, and know when to take in the sail, and to read the signs in the firmament over all. It matters not whether the solitary voyager is man or woman; nature, having endowed them equally, leaves them to their own skill and judgment in the hour of danger, and, if not equal to the occasion, alike they perish.[13]

At the March 18, 1892, Connecticut Woman Suffrage Association annual meeting, Isabella presided over renaming the group the Connecticut Woman Suffrage Society for the Study of Political Science.[14] Local clubs had kept suffrage before the public, and a suffrage tent had been erected at the state fair held in Meriden, with one day set aside as Woman's Day. Around the state, women were being allowed to hold municipal positions (though not elected ones) and seats in ecclesiastical societies.[15] The name change reflected the group's broadening interests.

In May 1892, delegates of the National American Woman Suffrage Association gathered in Chicago to find the past come back to haunt them. Victoria Woodhull was there distributing campaign material and claiming to run for president with the endorsement of the association. Like Isabella, Woodhull had gone to Europe to escape public condemnation after the Tilton scandal. There, she'd met her second husband, John Martin, a member of a wealthy banking family. The couple returned to the United States not for a serious candidacy but to remove the lingering stain on Woodhull's reputation.[16] Her claim of endorsement was quickly denounced, though Woodhull's husband suggested his wife meet with Isabella, who'd stayed in touch and had let her old friend know she'd be in Chicago. Oddly, Woodhull refused, but Martin persisted and arranged to meet with Isabella in a Chicago hotel. He did not tell his wife of the meeting, and brought along a recording secretary, who took notes and later typed them up for posterity. Isabella, who had just turned seventy, seemed intent to talk about the past, and when Martin pressed the case for his wife's candidacy, Isabella reminded him that Woodhull had been away a long time, and perhaps a large cash donation to a leading Spiritualist publication would help restore her good name.[17] The two women did not meet. When she died in 1927, Woodhull's obituary identified her as "Victoria Martin," and her role in the Tilton affair was barely mentioned.[18]

That same year, Charlotte Perkins Gilman, Isabella's grandniece, published her semiautobiographical short story "The Yellow Wallpaper," an exploration of a fictional wife-narrator's recuperation for "temporary nervous depression — a slight hysterical tendency."[19] This was Gilman's utopian writing contrasted against "an essential vision of female constriction."[20] The narrator breaks down over her inability to fulfill her duties as a mother, and the tranquility and recuperation she is prescribed are ultimately her undoing. The narrator ends up "in a total mental break-down at the end of the novel, with the woman crawling around her room, desperately trying to rip off the 'wallpaper of contention' and free the woman she thinks is hiding behind it."[21] In a 1901 letter, Isabella called her grandniece a "noble woman of large gifts who has a history that can[']t be put into print." She also wrote, "I doubt if she can do much but write books." Why? Isabella spoke from hard-learned lessons: "[T]he world will not pardon peculiarities."[22]

In 1893, Isabella served on the Board of Lady Managers of the Chicago World's Fair, which drew 28 million visitors to buildings that stretched a third of a mile long and included the world's first Ferris wheel.[23] Designed in part by Frederick Law Olmsted, the May–October spectacle — called the "White City" for its marble finish on the temporary buildings' plaster facades — celebrated the anniversary of Christopher Columbus's arrival in the New World.[24]

In addition to her job with the Lady Managers, Isabella taught parliamentary procedures to Southern exposition delegates to help them "outmaneuver Bertha Honore Palmer."[25] Palmer was the director of the Board of Lady Managers who presided over the exhibits in the Woman's Building and was considered the queen of the fair.[26] Born in Kentucky and educated in Maryland, Palmer was a formidable leader.[27] And she was an avowed antisuffragist.[28]

Earlier, even before Chicago won the bid to host the fair, women who'd decided to focus attention on Queen Isabella — without whom Columbus would not have traveled — quickly became known as "Isabellas." Their membership included Frances Dickinson, a medical doctor who was Susan B. Anthony's cousin, and they pushed for input in the planning of the fair. Anthony and others had petitioned to include women on the planning committees. When they were ignored, they asked for a Board of Lady Managers, and the first meeting was convened in November 1890.[29] Isabella led the committee for permanent organization, which would dictate the duties of the Lady Managers. Isabella, who'd spent thirty-plus years steeped in parliamentary procedure and behind-the-scenes politicking, came prepared, though it was Palmer who negotiated $200,000 for a Woman's Building.[30] Palmer "viewed the Exposition as something broader than a passing spectacle. She believed it could help to improve the lot of women around the world."[31] And she ruled with an iron hand. Palmer fired the secretary of the Board of Managers, a Missouri attorney named Phoebe W. Couzins, for having "assailed everyone connected with the management of the Fair."[32]

Couzins sued and lost, and Isabella helped shepherd other organizers against Palmer's leadership.[33] Isabella argued against the secretary's dismissal and for greater inclusion of Southern states' representation in the proceedings. The *Hartford Courant* reported on April 23, 1891, that Secretary of the Treasury Charles Foster received a letter from Isabella asking who within the Board of Lady Managers would receive a congressional allocation of $36,000. She also complained about Palmer, saying she'd usurped authority. Isabella's detractors worried that she, the veteran of many political discussions, would use her knowledge of parliamentary procedure to unseat Palmer, though that didn't happen.[34]

Isabella also made a point of getting to know the women delegates from Utah — most of whom were Mormons and many of them determinedly nonpolygamist. Isabella told an excited reporter that "if half she had heard was true, she wanted to come to Utah and remain."[35] She also spoke up for the Mormon women at one session, and one Mormon youth said Isabella had expressed her "surprise and pleasure over the exalted, refined, and pure sentiments uttered by our young girls."[36] The fair was an early engagement of Mormons in the non-Mormon world, and most non-Mormons, like Isabella, were impressed with the women's comparatively equal treatment in their home state. Involvement in this and other fairs "caused many Americans to readjust their views on Mormonism and its believers."[37]

Isabella also organized a ceremony that included the unveiling of a marble bust of her sister Harriet, who was in failing health. The sculptor was Anne Whitney, who in 1875 had lost a commission to sculpt a likeness of Charles Sumner because she was a woman.[38] No less a dignitary than Frederick Douglass asked to pose as Uncle Tom at the event.[39]

But if Douglass could pose out of respect for the beloved Harriet, he and others felt the fair, overall, was demeaning to African Americans. Managers planned August 25 to be Colored People's Day, which angered African Americans — particularly Ida B. Wells, who called it "Nigger Day."[40]

If the World's Fair was fraught with political sandpits, the push for suffrage was even more so. An April 20, 1893, *Courant* article said Isabella had conducted an "interesting hearing" before the Committee for Woman Suffrage at the House of Representatives in Washington, where members had turned their meeting over to the "veteran champion of equal rights." Because of the room's configuration, committee members were seated behind her, and she told those gathered that she didn't like speaking to people she couldn't see, and so committee members gamely left their seats and moved to sit with the rest of the crowd. She told the group that she "used to be a black Republican," but that party had abused its power and abandoned women, and now she was "trying to be a white democrat." Former Connecticut governor Thomas M. Waller, a recent convert to the suffrage cause, came in late. Isabella called on him, and he responded that he was still enough of a politician to avoid committing himself wholeheartedly to the cause, but that he was "enough of a man" to say that women should be given more rights and greater responsibilities. And in 1893, the Connecticut legislature allowed women to vote in school elections and made them eligible for membership on local school boards, following in the footsteps of Kentucky, which in 1838 had given some women — including widows with property — the right to vote in school elections.[41] The bill passed the state House but stalled in the Senate until the Hartford Equal Rights Club lobbied hard for its passage. Gov. Luzon B. Morris signed it into law, and despite several attempts for repeal, it remained on the books.[42]

Isabella threw herself into state activities, such as lunches held for the new generation of suffragists that included training in public speaking. She printed and distributed 50,000 copies of an equal rights tract to be sent to every Connecticut town. And in June 1894, the Equal Rights Club of Hartford decorated the graves of local suffragists, including the Smith sisters and Nathaniel Burton. A newspaper account of the ceremony said Isabella "spoke with the old-time enthusiasm and fervor."[43]

If Isabella still had the fire, her old neighborhood of Nook Farm was fading, as were its formerly illustrious residents. At age seventy-eight, John Hooker resigned as reporter of the state Supreme Court, effective January 1, 1894. He'd held the position for thirty-six years, and, according to the *Courant*, his work was "recognized on all sides as admirable illustrations of how that sort of work should and could be done."[44] Francis Gillette, the old abolitionist, had died in 1879, and his wife, Elisabeth, in 1893. Their son William, who more than anyone had brought the role of Sherlock Holmes to the American theatergoing public, was traveling the country performing and pursuing the good health that eluded him.[45] Mark Twain's finances had upended, and he was trying to figure out a way to tell the family, who so loved their brick mansion on Farmington Avenue, that they would never again be able to afford to live there.[46] Harriet had slipped into dementia and was fond of wandering the local properties and plucking flowers — roots and all. She especially liked the posies in Twain's greenhouse.[47]

When Harriet died on July 1, 1896, Isabella was with her, and a simple funeral service was planned.[48] When Henry Ward's wife, Eunice, came to Hartford to attend the funeral, she and Isabella avoided each other.[49] Harriet's former lecture tour manager, J. B. Pond, described the funeral for Mark Twain, who was traveling in Europe. All the Nook Farm neighbors were there — at least those who survived, including Susy Clemens, Twain's daughter, who was visiting Hartford at the time. "Mrs. Hooker was at the funeral, but she and Mrs. Beecher did not meet, — a very pathetic condition of affairs," according to Pond. Older sister Mary Perkins was there — unable to hear the proceedings but "brilliant and sparkling as ever." Harriet's body was then taken to Andover, Massachusetts, to be buried next to her husband, Calvin, who'd died in August 1886.[50]

Isabella later wrote a biography of her sister, and sold it along with a com-

Isabella with daughter Alice. *Courtesy of the Harriet Beecher Stowe Center, Hartford, Connecticut.*

memorative spoon. Isabella explained, "In the latter years of her life Mrs. Stowe was unable to aid the benevolent objects which had greatly interested her, by reason of the failure of the receipts from *Uncle Tom's Cabin,* the copyright having expired." She pronounced that she'd use the proceeds on "objects that always had her sister's sympathy."[51]

In 1898, Isabella published a suffrage leaflet titled "Are Women Too Ignorant?" in which she addressed the concern that adding women to the voting rolls would only add more ignorant votes. It was similar in tone to Thomas Wentworth Higginson's long-ago *Atlantic Monthly* article on women's rights that had so ignited Isabella.

For her article, Isabella "cited working-class and black women's benevolent associations and clubs as well as the large numbers of women pursuing higher education as evidence that women from every rank and walk of life wanted to vote and were actively preparing themselves for this civil responsibility."[52]

In June 1899, Isabella's son-in-law John Calvin Day died after years of ill health. He left Alice and their two daughters, neither of whom was married at the time of his death, financially comfortable and Isabella and John free to establish a relationship with the grandchildren they barely knew.

12

THE END,

AND A LEGACY

This is a sad chapter. It is sad not only because the life of this complicated and interesting woman was nearing its end but also because she was leaving this world without fulfilling her most fervent wish, to cast a vote. The hordes of women similarly disenfranchised must gather somewhere in the netherworld and talk about their disappointment. I hope they have a sense of humor about it. I'm not sure I would.

Nearing her seventy-eighth birthday, Isabella's hair had completely whitened, and her piercing eyes could still bore through wood. She'd stepped back from public engagement, though she still wrote the occasional letter to her local newspaper and still hosted the infrequent suffrage meeting.

Her desire to vote still burned. In early February 1900, the National American Woman Suffrage Association met in Washington, where it was announced, among other things, that the former Connecticut Woman Suffrage Association, now the Connecticut Woman Suffrage Society for the Study of Political Science, had moved its annual meeting from October to March to take advantage of the state legislature's session. The official record said Isabella was "presiding in her usual happy manner, making many bright little off-hand speeches, showing that time has not yet tucked her away on the shelf of the incompetents."[1] There must have been some comfort in Isabella's steadfastness, as suffrage work in the state had mostly stalled. The report of activity in Connecticut from the previous year, as recorded by Frances Ellen Burr, was desultory at best. From her notes: The Political Equality Club of Meriden had been inactive, but there were hopes members had recently found a new lease on life. The Equal Rights Club of Hartford continued "to keep the ark in motion with more or less spirit, according to times, seasons and occasions."[2]

On May 7, 1900, the *Courant* carried a short story about Adelaide Johnson, of Washington, D.C., who came to Hartford to make a clay bust of Isabella to add to her collection of famous women suffragists, a group that included Susan B. Anthony and Lucretia Mott. The two women must have enjoyed each other's company — Johnson, too, was a Spiritualist. She saw her sculpting as a mission to "record and immortalize the history" of the suffrage movement, and felt some urgency to capture a likeness of Isabella before she died.[3] Johnson had hoped the National American Woman Suffrage Association would fund the project and that her work would be displayed in the U.S. capitol. Anthony hoped the women's busts would be placed in the Library of Congress.[4] The work was eventually funded by the National Woman's Party, a rival group formed by Alice Paul.[5]

By the 1900s, both Isabella and John had vastly restricted their public appearances. They still read and discussed issues of the day, but as more loved ones died, Isabella's attention turned almost exclusively to Spiritualism and to communing with the dead.

She was not alone in her interest. In May 1900, Samuel and Olivia Clemens contacted a medium in hopes of speaking with their daughter Susy, who'd died of spinal meningitis in 1896. Staying in a cottage at Saranac Lake, New York, the couple took one of their daughter's brooches to a medium, who said Susy wanted a biography she'd written of her father to be published. The family was coming to terms with the idea of selling its Hartford house, which by then existed mostly as a memorial to Susy.[6]

From Isabella's journal dated January to May 1901, the first page quotes Luke 1:28 — the angel Gabriel's greeting to Mary, calling her "highly favored"— and Luke 2:19, a snippet of a verse that says, "But Mary treasured up all these things and pondered them in her heart." And then, in a faint hand, she wrote the simple note: "He died Feb. 12, 1901."

John Hooker had been failing, and as her lover-husband slipped away, Isabella appears to have spent more time contacting the spirit world. From her notebooks, she was particularly interested in pursuing spirit writing, in which she would take up a pen and wait to be inspired or moved to write by the spirits. With spirit writing, the writer does not know what he or she is recording until the event is over, and the handwriting itself may bear no resemblance to that of the writer.[7] In Isabella's notebooks, the handwriting

John Hooker, 1891. *Courtesy of the Harriet Beecher Stowe
Center, Hartford, Connecticut.*

varies from her no-nonsense right-slanted writing to a loopy, back-leaning script.

On January 7, 1901, Isabella settled in for an entire day to wait for guidance. She opened the notebook the next day and wrote: "Nothing comes — strange. I will go for my trolley ride."

Two days later, she wrote — most likely seeking her daughter Mary's spirit: "Darling — any news this morning? I am stupid — but have not eaten any breakfast." Two days later, she wrote, "This morning feel dull as usual before breakfast and conclude my brain couldn't be used before breakfast — any better than after — so inclined to give it all. (Mary dear — you don't seem able to watch the voyages and respond — what is the reason?) — no reply, so I give it up."

On January 15, she wrote, with the phrases in parentheses her own voice and the rest the voice of a spirit she hardly anticipated channeling, Napoleon Bonaparte, who'd died in 1821, the year before she was born:

"Here comes a new spirit with a new message — hear him finish. Hilarious — speak . . . — Yes, I am used to talking! [Unclear] that writing is also familiar, using another brain than your own."

And here, the handwriting changes markedly in a stream of consciousness/conversation:

"And that brain a woman's! I never thought I should come to that! Well. Such is life, life eternal they say it is — life eternal and [unclear] changes everlasting but life, no, that's not desirable, here on this particular planet, no. . . . Still, a visit now and there with a message, I don't mind that."

"(Have you a message for us this morning?)"

"That's the way it looks."

"(Let us hear it.)"

"I seem to be a poor messenger. The door is wide open but I can't — get in — I can't get in, what is the reason? I can't do it."

"(Shall you try again and write thro' her?)"

"Shakes head. Give it up, try again another time, not used to being balked so. I am Napoleon the Great.

(You'll get it after a while.)

Do you know who I am."

"(I do, could you find any one who does not know?)"

"And — this woman — [unclear] my soul, what a fool I was! What a fool I am. I asked this privilege but find it a burden. Adieu, Adieu."

The conversation, in radically different handwriting, stretches for four pages and is followed by — in Isabella's writing:

"All this was a great surprise — I cannot describe the interior sensation — must think about it. It seemed very strange to me that so many came to me from the other world when I could make so little use of their communications — but the impression was strong that I ought to work in faith — and that he also was calling to work."

She came back to the notebook a day later, a Wednesday morning, and wrote: "Are you ready? I feel bound to open this letter from Alice, tho' I don't see why I should."

And: "All day yesterday I was pondering and could not make up my mind whether to invite another interview." But she'd spent the previous evening reading about Napoleon and found he was, she wrote, "patient, gentle and good." She'd thought to discuss the previous day's chat with "Lilly"— perhaps Lilly Gillette Warner, Charles Dudley Warner's sister-in-law, or perhaps Lilly G. Foote, who was staying in the Hooker house at the time — but decided not to bother.

And then comes new handwriting, rounder and less slanted: *"Pardon, Mademoiselle, je suis — madame* cannot speak French. . . . What has my Josephine been doing? Everything and nothing! I can't explain I shall have to live it up for the present. Mrs. Hooker is so interested she can't let go, and it can't get hold til she does. What do you think it's been doing?"

Napoleon then tried to explain that he came to Mrs. Hooker because she was open, because she knew what to do with his communications.

Within the week, Isabella decided that her first duty of the day, just as soon as she was up and dressed, would be spirit writing. She was writing for her mother — or perhaps for herself — when she wrote:

You are a big battery — and always have been — you are constantly being tapped for useful purposes which can't be explained at present but some day you will be satisfied. This makes you think of the old scripture "I shall be satisfied when I awake in thy likeness" which used to be comforting but now you can't find whose likeness it is that is to be satisfying to your soul.

I can't help you in these matters — they are beyond me. The life I am now living is satisfactory to me in every respect and I am not even curious about the future — probably because relief from past suffering is all sufficient as the environment here is charming. The "battery" is pretty heavy for one alone.

By January 24, Isabella was eating only sporadically and was concentrating almost entirely on spirit writing. At one point, John was well enough to come into her room with the *Courant* and he reported some news of the day. "Is that the good news?" she asked the spirits, in her notebook. That John was up and reading the newspaper?

On February 8, 1901, Isabella thought there was room for hope for her husband's recovery, and she wrote Mary: "Well, darling, here we are; your father getting so well so far it is simply amusing."

That was a Friday, and by the following Monday, things looked dire. Isabella wrote:

> . . . not much changed as to vitality but lungs filling and much coughing at intervals all day. Slept [unclear] and wanted to talk to all of us by turns — mind clear and sometimes voice strong — tho' occasionally talking of business or something not clear to us. At noon he was quiet for a little and I gather all — I repeated psalms and hymns. Afternoon cough grew and more frequent and more painful. Alice could not bear it and begged Ned to soothe it as he did for Mary. And . . . he consented and left him asleep at about nine and he never waked. All suffering ended and this Tuesday morning at seven he gently, quietly closed . . . own life.

"He died Feb. 12, 1901."

But John's death could not keep Isabella from her husband, and four days later she wrote, "After dinner saw him alone — he took both hands and earnestly asked . . . no one allowed in his bed, nothing moved. I was glad and promised." His memorial in the state *Connecticut Reports* said that he possessed a "quick, acute, logical and analytical mind" and that he'd abandoned orthodox creed later in life, "but the fatherhood of God and the brotherhood of man grew more vivid and precious."[8]

Isabella and John
Hooker, 1891. *Courtesy
of the Harriet Beecher
Stowe Center, Hartford,
Connecticut.*

John Hooker, 1898–1901. *Courtesy of the Harriet
Beecher Stowe Center, Hartford, Connecticut.*

News of his death was not unexpected — John was in his ninth decade — and he was mourned throughout the state. The *Courant* said the "state lost one of its eminent citizens" and added he'd once told the article's unnamed author that "it was a curious turn of fate that he who loved peace above all else and hated contention had been struggling and fighting all his life"— first for the abolition of slavery and then for the enfranchisement of women.[9] He was called an "old school gentleman, patriot, and agitator such as modern days do not seem to produce."[10] His will, which had been witnessed by, among others, his sister-in-law Harriet, left everything to Isabella. She would enjoy a comfortable widowhood.

But without the input of her lover-husband, Isabella over time would not perform the smallest of tasks without consulting the spirits. Just as Harriet had fictitiously portrayed Isabella in *My Wife and I*, her younger sister had slipped into "a dream world" where "the most ordinary actions required permission or confirmation from the spirits."[11]

Six days later, on February 18, her handwriting nearly unrecognizable, she wrote:

"Now I feel as if I had hold of his hand and saying dear father, this sacred spot is your mountain of transfiguration — and he says yes . . . surrounded by those I loved best on earth I put off the mortal — and as I put on the universal, as my spirit was clothed in . . . I found that I loved the best in heaven. . . ."

There followed a round of visitors, and she barely had time to write — or talk with her dead husband and daughter. She also made time for her suffrage work.

The Connecticut Woman Suffrage Society for the Study of Political Science meeting was held on March 21, 1901, at Unity Hall in Hartford. Still in mourning, Isabella nevertheless spoke briefly about women's votes. She had the respect of all, but she did not have the vote. Interest in suffrage had dipped, and the treasurer's report for the Connecticut group said only $21.75 had been spent to further the cause that year. Frances E. Burr reported, "The work of the association is confined to the annual fall convention and the legislative hearing."[12]

In early 1902, a constitutional convention was held in Hartford and Isabella prepared and presented "A Memorial from the Connecticut Woman's Suffrage Association," stating, as told in Isabella's *Connecticut* magazine article, that "women are tired of being classed with minors, criminals and idiots, as proper subjects for disenfranchisement and asking that the word 'male' be stricken from article 6, section 2 of the old constitution." Not much lobbying was accomplished, though the association was able to get a room at the capitol in Hartford. Isabella's memorial was presented, but committee members would not grant a hearing to the suffragists.[13]

In 1903, a young suffragist wrote to Isabella decrying her lack of recognition in the post-unification movement. Sick in bed, Isabella took time to respond:

> I am not forgotten. The truth is ever since the World[']s Fair at Chicago
> I have often been ignored and never treated with old time courtesy and
> appreciation of the value of my devoted services. . . . And to this day it has
> never been suggested that my name should appear with Mrs[.] Stanton's
> and Miss Anthony's as Honorary Pres[iden]ts although in the earlier days
> I carried the Convention for them one year when they dared not have their
> names used. . . .[14]

In fact, with Isabella withdrawing from public lobbying, interest in suffrage in the state seemed to wane with each year, and annual expenditures from Connecticut's suffrage association never amounted to more than $200.[15] Membership dwindled as well. From the *Courant*, dated July 8, 1904, came the report that Isabella was opening her summer cottage on Maple Avenue in Norfolk, where she intended to spend several months. She did not attend the state's convention for two years.

In the spring of 1905, Isabella took a moment to look back at her eighty-three years for her *Connecticut* magazine article, "The Last of the Beechers." In it, she paid tribute to her "lover husband" and quoted from John Greenleaf Whittier's poem "My Triumph":

> Others shall sing the song,
> Others shall right the wrong,
> Finish what I begin,
> And all I fail of — win.

That issue of the magazine contained other articles that praised Isabella. The Beecher-Tilton scandal was forgotten, or, at least, people who remembered her controversial public stands could also look at the elderly lady and appreciate her efforts. In the article, she avoided any reference to the tensions between her social roles — public and private — though tensions most assuredly existed. As for the sister who never quite forgave her for her role in her brother's scandal, Mary, Isabella wrote only that she'd married an "eminent" local lawyer. Gone was evidence of Mary's anger at Isabella's breaking rank, but gone, too, were stories of Mary's influence, her advocacy in favor of John's law career, and her steady support of her sisters and brothers from her comfortable life in Hartford.

In 1905, Isabella sent for a Mrs. Lazarro, a Hartford medium, to come to her summer cottage in Norfolk so that she could correspond with John.[16] It is not recorded whether she was successful. That same year, she suffered a small stroke.

Her old friend and ally Anthony made one of her last public statements about suffrage at a gathering for her own eighty-sixth birthday in February 1906. She said, "With such women consecrating their lives, failure is impossible." That last part became the suffragists' motto.[17] Anthony died a month later, having never cast a legal vote. Stanton had died at her home in New York in 1902, also without casting a vote.

Isabella's name continued to show up in the local newspaper. Her letters to the editor ranged in topic from suffrage to where to buy the best dahlias in town. On November 2, 1906, Isabella sent a letter to the Connecticut Woman Suffrage Society for the Study of Political Science — which was holding its annual meeting in Meriden that year — and quoted from an 1888 speech she gave in Washington in which she said, "Prejudice and precedent, culture and blind conservatism are the only barriers against women in government today." She acknowledged that she was no longer as active, but prayed for and encouraged "my sisters who are still laboring for that which shall save our nation." She remained honorary president of the state suffrage association, but left her house less and less often.

On January 13, 1907, Isabella suffered another stroke.[18] She lingered nearly two weeks, and died at home on a bitterly cold January 25. The *Courant* headline said "Last of Beecher Family Is Dead." The obituary said she was the daughter of Lyman, "the famous divine made more famous by the genius of his children." Isabella, said the story, "had her fair share of the ability and originality which characterized Mrs. Stowe and Henry Ward Beecher. . . . It was a family with ideas and convictions" and family members "never hesitated from expressing their convictions" and the "popularity of the ideas was not taken into account."

"They followed no paths but made their own," the piece concluded.

The obituary also said that though neither John nor Isabella held "to the orthodox beliefs in which they were reared, both of them held to their belief in God and a future life as intensely as in their earlier years and many of the clergymen of the city were proud of Mrs. Hooker's friendship." The obituary also mentioned that "many families in the city have occasion to think of her ministrations with gratitude."

Ironically, the unnamed obituary writer semi-chided Isabella for what "we may almost say . . . was an agony of personality."

Her friend and recording secretary, Frances E. Burr, responded with a letter the next day and called Isabella "one of the most original and picturesque characters of the time." Burr recalled how she'd visited Isabella in the fall of 1867 at her Nook Farm home. The rooms were filled, wrote Burr, with "chatty guests," and once Isabella made up her mind about women's suffrage, she moved forward with an assurance and moral courage her brother Henry Ward and sister Harriet lacked.

The January 29, 1907, *Courant* headline said "Her Disappointment Borne with Serenity"—though using *serenity* was probably more a matter of not speaking ill of the dead. Isabella was not serene. Her rougher edges might have been worn down by the slowing of her mind, but she was not serene.

The funeral was conducted by three ministers, including her nephew, the Reverend Charles E. Stowe, of Bridgewater, Massachusetts. Honorary pallbearers included judges and Samuel L. Clemens. She was buried in Hartford's Cedar Hill Cemetery, the final resting place for many of Hartford's boldfaced names, including the financier J. P. Morgan and — eventually — the actress Katharine Hepburn. To her right was her lover-husband, John. A bit off to her left was the Reverend Nathaniel J. Burton, former head of the Connecticut Woman Suffrage Association. Beloved daughter Mary was buried just to John Hooker's right, and behind the three, within the family plot, was a table monument carved with the name Hooker.

At the 1907 state convention of the Connecticut suffrage association, held again at Hartford's Unity Hall, an entire afternoon session was devoted to its founder. According to Burr, Isabella was too modest to speak at the first two annual meetings, but "she soon got over that." Association member Mrs. E. J. Warren said that Isabella's heart, soul, purse, and home were open to the "destitute and friendless." The women then accorded Isabella a Chautauqua salute, the waving of white handkerchiefs, a "token of special honor," sparingly given.[19]

Frances Burr followed up with another *Courant* article on October 30, 1907, and said that Isabella "could not make any move on ordinary lines, or in any ordinary way." She also suggested future generations call her by her birth name, Isabella Beecher, "for the strong points always came from the Beecher font of originality."

And then while Isabella might have slipped into the other world to commune with the other spirits, there was the tawdry matter of her will, and a public reminder of her Spiritualism.

A March 20, 1908, *Courant* story carried the headline "Mrs. Hooker's Talks with Spirits." The trial discussed in the piece centered on Isabella's will, and whether she intended to give an estranged granddaughter, Katherine Burton Powers, a share in Isabella's roughly $60,000 estate. Powers, the granddaughter Isabella had sought to save from abduction after a spirit warning, was the daughter of Isabella's beloved Mary, who had been estranged from her husband when she died in 1886.

The death of his wife had not softened Burton's feelings toward his in-laws, particularly Isabella, and there were no post-Mary reunions between grandmother and granddaughter. Powers sought to set aside the will entered into court after her grandmother's death, which left her nothing, and her lawyers argued that Isabella was not of right mind when she wrote the will.

Throughout the trial, members of Hartford's Equal Rights Club sat in attendance. This was one of their own, and they got an earful.

Judge Milton Adelbert Shumway, a former Connecticut senator, presided over the case. Both sides agreed that the trouble between Isabella and Burton would not be discussed in court. Lilly G. Foote, a member of one of Isabella's Spiritualism classes, was one of the witnesses. Foote said the classes were held irregularly and that she once observed Isabella spirit-writing a letter from a dead Dr. Richardson, an English physician, in which the text was peppered with parenthetical phrases that — as did her journal around the time of her husband's death — separated her conversation from that of the spirit with which she was communicating. Isabella's son-in-law died in 1904, around the same time Isabella was writing to the dead Dr. Richardson.

Richardson wasn't the only deceased medical practitioner with whom Isabella corresponded. She also spoke with a Dr. Buck about a medical case her son, a homeopathic doctor, was handling.

The trial — followed slavishly by the local newspapers — moved an unnamed writer at a Congregationalist newspaper to muse: "It is interesting to note how money matters continue to influence folks in the next world. . . . But if departed relatives are allowed to be parties to lawsuits, there ought to be some means of bringing them into court to testify in their own behalf."[20]

However, testimony said that Isabella always advised acolytes not to follow a spirit's advice if it ran counter to their own judgment.

Another witness, a family friend named Mrs. Cynthia M. Fuller, of New London, speculated from the stand that Powers was omitted from the will because of "her neglect of her filial duty to her grandmother."

From the testimony, Powers, who was married to a doctor, hadn't seen her grandmother since 1888 and hadn't written her since October 1906. Son Ned said that his mother had continued her suffrage work fairly steadily until her first stroke in 1905. The will in question was executed in November 1904, three weeks after the death of Henry Eugene Burton. Ned said that his mother had hoped Kate would reconcile with her, but she did not. Ned said Isabella told him that if she couldn't have the love of her granddaughter, her granddaughter would receive nothing upon her death. Isabella talked, instead, of establishing a memorial to the Beecher and Hooker families, but nothing came of that. Powers's lawyers asked Ned if he'd tried to persuade his mother either way on the will question — if Powers received nothing, the remaining heirs, including Ned, stood to receive more. He insisted that neither he nor the spirits had sought to remove Kate from the will. The decision had been Isabella's.

The court decided for Powers, and Ned Hooker appealed, but in June 1908 he withdrew his appeal and agreed to grant Powers $10,000. The rest of the will was divided among family and a family servant, including $3,000

Isabella B. Hooker, 1902. *Courtesy of the Harriet Beecher Stowe Center, Hartford, Connecticut.*

in a trust for Ned's three children and — ever mindful of a married woman's standing in society — $5,000 to her daughter-in-law, Martha K. Hooker, "to be her sole and separate property." Daughter Alice received no share, "because she and her children are so amply provided for by the estate of her late husband." The rest of the estate went to Ned, according to a *Courant* story from June 11, 1908.

In October 1909, the notorious English suffragist Emmeline Pankhurst came to speak in Hartford and helped reignite the flame. Activists — including Katharine Houghton Hepburn, mother of the actress — began to organize campaigns using automobiles, and the first suffrage parade took place in Hartford on May 2, 1914.[21] The movement picked up steam — both in New England and elsewhere — but when Tennessee became the thirty-sixth state to ratify the Nineteenth Amendment in 1920, it was too late for Isabella, and for Elizabeth Cady Stanton, and Susan B. Anthony, and Lucretia Mott, and all the others. Some have been remembered and honored. Others — like Isabella — were cast aside.

So much for serenity. This complicated, openhearted, whole-souled, tempest-tossed woman bore little with serenity. From the beginning, she wanted more, she wanted it all, and she wanted it all at the same time. She'd tried to fit into the cultural ideal of womanhood, found the role too constricting, and set out to create her own path. She lived and died, exalted by some and misunderstood by most. When a civil rights movement was floundering, she stepped into the breach, a little nervous and a lot exhilarated. She risked public ridicule to stand by her beliefs. The condemnation stung, but she did not waiver. The last entry in her final journal, written in a spidery scrawl several months before she died, heralded family events and her own hope for a happy future: "But not until after I am gone over," she wrote.

We could learn from this woman.

NOTES

1. THE WORLD THAT AWAITED BELLE

1. *The Congregationalist and Christian World* (Cleveland: Pilgrim Press, 1907), 1: 137.

2. Edward F. Hayward, *Lyman Beecher* (Boston: Pilgrim Press, 1904), 1.

3. Edwin J. Perkins, *The Economy of Colonial America* (New York: Columbia University Press, 1988), 7.

4. Charles Beecher, *Autobiography, Correspondence, Etc., of Lyman Beecher, D.D.* (New York: Harper and Bros., 1865), 21.

5. Alan Bewell, *Romanticism and Colonial Disease* (Baltimore: Johns Hopkins University Press, 2003), 186.

6. Charles Beecher, *Autobiography*, 22.

7. Hayward, *Lyman Beecher*, 11.

8. George C. Kohn, *Encyclopedia of Plague and Pestilence* (New York: Infobase Publishing, 2010), 273.

9. Charles Beecher, *Autobiography*, 43.

10. Ibid., 45.

11. Hayward, *Lyman Beecher*, 12.

12. Walter Seth Logan, *Thomas Hooker: The First American Democrat* (Whitefish, MT: Kessinger Publishing, 2004), 19.

13. Charles Beecher, *Autobiography*, 53.

14. Mary Kelley, *Private Woman, Public Stage: Literary Domesticity in Nineteenth Century America* (Chapel Hill: University of North Carolina Press, 2002), 45.

15. Charles Beecher, *Autobiography*, 80.

16. Ibid., 76.

17. Jonathan Edwards, *Sinners in the Hands of an Angry God, and Other Puritan Sermons* (North Chelmsford, MA: Courier Dover Publications, 2005), v.

18. Lyman Beecher, "The Government of God Desirable: A Sermon," delivered at Newark, New Jersey, October 1808 (Boston: T. R. Marvin, 1827), 27.

19. Milton Rugoff, *The Beechers: An American Family in the Nineteenth Century* (New York: Harper & Row, 1981), 116.

20. Charles Kupchan, *The End of the American Era: U.S. Foreign Policy and the Geopolitics of the Twenty-First Century* (New York: Random House Digital, 2002), 315.

21. Joseph F. Healey, *Diversity and Society: Race, Ethnicity, and Gender* (New York: Pine Forge Press, 2009), 142.

22. Alan Heimert and Andrew Delbanco, *The Puritans in America: A Narrative Anthology* (Cambridge: Harvard University Press, 1985), 20.

23. George McKenna, *The Puritan Origins of American Patriotism* (New Haven: Yale University Press, 2007), 177.

24. James Hastings, John Alexander Selbie, and Louis Herbert Gray, *Encyclopedia of Religion and Ethics* (New York: T&T Clark, 1919), 10: 514.

25. Betsy Krieg Salm, *Women's Painted Furniture, 1790–1830* (Lebanon, NH: University Press of New England, 2010), 112.

26. Paxton Hibben and Sinclair Lewis, *Henry Ward Beecher: An American Portrait* (Whitefish, MT: Kessinger Publishing, 2003), 16.

27. National Bureau of Economic Research, *Trends in the American Economy in the Nineteenth Century*, Conference on Research in Income and Wealth, 1920, www.nber.org/books/unkn60-1.

28. Emily Noyes Vanderpol, *Chronicles of a Pioneer School from 1792 to 1833* (Lanham, MD: University Press, 1903), 259.

29. Christine Bolt, *The Women's Movements in the United States and Great Britain from the 1790s to the 1920s* (Amherst: University of Massachusetts Press, 1993), 41.

30. Margaret Beetham, *A Magazine of Her Own? Domesticity and Desire in the Woman's Magazine, 1800–1914* (Florence, KY: Psychology Press, 1996), 26.

31. K. H. Adler and Carrie Hamilton, *Homes and Homecomings: Gendered Histories of Domesticity and Return* (Hoboken, NJ: John Wiley & Sons, 2011), 69.

32. Michael Kazin, Rebecca Edwards, and Adam Rothman, *The Concise Princeton Encyclopedia of American Political History* (Princeton, NJ: Princeton University Press, 2011), 1:261.

33. Nancy F. Cott, *The Bonds of Womanhood: "Woman's Sphere" in New England, 1780–1835* (New Haven: Yale University Press, 1997), 104.

34. Cott, *The Bonds of Womanhood*, 64.

35. Heidi Brayman Hackle and Catherine E. Kelly, *Reading Women: Literacy, Authorship, and Culture in the Atlantic World, 1500–1800* (Philadelphia: University of Pennsylvania Press, 2009), 139.

36. Lyman Beecher, *A Plea for the West* (Cincinnati: Truman and Smith, 1835), 7.

37. Charles Beecher, *Autobiography*, 70.

38. Ibid., 10.

39. Charles Beecher, *Autobiography*, 11.

40. Jeanne Boydston, Mary Kelley, and Anne Throne Margolis, *The Limits of Sisterhood: The Beecher Sisters on Women's Rights and Woman's Sphere* (Chapel Hill: University of North Carolina Press, 1988), 20.

41. Susan Belasco, *Stowe in Her Own Time: A Biographical Chronicle of Her Life, Drawn from Recollections, Interviews, and Memoirs by Family, Friends, and Associates* (Iowa City: University of Iowa Press, 2009), xxxviii.

42. Hibben, *Henry Ward Beecher*, 10.

43. Barbara A. White, *The Beecher Sisters* (New Haven: Yale University Press, 2003), 4.

44. Debby Applegate, *The Most Famous Man in America: The Biography of Henry Ward Beecher* (New York: Doubleday, 2006), 31.

45. Lyman Beecher Stowe, *Saints, Sinners and Beechers* (Indianapolis: Bobbs-Merrill Co., 1934), 28.

46. Applegate, *The Most Famous Man in America*, 27.

47. Charles Beecher, *Autobiography*, 358.

48. Applegate, *The Most Famous Man in America*, 32.

49. Ibid., 32.

50. L. Stowe, *Saints, Sinners*, 45.

51. Ibid., 45.

52. Hayward, *Lyman Beecher*, 33–34.

53. Charles Beecher, *Autobiography*, 365.

54. L. Stowe, *Saints, Sinners*, 46.

55. John R. Howard, "Harriet Beecher Stowe: A Sketch," *The Outlook*, vol. 54 (1896), 138.

56. L. Beecher, *Saints, Sinners*, 424.

57. Samuel Agnew Schreiner, *The Passionate Beechers: A Family Saga of Sanctity and Scandal That Changed America* (Hoboken, NJ: John Wiley & Sons, 2003), 45.

58. Schreiner, *The Passionate Beechers*, 46.

59. Forrest Wilson, *Crusader in Crinoline: The Life of Harriet Beecher Stowe* (Philadelphia: J. B. Lippincott Co., 1941), 56.

60. Martha Foote Crow, *Harriet Beecher Stowe: A Biography for Girls* (New York: D. Appleton and Co., 1913), 54.

61. Harriet Beecher Stowe, *Life and Letters of Harriet Beecher Stowe* (New York: Houghton, Mifflin and Co., 1898), 30.

2. TRAINING TO BE A BEECHER

1. "Childbirth in Early America," Digital History, October 23, 2012, www.digitalhistory.uh.edu/historyonline/childbirth.cfm.

2. Janet Farrell Brodie, *Contraception and Abortion in Nineteenth-Century America* (Ithaca, NY: Cornell University, 1997), 5.

3. Nancy M. Theriot, *Mothers and Daughters in Nineteenth Century America: The Biosocial Construction of Femininity* (Lexington: University Press of Kentucky, 1996), 61.

4. Shirley Samuels, *Romances of the Republic: Women, the Family and Violence in the Literature of the Early American Nation* (New York: Oxford University Press, 1996), 150.

5. Ralph D. Gray and Michael A. Morrison, *New Perspectives on the Early Republic: Essays from the "Journal of the Early Republic," 1981–1991* (Champaign: University of Illinois Press, 1994), 466.

6. Forrest Wilson, *Crusader in Crinoline: The Life of Harriet Beecher Stowe* (Philadelphia: J. B. Lippincott Co., 1941), Wilson, 57.

7. Wilson, *Crusader in Crinoline*, 90.

8. Andrea Walton, *Women and Philanthropy in Education* (Bloomington: Indiana University Press, 2005), 39.

9. Walton, *Women and Philanthropy*, 40.

10. Valerie Finholm, "Pioneer Educator Unshuttered Young Women's Minds," *Hartford Courant*, January 15, 2002, http://articles.courant.com/2002-01-15/news/0201150767_1_calvin-stowe-lyman-beecher-catharine-beecher/3.

11. Walton, *Women and Philanthropy*, 46.

12. June Edwards, *Women in American Education, 1820–1955* (Westport, CT: Greenwood Publishing, 2002), 3.

13. Catharine Esther Beecher, *Educational Reminiscences and Suggestions* (New York: J. B. Ford and Co., 1874), 21.

14. Edward F. Hayward, *Lyman Beecher* (Boston: Pilgrim Press, 1904), 39.

15. Richard Joseph Purcell, *Connecticut in Transition, 1775–1818* (Connecticut: American Historical Association, 1918), 23.

16. Hayward, *Lyman Beecher*, 40.

17. James C. White, *Personal Reminiscences of Lyman Beecher* (New York: Funk & Wagnalls, 1882), 4.

18. J. White, *Personal Reminiscences*, 4.

19. Ibid., 5.

20. Ibid., 6.

21. Lyman Beecher and Joshua Lacy Wilson, *Trial and Acquittal of Lyman Beecher, D.D.* (Cincinnati: Eli Taylor, 1835), 33.

22. Charles Williams Wendte, D.D., *The Unitarian Register*, vol. 101 (Boston: American Unitarian Association, 1922), 399.

23. Lowell Mason and Michael Broyles, *A Yankee Musician in Europe: The 1837 Journals of Lowell Mason* (Rochester, NY: University of Rochester Press, 1990), 1.

24. Carol Ann Pemberton, *Lowell Mason: His Life and Work* (Ann Arbor, MI: UMI Research Press, 1985), 44.

25. Barbara A. White, *The Beecher Sisters* (New Haven: Yale University Press, 2003), 10–11.

26. Debby Applegate, *The Most Famous Man in America: The Biography of Henry Ward Beecher* (New York: Doubleday, 2006), 46.

27. B. White, *The Beecher Sisters*, 76.

28. William Constantine Beecher, Samuel Scoville, and Mrs. Henry Ward Beecher, *A Biography of Rev. Henry Ward Beecher* (London: S. Low, Marston, 1891), 54.

29. B. White, *The Beecher Sisters*, 18.

30. John Henry Barrows, *Henry Ward Beecher: The Shakespeare of the Pulpit* (New York: Funk & Wagnalls, 1893), 22.

31. David S. Reynolds, *Mightier than the Sword: "Uncle Tom's Cabin" and the Battle for America* (New York: W. W. Norton & Co., 2012), 4.

1. Federal Writers' Project, *Cincinnati: A Guide to the Queen City and Its Neighbors* (Washington, DC: U.S. History Publishers), xxi.

2. Lane Theological Seminary, *Pamphlet Souvenir of the Sixtieth Anniversary in the History of Lane Theological Seminary* (Cincinnati: Lane, 1890), 7.

3. Harriet Beecher Stowe, *Life of Harriet Beecher Stowe* (New York: Houghton, Mifflin and Co., 1891), 54.

4. Forrest Wilson, *Crusader in Crinoline: The Life of Harriet Beecher Stowe* (Philadelphia: J. B. Lippincott Co., 1941), 90.

5. Daniel Drake, *A Systemic Treatise, Historical, Etiological and Practical, on the Principal Diseases of North America* (Cincinnati: Winthrop B. Smith & Co., 1854), 392.

6. Daniel Drake, *The Western Journal of the Medical and Physical Sciences*, vol. 7 (1834), 172.

7. Edward Deering Mansfield, *Memoirs of the Life and Services of Daniel Drake, M.D., Physician, Professor, and Author* (Cincinnati: Applegate & Co., 1855), 219.

8. Debby Applegate, *The Most Famous Man in America: The Biography of Henry Ward Beecher* (New York: Doubleday, 2006), 110.

9. Henry Howe, *Historical Collections of Ohio: An Encyclopedia of the State* (Norwalk, OH: Laning Printing Co., 1896), 822.

10. Barbara A. White, *The Beecher Sisters* (New Haven: Yale University Press, 2003), 14.

11. John A. Jakle, "Cincinnati in the 1830s: A Cognitive Map of Travelers' Landscape Impressions," *Environmental Review* (Spring 1979), 2.

12. James L. Roark, Michael P. Johnson, Patricia Cline Cohen, Sarah Stage, and Susan M. Hartmann, *The American Promise*, vol. 1: *To 1877: A History of the United States* (New York: MacMillan, 2008), 381.

13. Nikki Marie Taylor, *Frontiers of Freedom: Cincinnati's Black Community, 1802–1868* (Athens: Ohio University Press, 2005), 56.

14. Taylor, *Frontiers of Freedom*, 56.

15. Ousmane Kirumu Greene, *Against Wind and Tide: African Americans' Response to the Colonization Movement and Emigration, 1770–1865* (Amherst: University of Massachusetts Press, 2007), 194.

16. Peter P. Hinks, John R. McKivigan, and R. Owen Williams, *Encyclopedia of Rights and Abolition* (Chapel Hill: University of North Carolina Press, 2004), 2:403.

17. Owen W. Muelder, *Theodore Dwight Weld and the American Anti-Slavery Society* (Jefferson, NC: McFarland, 2011), 54.

18. Hinks, *Encyclopedia*, 404.

19. Robert S. Fletcher, *A History of Oberlin College from Its Foundation through the Civil War* (Oberlin, OH: Oberlin College, 1943), 158–160.

20. Paxton Hibben and Sinclair Lewis, *Henry Ward Beecher: An American Portrait* (Whitefish, MT: Kessinger Publishing, 2003), 49.

21. Jeanne Boydston, Mary Kelley, and Anne Throne Margolis, *The Limits of*

Sisterhood: The Beecher Sisters on Women's Rights and Woman's Sphere (Chapel Hill: University of North Carolina Press, 1988), 3.

22. Fifth Annual Report of the Trustees of the Cincinnati Lane Seminary (Cincinnati: F. S. Benton, 1834), 2.

23. B. White, The Beecher Sisters, 16.

24. Joan D. Hedrick, Harriet Beecher Stowe: A Life (New York: Oxford University Press, 1995), 109.

25. Hedrick, Harriet Beecher Stowe, 109.

26. Isabella Beecher Hooker, "The Last of the Beechers: Memories on My 83rd Birthday," Connecticut (Spring 1905), 288.

27. James Miller, The Christian Examiner, vol. 19, 117.

28. Applegate, The Most Famous Man in America, 122.

29. Arthur Joseph Stansbury, Trial of the Rev. Lyman Beecher, D.D., before the Presbytery of Cincinnati on the Charge of Heresy (New York, 1835), 1.

30. E. Polk Johnson, A History of Kentucky and Kentuckians: The Leaders and Representative Men in Commerce, Industry, and Modern Activities (Chicago: Lewis Publishing Co., 1912), 3: 1256.

31. Zebulon Crocker, The Catastrophe of the Presbyterian Church (New Haven: B&W Noyes, 1838), 75.

32. Hedrick, Harriet Beecher Stowe, 122.

33. B. White, The Beecher Sisters, 19.

34. Anne Throne Margolis and Margaret Granville Mair, eds., Guide to the Isabella Beecher Hooker Project (Hartford: Stowe-Day Foundation, 1979), 10.

35. Dale Patrick Brown, Literary Cincinnati: The Missing Chapter (Athens: Ohio University Press, 2011), 22.

36. Susan Belasco, Stowe in Her Own Time: A Biographical Chronicle of Her Life, Drawn from Recollections, Interviews, and Memoirs by Family, Friends, and Associates (Iowa City: University of Iowa Press, 2009), 33.

37. Catharine Esther Beecher, Educational Reminiscences and Suggestions (New York: J. B. Ford and Co., 1874), 84.

38. Alisse Portnoy, Their Right to Speak: Women's Activism in the Indian and Slave Debates (Cambridge: Harvard University Press, 2005), 187.

39. Belasco, Stowe in Her Own Time, 30.

40. B. White, The Beecher Sisters, 17.

41. Ibid., 18.

42. Wilson, Crusader in Crinoline, 155.

43. Ibid., 155.

44. Lyman Beecher, A Plea for the West (Cincinnati: Truman and Smith, 1835), 410.

45. B. White, The Beecher Sisters, 21.

46. Hedrick, Harriet Beecher Stowe, 22.

47. B. White, The Beecher Sisters, 19.

48. Ibid., 21.

49. Ibid., 20.

50. Ibid., 21.

51. Ibid.

52. Ibid., 25.

53. Conrad Reno and Leonard Augustus Jones, *Memoirs of the Judiciary and the Bar of New England of the Nineteenth Century* (Post Falls, ID: Century Memorial Publishing Co., 1901), 1: 125.

54. B. White, *The Beecher Sisters*, 25.

55. Cynthia J. Davis, *Charlotte Perkins Gilman: A Biography* (Palo Alto, CA: Stanford University Press, 2010), 259.

56. Charlotte Perkins Gilman and Larry Ceplair, *Charlotte Perkins Gilman: A Nonfiction Reader* (New York: Columbia University Press, 1991), ix.

57. Lyman Beecher Stowe, *Saints, Sinners and Beechers* (Indianapolis: Bobbs-Merrill Co., 1934), 344.

4. ISABELLA IN LOVE

1. Michiyo Morita, *Horace Bushnell on Women in Nineteenth Century America* (Lanham, MD: University Press of America, 2004), 4.

2. Paul S. Boyer et al., *The Enduring Vision: A History of the American People since 1863* (Independence, KY: Cengage Learning, 2012), 216.

3. Perry Miller, *Errand into the Wilderness* (Cambridge: Harvard University Press, 1956), 17.

4. Samuel Agnew Schreiner, *The Passionate Beechers: A Family Saga of Sanctity and Scandal That Changed America* (Hoboken, NJ: John Wiley & Sons, 2003), 195.

5. Barbara A. White, *The Beecher Sisters* (New Haven: Yale University Press, 2003), 242.

6. Lydia Hewes, *A Short History of Farmington, Conn.* (Farmington Committee of the Connecticut Tercentenary, 1935), 21.

7. Joshua Lawrence Chamberlain, ed., *Universities and Their Sons: History, Influence, and Characteristics of American Universities, with Biographical Sketches and Portraits of Alumni and Recipients of Honorary Degrees* (Boston: R. Herndon Co., 1900), 4: 495.

8. *Hartford Courant*, Nov. 16, 1927.

9. John Hooker, *Reminiscences of a Long Life: With a Few Articles on Moral and Social Subjects of Present Interest* (Hartford: Case, Lockwood & Brainard Co., 1899), 145.

10. Ibid., 114.

11. B. White, *The Beecher Sisters*, 37.

12. Jeanne Boydston, Mary Kelley, and Anne Throne Margolis, *The Limits of Sisterhood: The Beecher Sisters on Women's Rights and Woman's Sphere* (Chapel Hill: University of North Carolina Press, 1988), 337.

13. Boydston, *The Limits of Sisterhood*, 338.

14. Ibid., 339.

15. Schreiner, *The Passionate Beechers*, 108–109.

16. Debby Applegate, *The Most Famous Man in America: The Biography of Henry Ward Beecher* (New York: Doubleday, 2006), 165.

17. Applegate, *The Most Famous Man in America*, 166.

5. ISABELLA MARRIES, AND FACES A CONUNDRUM

1. Francesca M. Cancian, *Love in America: Gender and Self-Development* (New York: Cambridge University Press, 1990), 18.

2. Cancian, *Love in America*, 19.

3. Elizabeth C. Stevens, *Elizabeth Buffum Chace and Lillie Chace Wyman: A Century of Abolitionist, Suffragist, and Workers' Rights Activism* (Jefferson, NC: McFarland, 2003), 8.

4. John S. C. Abbott, *The Mother at Home; or, Principles of Maternal Duty* (Boston: Crocker & Brewster, 1835), 78.

5. Rima Dombrow Apple, *Perfect Motherhood: Science and Childrearing in America* (Piscataway Township, NJ: Rutgers University Press, 2006), 4.

6. John Hooker, *Reminiscences of a Long Life: With a Few Articles on Moral and Social Subjects of Present Interest* (Hartford: Case, Lockwood & Brainard Co., 1899), 128.

7. Barbara A. White, *The Beecher Sisters* (New Haven: Yale University Press, 2003), 34.

8. Sir William Blackstone, *Commentaries on the Laws of England* (Chicago: Callaghan and Co., 1884), 1:289.

9. Anne Throne Margolis and Margaret Granville Mair, eds., *Guide to the Isabella Beecher Hooker Project* (Hartford: Stowe-Day Foundation, 1979), 12.

10. Michael Grossberg and Christopher L. Tomlins, *The Cambridge History of Law in America: Early America, 1580–1815* (New York: Cambridge University Press, 2008), 318.

11. Isabella Beecher Hooker, "The Last of the Beechers: Memories on My 83rd Birthday," *Connecticut* (Spring 1905), 291.

12. J. Hooker, *Reminiscences*, 10.

13. Kathleen Anne McHugh, *American Domesticity: From How-To Manual to Hollywood Melodrama* (New York: Oxford University Press, 1999), 5.

14. Jeanne Boydston, Mary Kelley, and Anne Throne Margolis, *The Limits of Sisterhood: The Beecher Sisters on Women's Rights and Woman's Sphere* (Chapel Hill: University of North Carolina Press, 1988), 82.

15. B. White, *The Beecher Sisters*, 34.

16. Sarah Frances Smith, *"She Moves the Hands That Move the World": Antebellum Childrearing* (Minneapolis: University of Minnesota Press, 2006), 111.

17. Mary P. Ryan, *The Empire of the Mother: American Writing about Domesticity, 1830 to 1860* (Florence, KY: Psychology Press, 1982), 56.

18. Julia Grant, *Raising Baby by the Book: The Education of American Mothers* (New Haven: Yale University Press, 1998), 23.

19. Margolis, *Guide*, 12.

20. John S. Haller, *The History of American Homeopathy: The Academic Years, 1820–1935* (Florence, KY: Psychology Press, 2005), 48.

21. Margolis, *Guide*, 13.

22. Susan Cayleff, *Wash and Be Healed: The Water-Cure Movement and Women's Health* (Philadelphia: Temple University Press, 1991), 17.

23. Martha H. Verbrugge, *Able-Bodied Womanhood: Personal Health and Social Change in Nineteenth-Century Boston* (New York: Oxford University Press, 1988), 24.

24. *The Water-Cure Journal*, vols. 17–20 (New York: Fowler and Wells, 1854), 109.

25. Cayleff, *Wash and Be Healed*, 63.

26. Ibid., 73.

27. Judith Walzer Leavitt, *Women and Health in America: Historical Readings* (Madison: University of Wisconsin Press, 1999), 177.

28. Stacey M. Robertson and Parker Pillsbury: Radical Abolitionist, Male Feminist (Ithaca, NY: Cornell University, 2007), 172.

29. Catharine E. Beecher, "The Water Cure," *The National Era* v, no. 226, 71.

30. Laura E. Skandera Trombley, *Mark Twain in the Company of Women* (Philadelphia: University of Pennsylvania Press, 1997), 78.

31. H. F. Phinney, *The Water Cure in America: Over Three Hundred Cases of Various Diseases Treated with Water* (New York: Fowler and Wells, 1852), 326.

32. Marybetts Sinclair, *Modern Hydrotherapy for the Massage Therapist* (Philadelphia: Lippincott Williams & Wilkins, 2007), 13.

33. Sarah Robbins, *The Cambridge Introduction to Harriet Beecher Stowe* (New York: Cambridge University Press, 2007), 5.

34. Marilyn T. Williams, *Washing "The Great Unwashed": Public Baths in Urban America, 1840–1920* (Columbus: Ohio State University Press, 1991), 13.

35. B. White, *The Beecher Sisters*, 37.

36. Henry Elliot, *Harriet Beecher Stowe: The Voice of Humanity in White America* (New York: Crabtree Publishing Co., 2009), 18.

37. Paxton Hibben and Sinclair Lewis, *Henry Ward Beecher: An American Portrait* (Whitefish, MT: Kessinger Publishing, 2003), 48.

38. Hibben, *Henry Ward Beecher*, 48.

39. Gary J. Dorrien, *The Making of American Liberal Theology: Imagining Progressive Religion, 1805–1900* (Louisville: Westminster John Knox Press, 2001), 182.

40. J. Hooker, *Reminiscences*, 22.

41. Linda Carlson Johnson, "Isabella Beecher Hooker: The Suffragists' Preacher" (master's thesis, Hartford Seminary, September 1998), 6.

42. Mason I. Lowance, *Against Slavery: An Abolitionist Reader* (New York: Penguin, 2000), xxix.

43. Grossberg, *The Cambridge History of Law*, 302.

44. Jean Fagan Yellin and John C. van Horne, *The Abolitionist Sisterhood: Women's Political Culture in Antebellum America* (Ithaca, NY: Cornell University Press, 1994), 301.

45. Karen P. O'Connor, *Gender and Women's Leadership: A Reference Handbook* (Thousand Oaks, CA: Sage Publications, 2010), 182.

46. Lee Ann Banaszak, *Why Movements Succeed or Fail: Opportunity, Culture, and the Struggle for Woman Suffrage* (Princeton, NJ: Princeton University Press, 1996), 68.

47. Lisa Tendrich Frank, *Women in the Civil War* (Santa Barbara, CA: ABC-CLIO, 2008), 1:8.

48. Kathryn Cullen-DuPont, *Women's Suffrage in America* (New York: Infobase Publishing, 2005), 58.

49. Peter P. Hinks, John R. McKivigan, and R. Owen Williams, *Encyclopedia of Rights and Abolition* (Chapel Hill: University of North Carolina Press, 2004), 2: 761.

50. Linda Carlson Johnson, "Isabella Beecher Hooker," 6.

51. Marie Caskey, *Chariots of Fire: Religion and the Beecher Family* (New Haven: Yale University Press, 1978), 112.

52. Paul Finkelman, ed., *Encyclopedia of African American History, 1619–1895* (New York: Oxford University Press, 2006), 275.

53. Darcy G. Robinson, *Others: Third Party Politics from the Nation's Founding to the Rise and Fall of the Greenback-Labor Party* (iUniverse, 2004), 104.

54. Kevin Murphy, *Water for Hartford: The Story of the Hartford Water Works and the Metropolitan District Commission* (Middletown, CT: Wesleyan University Press, 2010), 38.

55. James L. Sundquist, *Dynamics of the Party System: Alignment and Realignment of Political Parties in the United States* (Washington, DC: Brookings Institution Press, 1983), 58.

56. Emma Hardinge Britten, *Modern American Spiritualism: A Twenty Years' Record of the Communion between Earth and the World of Spirits* (New Hyde Park, NY: University Books, 1870), 155.

57. Mark Twain, "Schoolhouse Hill," *Huck Finn and Tom Sawyer among the Indians, and Other Unfinished Stories* (Berkeley: University of California Press, 1989), 245.

58. Barbara Goldsmith, *Other Powers: The Age of Suffrage, Spiritualism, and the Scandalous Victoria Woodhull* (New York: Harper Perennial, 1999), 69.

59. Harriet Elinor Smith, ed., *Autobiography of Mark Twain* (Berkeley: University of California Press, 2010), 1: 356.

60. H. Smith, *Autobiography of Mark Twain*, 356.

61. David S. Reynolds, *Mightier than the Sword: "Uncle Tom's Cabin" and the Battle for America* (New York: W. W. Norton & Co., 2011), 19.

62. Susan B. Martinez, *The Psychic Life of Abraham Lincoln* (Pompton Plains, NY: Career Press, 2007), 161.

63. Molly McGarry, *Ghosts of Futures Past: Spiritualism and the Cultural Politics of the Nineteenth Century* (Berkeley: University of California Press, 2008), 4.

64. Ann Braude, *Radical Spirits: Spiritualism and Women's Rights in Nineteenth Century America* (Boston: Beacon Press, 1989), 78.

65. Mary Gabriel, *Notorious Victoria: The Life of Victoria Woodhull, Uncensored* (New York: Algonquin Books, 1998), 29.

66. Matthew Warshauer, *Connecticut in the American Civil War: Slavery, Sacrifice, and Survival* (Middletown, CT: Wesleyan University Press, 2011), 24.

67. Boydston, *The Limits of Sisterhood*, 83.

68. Ibid., 91.

6. MOTHERHOOD, AND CONFUSION

1. Christopher Benfey, *A Summer of Hummingbirds: Love, Art and Scandal in the Intersecting Worlds of Emily Dickinson, Mark Twain, Harriet Beecher Stowe and Martin Johnson Heade* (New York: Penguin Press, 2008), 226.

2. Emory Elliott, *Columbia Literary History of the United States* (New York: Columbia University Press, 1988), 765.

3. Samuel May, *The Fugitive Slave Law and Its Victims* (Boston: American Anti-Slavery Society, 1861), 8.

4. William Craft and Ellen Craft, *Running a Thousand Miles for Freedom* (Teddington, UK: Echo Library, 2009), 16.

5. John M. Murrin, Paul E. Johnson, James M. McPherson, Alice Fahs, and Gary Gerstle, *Liberty, Equality, Power*, vol. 2: *A History of the American People since 1863* (Independence, KY: Cengage Learning, 2011), 365.

6. Murrin, *Liberty, Equality, Power*, 365.

7. Allen Johnson, ed., *Readings in American Constitutional History, 1776–1876* (New York: Houghton Mifflin Co., 1912), 416.

8. Junius P. Rodriguez, *Slavery in the United States: A Social, Political, and Historical Encyclopedia* (Santa Barbara, CA: ABC-CLIO, 2007), 2:424.

9. John R. McKivigan, *Abolitionism and the Law* (Florence, KY: Taylor & Francis, 1999), 199.

10. Clarence Edwin Carter, *The Struggle in Congress over Abolition Petitions* (Madison: University of Wisconsin–Madison, 1906), 47.

11. Rodriguez, *Slavery in the United States*, 425.

12. May, *The Fugitive Slave Law*, 5.

13. Ibid., 5.

14. John Hooker, *Reminiscences of a Long Life: With a Few Articles on Moral and Social Subjects of Present Interest* (Hartford: Case, Lockwood & Brainard Co., 1899), 38.

15. Barbara A. White, *The Beecher Sisters* (New Haven: Yale University Press, 2003), 15.

16. B. White, *The Beecher Sisters*, 16.

17. Jeffrey Schultz, John West, and Iain Maclean, *Encyclopedia of Religion in American Politics* (Westport, CT: Greenwood Publishing Group, 1998), 23.

18. Tim McNeese, *America's Civil War* (Dayton, OH: Lorenz Educational Press, 2003), 20.

19. Joan D. Hedrick, *Harriet Beecher Stowe: A Life* (New York: Oxford University Press, 1995), 206–7.

20. B. White, *The Beecher Sisters*, 16.

21. Elsa Dixler, *Harriet Beecher Stowe's "Uncle Tom's Cabin"* (Hauppauge, NY: Barron's Educational Series, 1985), 105.

22. Mason I. Lowance and Ellen E. Westbrook, *The Stowe Debate: Rhetorical Struggles in "Uncle Tom's Cabin"* (Amherst: University of Massachusetts Press, 1994), 262.

23. David W. Blight, *Frederick Douglass' Civil War: Keeping Faith in Jubilee* (Baton Rouge: Louisiana State University Press, 1991), 127.

24. Eric J. Sundquist, *New Essays on "Uncle Tom's Cabin"* (New York: Cambridge University Press, 1986), 142.

25. Blight, *Frederick Douglass' Civil War*, 7.

26. Alfred Bendixen, *A Companion to the American Novel* (Hoboken, NJ: John Wiley & Sons, 2012), 414.

27. Christopher L. Webber, *American to the Backbone: The Life of James W. C. Pennington, the Fugitive Slave Who Became One of the First Black Abolitionists* (New York: Open Road Media, 2011), i.

28. Lyman Beecher, *A Plea for the West* (Cincinnati: Truman and Smith, 1835), 541.

29. Jeanne Boydston, Mary Kelley, and Anne Throne Margolis, *The Limits of Sisterhood: The Beecher Sisters on Women's Rights and Woman's Sphere* (Chapel Hill: University of North Carolina Press, 1988), 139.

30. Hedrick, *Harriet Beecher Stowe*, 221.

31. Claire Parfait, *The Publishing History of "Uncle Tom's Cabin," 1852–2002* (London: Ashgate Publishing Co., 2007), 17.

32. Robert B. Downs, *Books That Changed the World* (New York: Penguin, 2004), 266.

33. Downs, *Books*, 266.

34. Ibid., 273.

35. Edward T. James and Janet Wilson James, *Notable American Women: A Biographical Dictionary* (Cambridge: Belknap Press, 1971), 80.

36. Catharine E. Beecher, *The American Woman's Home* (New York: J. B. Ford & Co., 1872), 466.

37. June Edwards, *Women in American Education, 1820–1955* (Westport, CT: Greenwood Publishing, 2002), 8.

38. Frederick Rudolph and John R. Thelin, *The American College and University: A History* (Athens: University of Georgia Press, 1962), 312.

39. Catharine Esther Beecher and Harriet Beecher Stowe, *The American Woman's Home,* ed. Nicole Tonkovich (Piscataway Township, NJ: Rutgers University Press, 2002), xvi.

40. Gregg Lee Carter, *Guns in American Society* (Santa Barbara, CA: ABC-CLIO, 2002), 58.

41. Lyman Beecher Stowe, *Saints, Sinners and Beechers* (Indianapolis: Bobbs-Merrill Co., 1934), 283.

42. John Bach McMaster, *A History of the People of the United States: From the Revolution to the Civil War* (New York: D. Appleton, 1913), 8: 256.

43. Paul Finkelman, ed., *Encyclopedia of African American History, 1619–1895* (New York: Oxford University Press, 2006), 122.

44. Boydston, *The Limits of Sisterhood*, 84.

45. J. Hooker, *Reminiscences*, 170.

46. Joseph S. Van Why and Earl French, eds., *Nook Farm* (Hartford: Stowe-Day Foundation, 1975), 9.

47. Anne Throne Margolis and Margaret Granville Mair, eds., *Guide to the Isabella Beecher Hooker Project* (Hartford: Stowe-Day Foundation, 1979), 13.

48. Margolis, *Guide*, 13.

49. Kenneth Richmond Andrews, *Nook Farm: Mark Twain's Hartford Circle* (Cambridge: Harvard University Press, 1950), xi.

50. Mary P. Ryan, *The Empire of the Mother: American Writing about Domesticity, 1830 to 1860* (Sussex, UK: Psychology Press, 1982), 97.

51. Amy Kaplan, *The Anarchy of Empire in the Making of U.S. Culture* (Cambridge: Harvard University Press, 2005), 28.

52. Julia T. Wood, *Gendered Lives: Communication, Gender & Culture* (Independence, KY: Cengage Learning, 2010), 71.

53. D. Margaret Costa and Sharon Ruth Guthrie, *Women and Sport: Interdisciplinary Perspectives* (Champaign, IL: Human Kinetics, 1994), 66.

54. Nancy F. Cott, *The Bonds of Womanhood: "Woman's Sphere" in New England, 1780–1835* (New Haven: Yale University Press, 1997), 126.

55. Boydston, *The Limits of Sisterhood*, 84.

56. Benfey, *A Summer of Hummingbirds*, 17.

57. Beverly Ann Zink-Sawyer, *From Preachers to Suffragists: Woman's Rights and Religious Conviction in the Lives of Three Nineteenth-Century Clergywomen* (Louisville: Westminster John Knox Press, 2003), 15.

58. Mary Potter Thacher Higginson, *Thomas Wentworth Higginson: The Story of His Life* (New York: Houghton Mifflin Co., 1914), 73.

59. Thomas Wentworth Higginson, "Ought Women to Learn the Alphabet?" *Atlantic Monthly*, February 1859.

60. Henry Ward Beecher, *Woman's Influence in Politics* (Boston: R. F. Wallcut, 1869), 8.

61. Linda Carlson Johnson, "Isabella Beecher Hooker: The Suffragists' Preacher," master's thesis (Hartford Seminary, September 1998), 16.

62. B. White, *The Beecher Sisters*, 74.

63. Boydston, *The Limits of Sisterhood*, 108–9.

64. Ibid., 111.

65. Margolis, *Guide*, 16.

66. Ibid., 16.

67. Brenda Wineapple, *White Heat: The Friendship of Emily Dickinson and Thomas Wentworth Higginson* (New York: Random House Digital, 2009), 33.

68. Vivian Gornick, *The Solitude of Self: Thinking about Elizabeth Cady Stanton* (New York: Macmillan, 2006), 86.

69. Margolis, *Guide*, 15.

7. ABOLITION, AND AN AWAKENING

1. Daniel Coit Gilman, Harry Thurston Peck, and Frank Moore Colby, *The New International Encyclopedia*, vol. 20 (New York: Dodd, Mead and Co., 1909), 622.

2. Patricia A. Cunningham, *Reforming Women's Fashion, 1850–1920: Politics, Health, and Art* (Kent, OH: Kent State University Press, 2003), 33.

3. Laura E. Skandera Trombley, *Mark Twain in the Company of Women* (Philadelphia: University of Pennsylvania Press, 1997), 81.

4. Linda M. Scott, *Fresh Lipstick: Redressing Fashion and Feminism* (New York: Macmillan, 2006), 58.

5. Mary J. Lickteig, *Amelia Bloomer: A Photo-Illustrated Biography* (North Mankato, MN: Capstone Press, 1998), 15.

6. Cunningham, *Reforming Women's Fashion*, 61.

7. Beverly Ann Zink-Sawyer, *From Preachers to Suffragists: Woman's Rights and Religious Conviction in the Lives of Three Nineteenth-Century Clergywomen* (Louisville: Westminster John Knox Press, 2003), 15.

8. Henry Ward Beecher, *Woman's Influence in Politics: An Address Delivered by Henry Ward Beecher, at Cooper Institute, New York, Thursday Evening, Feb. 2d, 1860* (New York: R. F. Wallcut Co., 1860), 8.

9. Paxton Hibben and Sinclair Lewis, *Henry Ward Beecher: An American Portrait* (Whitefish, MT: Kessinger Publishing, 2003), 176.

10. Karlyn Kohrs Campbell, *Women Public Speakers in the United States, 1800–1925* (Santa Barbara, CA: ABC-CLIO, 1993), 156.

11. Bellee Squire, *The Woman Movement in America: A Short Account of the Struggle for Equal Rights* (Chicago: A. C. McClurg & Co., 1911), 103.

12. John Stuart Mill and Harriet Taylor Mill, *Essays on Sex Equality*, ed. Alice S. Rossi (Chicago: University of Chicago Press, 1970), 41.

13. Harriet Taylor Mill, "The Enfranchisement of Women," *Westminster Review,* July 1851.

14. Anne Throne Margolis and Margaret Granville Mair, eds., *Guide to the Isabella Beecher Hooker Project* (Hartford: Stowe-Day Foundation, 1979), 19.

15. Barbara A. White, *Visits with Lincoln: Abolitionists Meet the President at the White House* (Lanham, MD: Lexington Books, 2001), 51.

16. Mark A. Noll, *America's God: From Jonathan Edwards to Abraham Lincoln* (New York: Oxford University Press, 2002), 326.

17. Elizabeth Cady Stanton and Harriot Stanton Blatch, *Elizabeth Cady Stanton as Revealed in Her Letters, Diary and Reminiscences* (New York: Harper and Bros., 1922), 38.

18. Lori D. Ginzberg, *Elizabeth Cady Stanton: An American Life* (New York: Macmillan, 2010), 108.

19. Joseph S. Van Why and Earl French, eds., *Nook Farm* (Hartford: Stowe-Day Foundation, 1975), 20.

20. Gordon Morris Bakken and Brenda Farrington, *Encyclopedia of Women in the American West* (New York: SAGE, 2003), 257.

21. Mrs. John A. Logan, *The Part Taken by Women in American History* (Wilmington, DE: Perry-Nalle Publishing Co., 1912), 415.

22. Logan, *The Part Taken by Women*, 415.

23. Margolis, *Guide*, 20.

24. Matthew Warshauer, *Connecticut in the American Civil War: Slavery, Sacrifice, and Survival* (Middletown, CT: Wesleyan University Press, 2011), 254.

25. Warshauer, *Connecticut in the American Civil War*, 62.

26. Jeanne Boydston, Mary Kelley, and Anne Throne Margolis, *The Limits of Sisterhood: The Beecher Sisters on Women's Rights and Woman's Sphere* (Chapel Hill: University of North Carolina Press, 1988), 81.

27. Daniel R. Vollaro, "Lincoln, Stowe, and the 'Little Woman/Great War' Story: The Making, and Breaking of a Great American Anecdote," *Journal of the Abraham Lincoln Association* 30, no. 1 (Winter 2009).

28. B. White, *The Beecher Sisters*, 92.

29. Ellen Carol DuBois, *Feminism and Suffrage: The Emergence of an Independent Women's Movement in America, 1848–1869* (Ithaca, NY: Cornell University Press, 1999), 79.

30. Eleanor Flexner and Ellen Frances Fitzpatrick, *Century of Struggle: The Woman's Rights Movement in the United States* (Cambridge: Harvard University Press, 1996), 140.

31. Tom Slater, Tom Slater, and James L. Halperin, ed., *Heritage Political Memorabilia and Americana Auction Catalog* no. 659 (Heritage Capital Corp., 2007), 55.

32. DuBois, *Feminism and Suffrage*, 80.

33. Flexner, *Century of Struggle*, 139.

34. Faye E. Dudden, *Fighting Chance: The Struggle over Woman Suffrage and Black Suffrage in Reconstruction America* (New York: Oxford University Press, 2011), 11.

35. Carolyn Summers Vacca, *A Reform against Nature: Woman Suffrage and the Rethinking of American Citizenship, 1840–1920* (New York: Peter Lang, 2004), 49.

36. Deborah Kent, *Elizabeth Cady Stanton: Woman Knows the Cost of Life* (Berkeley Heights, NJ: Enslow Publishers, 2010), 69.

37. Sally G. McMillen, *Seneca Falls and the Origins of the Women's Rights Movement* (New York: Oxford University Press, 2009), 170.

38. McMillen, *Seneca Falls*, 171.

39. Elisabeth Griffith, *In Her Own Right: The Life of Elizabeth Cady Stanton* (New York: Oxford University Press, 1984), 130.

40. Dudden, *Fighting Chance*, 11.

41. Ann D. Gordon, ed., *The Selected Papers of Elizabeth Cady Stanton and Susan B. Anthony: National Protection for National Citizens, 1873 to 1880* (Piscataway Township, NJ: Rutgers University Press, 2000), 79.

42. Ann D. Gordon, ed., *The Selected Papers of Elizabeth Cady Stanton and Susan B. Anthony: Against an Aristocracy of Sex, 1866 to 1873* (Piscataway Township, NJ: Rutgers University Press, 2000), 246.

43. Boydston, *The Limits of Sisterhood*, 199.

44. Carol Faulkner, *Lucretia Mott's Heresy: Abolition and Women's Rights in Nineteenth Century America* (Philadelphia: University of Pennsylvania Press), 187.

45. Jean Fagan Yellin, *Harriet Jacobs: A Life* (Jackson, TN: Basic Civitas Book), 202.

46. Barbara Goldsmith, *Other Powers: The Age of Suffrage, Spiritualism, and the Scandalous Victoria Woodhull* (New York: Harper Perennial, 1999), 196.

47. Charles Howard Young, *The Sunny Life of an Invalid* (Hartford: Case, Lockwood & Brainard, 1897), 104.

48. Carole Nichols, *Votes and More for Women: Suffrage and After in Connecticut* (Florence, KY: Psychology Press, 1983), 6.

49. Nichols, "Votes and More for Women," 6.

50. Linda Carlson Johnson, "Isabella Beecher Hooker," 23.

51. Ibid., 28.

52. Isabella Beecher Hooker, "A Mother's Letters to a Daughter on Woman Suffrage," www.connhistory.org/Isabella_readings.htm.

53. Boydston, *The Limits of Sisterhood*, 81.

54. Linda Carlson Johnson, "Isabella Beecher Hooker," 39.

55. Andrea Moore Kerr, *Lucy Stone: Speaking Out for Equality* (Piscataway Township, NJ: Rutgers University Press, 1992), 138.

56. Alexander Tsesis, *We Shall Overcome: A History of Civil Rights and the Law* (New Haven: Yale University Press, 2008), 149.

57. Ellen Carol DuBois and Richard Candida Smith, *Elizabeth Cady Stanton, Feminist as Thinker: A Reader in Documents and Essays* (New York: New York University Press, 2007), 142.

58. DuBois and Smith, *Elizabeth Cady Stanton*, 139.

59. Ibid., 136.

60. Linda Carlson Johnson, "Isabella Beecher Hooker," 38.

61. DuBois, *Feminism and Suffrage*, 169.

62. Kathleen Hall Jamieson, *Eloquence in an Electronic Age: The Transformation of Political Speechmaking* (New York: Oxford University Press, 1990), 110.

63. Elizabeth Cady Stanton, ed., *History of Woman Suffrage* (New York: Fowler and Wells, 1882), 6: 383.

64. Dudden, *Fighting Chance*, 163.

65. Ibid., 163.

66. Steven M. Buechler, *Women's Movements in the United States: Woman Suffrage, Equal Rights, and Beyond* (Piscataway Township, NJ: Rutgers University Press, 1990), 140.

67. David S. Reynolds, *Mightier than the Sword: "Uncle Tom's Cabin" and the Battle for America* (New York: W. W. Norton & Co., 2012), 53–54.

68. Linda Carlson Johnson, "Isabella Beecher Hooker," 40.

69. Michiyo Morita, *Horace Bushnell on Women in Nineteenth Century America* (Lanham, MD: University Press of America, 2004), 97.

70. Susan E. Marshall, *Splintered Sisterhood: Gender and Class in the Campaign against Woman Suffrage* (Madison: University of Wisconsin Press, 1997), 20.

71. Patricia Lyn Scott and Linda Thatcher, *Women in Utah History: Paradigm or Paradox?* (Logan: Utah State University Press, 2005), 371.

72. John R. Shook, *Dictionary of Modern American Philosophers* (New York: Continuum International Publishing Group, 2005), 1: 175.

73. Boydston, *The Limits of Sisterhood*, 352.

74. Linda Carlson Johnson, "Isabella Beecher Hooker," 69.

75. Ibid., 32.

76. Kathryn Cullen-DuPont, *Women's Suffrage in America* (New York: Infobase Publishing, 2005), 447.

77. David A. J. Richards, *Women, Gays, and the Constitution: The Grounds for Feminism and Gay Rights in Culture and Law* (Chicago: University of Chicago Press, 1998), 156.

78. Janet Todd, *Mary Wollstonecraft: A Revolutionary Life* (New York: Columbia University Press, 2002), ix.

79. Goldsmith, *Other Powers*, 208.

80. Stanton, ed., *History of Woman Suffrage*, 389.

81. Ibid., 386.

82. Judith E. Harper, *Women during the Civil War: An Encyclopedia* (Boca Raton, FL: CRC Press), 468.

83. Boydston, *The Limits of Sisterhood*, 187.

84. Kimberly Ann Hamlin, *Beyond Adam's Rib: How Darwinian Evolutionary Theory Defined Gender and Influenced American Feminist Thought, 1870–1920* (Ann Arbor, MI: ProQuest, 2007), 46.

85. Linda Carlson Johnson, "Isabella Beecher Hooker," 48.

86. Joan D. Hedrick, *Harriet Beecher Stowe: A Life* (New York: Oxford University Press, 1995), 358.

87. Nicholas H. Wolfinger, *Understanding the Divorce Cycle: The Children of Divorce in Their Own Marriages* (New York: Cambridge University Press, 2005), 117.

88. David Brion Davis, *Antebellum American Culture: An Interpretive Anthology* (University Park: Penn State University Press, 1979), 96.

89. *Annual Report of the Secretary of State of Ohio* (1873), 237.

90. Ann Field, ed., *Harriet Beecher Stowe: Life and Letters* (New York: Houghton, Mifflin, 1897), 303.

91. Horace Bushnell, *Women's Suffrage: The Reform against Nature* (New York: C. Scribner and Co., 1869), 5.

92. Morita, *Horace Bushnell*, 107.

93. Bushnell, *Women's Suffrage*, 21.

94. Ibid., 44.

95. Barbara A. White, *The Beecher Sisters* (New Haven: Yale University Press, 2003), 147.

96. Ida Husted Harper, *The Life and Work of Susan B. Anthony* (Indianapolis: Bowen-Merrill Co., 1898), 413.

97. Ellen Burr, recording sec., notes of the Connecticut Woman Suffrage Association, vol. 1 (1869), Connecticut State Library.

98. Edward Royall Tyler, *New Englander and Yale Review* (New Haven: W. L. Kingsley, 1888) 48: 321.

99. Boydston, *The Limits of Sisterhood*, 293.

100. Van Why, *Nook Farm*, 37.

101. Linda Carlson Johnson, "Isabella Beecher Hooker," 62.

102. Wendy Hamand Venet, *A Strong-Minded Woman: The Life of Mary Livermore* (Amherst: University of Massachusetts Press, 2005), 1.

103. Linda Carlson Johnson, "Isabella Beecher Hooker," 52.

104. Ibid., 54.

105. Michael Anthony Lawrence, *Radicals in Their Own Time: Four Hundred Years of Struggle for Liberty and Equal Justice in America* (New York: Cambridge University Press, 2010), 343.

106. Gordon, ed., *The Selected Papers*, 240.

107. I. Harper, *The Life and Work*, 362.

108. Sue Davis, *The Political Thought of Elizabeth Cady Stanton: Women's Rights and the American Political Traditions* (New York: New York University Press, 2008), 256.

109. Mary Chapman and Angela Mills, *Treacherous Texts: U.S. Suffrage Literature, 1846–1946* (Piscataway Township, NJ: Rutgers University Press, 2011), 26.

8. A WOMAN'S WORTH, A BROTHER'S SHAME

1. Linda Carlson Johnson, "Isabella Beecher Hooker: The Suffragists' Preacher," master's thesis (Hartford Seminary, September 1998), 69.

2. Elizabeth Cady Stanton, *The Woman's Bible* (Boston: Northeastern University Press, 1993), vii.

3. Jennifer Michael Hecht, *Doubt: A History* (New York: HarperCollins, 2004), 392.

4. Barbara Goldsmith, *Other Powers: The Age of Suffrage, Spiritualism, and the Scandalous Victoria Woodhull* (New York: Harper Perennial, 1999), 207.

5. Kathi Kern, *Mrs. Stanton's Bible* (Ithaca, NY: Cornell University Press, 2002), 120.

6. Jeanne Boydston, Mary Kelley, and Anne Throne Margolis, *The Limits of Sisterhood: The Beecher Sisters on Women's Rights and Woman's Sphere* (Chapel Hill: University of North Carolina Press, 1988), 184.

7. Lyman Abbott, *Henry Ward Beecher* (New York: Houghton, Mifflin and Co., 1903) 333–34.

8. Barbara A. White, *The Beecher Sisters* (New Haven: Yale University Press, 2003),, 152.

9. Joan D. Hedrick, *Harriet Beecher Stowe: A Life* (New York: Oxford University Press, 1995), 371.

10. Daniel McFarland, *The Richardson-McFarland Tragedy* (Philadelphia: Barclay & Co., 1870), 21.

11. Ann D. Gordon, ed., *The Selected Papers of Elizabeth Cady Stanton and Susan B. Anthony: National Protection for National Citizens, 1873 to 1880* (Piscataway Township, NJ: Rutgers University Press, 2003), 360.

12. Goldsmith, *Other Powers*, 207.

13. John M. Murrin, Paul E. Johnson, James M. McPherson, Alice Fahs, and Gary Gerstle *Liberty, Equality, Power*, vol. 2: *A History of the American People since 1863* (Independence, KY: Cengage Learning, 2011), 591.

14. John Hooker, *Reminiscences of a Long Life: With a Few Articles on Moral and Social Subjects of Present Interest* (Hartford: Case, Lockwood & Brainard Co., 1899), 91.

15. Ann Gordon, ed., *The Selected Papers of Elizabeth Cady Stanton and Susan B. Anthony: Against an Aristocracy of Sex, 1866 to 1873* (Piscataway Township, NJ: Rutgers University Press, 2000), 305.

16. Linda Carlson Johnson, "Isabella Beecher Hooker," 75.

17. Gordon, ed., *National Protection*, 380–81.

18. Ellen Burr, recording sec., notes of the Connecticut Woman Suffrage Association, vol. 1 (1870), Connecticut State Library.

19. Gordon, ed., *National Protection*, 391–92.

20. Anne Throne Margolis and Margaret Granville Mair, eds., *Guide to the Isabella Beecher Hooker Project* (Hartford: Stowe-Day Foundation, 1979), 28.

21. Lyman Beecher Stowe, *Saints, Sinners and Beechers* (Indianapolis: Bobbs-Merrill Co., 1934), 352.

22. Goldsmith, *Other Powers*, 246.

23. Ida Husted Harper, *The Life and Work of Susan B. Anthony* (Indianapolis: Bowen-Merrill Co., 1898), 371–77.

24. B. White, *The Beecher Sisters*, 247.

25. Ibid., 162.

26. *Woodhull & Claflin's Weekly,* January 14, 1871.

27. Catharine Beecher, *Woman's Profession as Mother and Educator: With Views in Opposition to Woman Suffrage* (New York: G. Maclean, 1872), 128.

28. Beecher, *Woman's Profession*, 130–31.

29. Kate Havelin, *Victoria Woodhull: Fearless Feminist* (Breckenridge, CO: Twenty-First Century Books, 2006), 44.

30. I. Harper, *The Life and Work*, 375.

31. Lois Beachy Underhill, *The Woman Who Ran for President: The Many Lives of Victoria Woodhull* (New York: Penguin Books, 1996), 101–2.

32. Underhill, *The Woman Who Ran*, 104.

33. Victoria Claflin Woodhull, *The Human Body the Temple of God; or, The Philosophy of Sociology* (London: Hyde Park Gate, 1890), 283.

34. Linda Carlson Johnson, "Isabella Beecher Hooker," 78.

35. Ibid., 80.

36. Amanda Frisken, *Victoria Woodhull's Sexual Revolution: Political Theater and the Popular Press in Nineteenth-Century America* (Philadelphia: University of Pennsylvania Press, 2011), 31–32.

37. Linda Carlson Johnson, "Isabella Beecher Hooker," 80.

38. Marion Meade, *Free Woman: The Life and Times of Victoria Woodhull* (New York: E-reads/E-rights, 2011), 82.

39. I. Harper, *The Life and Work*, 379.

40. Debby Applegate, *The Most Famous Man in America: The Biography of Henry Ward Beecher* (New York: Doubleday, 2006), 413.

41. Joseph S. Van Why and Earl French, eds., *Nook Farm* (Hartford: Stowe-Day Foundation, 1975), 40.

42. Boydston, *The Limits of Sisterhood*, 209.

43. Goldsmith, *Other Powers*, 215.

44. Ibid., 256.

45. Austin Sarat, Lawrence Douglas, and Martha Umphrey, eds., *Lives in the Law* (Ann Arbor, MI: University of Michigan Press, 2002), 72.

46. Emanie N. Sachs, *The Terrible Siren: Victoria Woodhull, 1838–1927* (New York: Harper and Bros., 1928), 113.

47. Frisken, *Victoria Woodhull's Sexual Revolution*, 31.

48. Bonnie G. Mani, *Women, Power, and Political Change* (New York: Lexington Books, 2007), 77.

49. Underhill, *The Woman Who Ran*, 179.

50. B. White, *The Beecher Sisters*, 187–88.

51. B. White, *The Beecher Sisters*, 188.

52. Goldsmith, *Other Powers*, 291.

53. Ibid., 291.

54. Underhill, *The Woman Who Ran*, 179–82.

55. Alana S. Jeydel, *Political Women: The Women's Movement, Political Institutions, the Battle for Women's Suffrage, and the ERA* (London: Psychology Press, 2004), 54.

56. Stanton, *The Woman's Bible*, 30.

57. Gordon, ed., *National Protection*, 481.

58. Frisken, *Victoria Woodhull's Sexual Revolution*, 67.

59. Philip Sheldon Foner, ed., *Frederick Douglass on Women's Rights* (Cambridge: Da Capo Press, 1992), 38.

60. Linda Carlson Johnson, "Isabella Beecher Hooker," 99.

61. Goldsmith, *Other Powers*, 320–21.

62. Carl M. Carpenter, ed., *Selected Writings of Victoria Woodhull: Suffrage, Free Love, and Eugenics* (Omaha: University of Nebraska Press, 2010), xiii.

63. I. Harper, *The Life and Work*, 415.

64. Ibid., 413.

65. Hedrick, *Harriet Beecher Stowe*, 375.

66. B. White, *The Beecher Sisters*, 169.

67. Goldsmith, *Other Powers*, 479.

68. Linda Carlson Johnson, "Isabella Beecher Hooker," 88.

69. Mary Chapman and Angela Mills, *Treacherous Texts: U.S. Suffrage Literature, 1846–1946* (Piscataway Township, NJ: Rutgers University Press, 2011), 51.

70. Chapman and Mills, *Treacherous Texts*, 61.

71. Hedrick, *Harriet Beecher Stowe*, 374.

72. B. White, *The Beecher Sisters*, 214.

73. Boydston, *The Limits of Sisterhood*, 298.

74. Kenneth Richmond Andrews, *Nook Farm: Mark Twain's Hartford Circle* (Cambridge: Harvard University Press, 1950), 139.

75. Boydston, *The Limits of Sisterhood*, 296.

76. B. White, *The Beecher Sisters*, 198.

77. Michael W. Perry, ed., *Lady Eugenist: Feminist Eugenics in the Speeches and Writings of Victoria Woodhull* (Seattle: Inkling Books, 2005), 120.

78. Frisken, *Victoria Woodhull's Sexual Revolution*, 94.

79. Linda Carlson Johnson, "Isabella Beecher Hooker," 103.

80. Ibid., 93.

81. Frisken, *Victoria Woodhull's Sexual Revolution*, 9.

82. Laura Hanft Korobkin, *Criminal Conversations: Sentimentality and Nineteenth-Century Legal Stories of Adultery* (New York: Columbia University Press, 1998), 61.

83. Korobkin, *Criminal Conversations*, 61.

84. Frisken, *Victoria Woodhull's Sexual Revolution*, 88.

85. David Sehat, *The American Moral Establishment: Religion and Liberalism in the Nineteenth Century* (Chapel Hill: University of North Carolina Press, 2007), 130.

86. Linda Carlson Johnson, "Isabella Beecher Hooker," 111.

87. B. White, *The Beecher Sisters*, 208.

88. J. E. P. Doyle, *Plymouth Church and Its Pastor; or, Henry Ward Beecher and His Accusers* (St. Louis: Bryan, Brand & Co., 1875), 13.

89. Doyle, *Plymouth Church*, 41.

90. Andrews, *Nook Farm*, 39.

91. Boydston, *The Limits of Sisterhood*, 298.

92. Applegate, *The Most Famous Man in America*, 424.

93. Ibid., 425.

94. Frances Elizabeth Willard and Mary Ashton Rice Livermore, *American Women: Fifteen Hundred Biographies with Over 1,400 Portraits* (Springfield, OH: Mast, Crowell & Kirkpatrick, 1897), 391.

95. Van Why, *Nook Farm*, 39–40.

96. Robert Shaplen, *Free Love and Heavenly Sinners* (New York: Alfred A. Knopf, 1954), 206–14.

97. B. White, *The Beecher Sisters*, 223.

98. Margolis, *Guide*, 34.

99. Applegate, *The Most Famous Man in America*, 425.

100. Ibid., 424.

101. B. White, *The Beecher Sisters*, 242.

102. Applegate, *The Most Famous Man in America*, 437.

103. Boydston, *The Limits of Sisterhood*, 298.

104. Ibid., 323.

105. Applegate, *The Most Famous Man in America*, 436.

106. B. White, *The Beecher Sisters*, 245.

107. Lori Merish, *Sentimental Materialism: Gender, Commodity Culture, and Nineteenth-Century Literature* (Durham, NC: Duke University Press, 2000), 145.

108. Wilson, *Crusader in Crinoline*, 571.

109. Boydston, *The Limits of Sisterhood*, 189.

110. Margolis, *Guide*, 36.

111. Samuel Agnew Schreiner, *The Passionate Beechers: A Family Saga of Sanctity and Scandal That Changed America* (Hoboken, NJ: John Wiley & Sons, 2003), 305.

112. Wilson, *Crusader in Crinoline*, 602.

113. Florence Marryat, *There Is No Death* (New York: Lovell, Coryell & Co., 1891), 243.

114. Edward T. James, Janet Wilson James, and Paul S. Boyer, *Notable American Women, 1607–1950: A Biographical Dictionary* (Boston: Harvard University Press, 1971), 2: 213.

115. David H. Fears, *Mark Twain Day by Day: 1835–1885* (Banks, OR: Horizon Micro Publishing, 2007), 561.

116. James, James, and Boyer, *Notable American Women*, 213.

117. Amy Dru Stanley, *From Bondage to Contract: Wage Labor, Marriage, and the Market in the Age of Slave Emancipation* (New York: Cambridge University Press, 1998), 184.

118. J. Hooker, *Reminiscences*, 56–57.

119. Ibid., 57.

120. Margolis, *Guide*, 40.

121. J. Hooker, *Reminiscences*, 57.

122. *Banking: Journal of the American Bankers Association*, vol. 12 (American Institute of Banking, 1919), 93.

123. *Connecticut Reports: Proceedings in the Supreme Court of the State of Connecticut* (Hartford: Connecticut Supreme Court of Errors, 1922), 88: 778.

124. William Jay Youmans, *Appleton's Popular Science Monthly*, vol. 49 (New York: D. Appleton and Co., 1896), 842.

125. Schreiner, *The Passionate Beechers*, 307.

126. Numbers 22:28–33 (New Revised Standard Version).

127. Margolis, *Guide*, 37.

128. Ibid., 39.

129. Mari Jo Buhle and Paul Buhle, *The Concise History of Woman Suffrage* (Champaign: University of Illinois Press, 2005), 307.

130. Robert Hubbard, *Glastonbury* (Mount Pleasant, SC: Arcadia Publishing, 2012), 21.

131. Linda K. Kerber, *No Constitutional Right to Be Ladies: Women and the Obligations of Citizenship* (New York: Macmillan, 1998), 84.

132. Kerber, *No Constitutional Right*, 87.

133. Antonia Petrash, *More than Petticoats: Remarkable Connecticut Women* (Guilford, CT: Globe Pequot Press, 2003), 18.

134. Petrash, *More than Petticoats*, 21.

135. Kathryn Cullen-DuPont, *Women's Suffrage in America* (New York: Infobase Publishing, 2005, 234.

136. June Purvis and Sandra Stanley Holton, *Votes for Women* (Florence, KY: Psychology Press, 2000), 16.

137. Ellen Carol DuBois, *Feminism and Suffrage: The Emergence of an Independent Women's Movement in America, 1848–1869* (Ithaca, NY: Cornell University Press, 1999), 134.

138. Lee Ann Banaszak, *Why Movements Succeed or Fail: Opportunity, Culture, and the Struggle for Woman Suffrage* (Princeton, NJ: Princeton University Press, 1996), 242.

139. Jeffrey Schultz, John West, and Iain Maclean, *Encyclopedia of Religion in American Politics* (Westport, CT: Greenwood Publishing Group, 1998), 247.

140. Rebecca Brooks Edwards, *Angels in the Machinery: Gender in American Party Politics from the Civil War to the Progressive Era* (New York: Oxford University Press, 1997), 51.

9. A SPIRITUAL DIGRESSION

1. Jean H. Baker, *Mary Todd Lincoln: A Biography* (New York: W. W. Norton & Co., 2008), 42.

10. IN THE THICK OF IT

1. Ida Husted Harper, ed., *The History of Woman Suffrage: 1900–1920* (Fowler and Wells, 1922), 453.

2. Marjorie Spruill Wheeler, *Votes for Women! The Woman Suffrage Movement in Tennessee, the South, and the Nation* (Knoxville: University of Tennessee Press, 1995), 13–14.

3. Ida Husted Harper, *The Life and Work of Susan B. Anthony* (Indianapolis: Bowen-Merrill Co., 1898), 1571.

4. Stephen B. Goddard, *Colonel Albert Pope and His American Dream Machines: The Life and Times of a Bicycle Tycoon Turned Automotive Pioneer* (Jefferson, NC: McFarland, 2000), 1.

5. William Corbett, *Literary New England: A History and Guide* (Boston: Faber and Faber, 1993), 11.

6. Tina Grant, *International Directory of Company Histories* (Chicago: St. James Press, 1996), 70.

7. Gillian M. Rodger, *Champagne Charlie and Pretty Jemima: Variety Theater in the Nineteenth Century* (Champaign: University of Illinois Press, 2010), 232.

8. Kevin Murphy, *Water for Hartford: The Story of the Hartford Water Works and the Metropolitan District Commission* (Middletown, CT: Wesleyan University Press, 2010), 156.

9. Anne Throne Margolis and Margaret Granville Mair, eds., *Guide to the Isabella Beecher Hooker Project* (Hartford: Stowe-Day Foundation, 1979), 7.

10. Lyman Beecher Stowe, *Saints, Sinners and Beechers* (Indianapolis: Bobbs-Merrill Co., 1934), 352.

11. Alan C. Swedlund, *Shadows in the Valley: A Cultural History of Illness, Death,*

and Loss in New England, 1840–1916 (Amherst: University of Massachusetts Press, 2010), 85.

12. Louisa Knapp, ed. *Ladies Home Journal and Practical Housekeeper*, vols. 5–6 (Indianapolis: Curtis Pub. Co., 1887), 215.

13. Ann Braude, *Radical Spirits: Spiritualism and Women's Rights in Nineteenth Century America* (Boston: Beacon Press, 1989), 24.

14. John Hooker, *Reminiscences of a Long Life: With a Few Articles on Moral and Social Subjects of Present Interest* (Hartford: Case, Lockwood & Brainard Co., 1899), 253.

15. J. Hooker, *Reminiscences*, 263.

16. Mary Chapman and Angela Mills, *Treacherous Texts: U.S. Suffrage Literature, 1846–1946* (Piscataway Township, NJ: Rutgers University Press, 2011), 115.

17. *Report of the International Council of Women* (Washington: R. H. Darby, 1888), 10.

18. Jeanne Boydston, Mary Kelley, and Anne Throne Margolis, *The Limits of Sisterhood: The Beecher Sisters on Women's Rights and Woman's Sphere* (Chapel Hill: University of North Carolina Press, 1988), 189.

19. *Report of the International Council of Women*, 303.

20. Gordon Morris Bakken and Brenda Gail Farrington, eds. *The American West* (Florence, KY: Psychology Press, 2000), 347.

21. Joan Iverson, *The Antipolygamy Controversy in U.S. Women's Movements, 1880–1925: A Debate on the American Home* (London: Taylor & Francis, 1997), 162.

22. Bakken, *The American West*, 347.

23. Allison L. Sneider, *Suffragists in an Imperial Age: U.S. Expansion and the Woman Question, 1870–1929* (New York: Oxford University Press, 2008), 10.

24. Ann D. Gordon, ed., *The Selected Papers of Elizabeth Cady Stanton and Susan B. Anthony: National Protection for National Citizens, 1873 to 1880* (Piscataway Township, NJ: Rutgers University Press, 2003), 343.

25. Wilma Mankiller, *The Reader's Companion to U.S. Women's History* (New York: Houghton Mifflin Harcourt, 1999), 577.

26. Debby Applegate, *The Most Famous Man in America: The Biography of Henry Ward Beecher* (New York: Doubleday, 2006), 466.

27. Samuel Agnew Schreiner, *The Passionate Beechers: A Family Saga of Sanctity and Scandal That Changed America* (Hoboken, NJ: John Wiley & Sons, 2003), 333.

28. Plymouth Church of the Pilgrims, *Henry Ward Beecher: A Memorial* (New York: Plymouth Church, 1887), 42.

29. Wilson, *Crusader in Crinoline: The Life of Harriet Beecher Stowe* (Philadelphia: J. B. Lippincott Co., 1941), 626.

30. Margolis, *Guide*, 40.

31. Susan Hodge Armitage, *The Women's West* (Norman: University of Oklahoma Press, 1987), 271.

1. Suzanne O'Dea Schenken, *From Suffrage to the Senate, A–M* (Santa Barbara, CA: ABC-CLIO, 1999), 1: 42.

2. Michael Burgan, *Elizabeth Cady Stanton: Social Reformer* (Minneapolis: Compass Point Books, 2005), 89.

3. Alice Stone Blackwell, *The Woman Citizen*, vol. 3 (New York: Leslie Woman Suffrage Commission, 1918), 1018.

4. Barbara A. White, *The Beecher Sisters* (New Haven: Yale University Press, 2003), 314.

5. Jeanne Boydston, Mary Kelley, and Anne Throne Margolis, *The Limits of Sisterhood: The Beecher Sisters on Women's Rights and Woman's Sphere* (Chapel Hill: University of North Carolina Press, 1988), 190.

6. Boydston, *The Limits of Sisterhood*, 190.

7. Ibid., 218.

8. John Hooker, ed., *An Account of the Reunion of the Descendants of Rev. Thomas Hooker* (Salem, MA: The Salem Press, 1890), 12.

9. *Transactions of the National Council of Women of the United States, Assembled in Washington, D.C., Feb. 22 to 25, 1891* (J. P. Lippincott, 1891), 42.

10. *Transactions*, 324.

11. Anne Throne Margolis and Margaret Granville Mair, eds., *Guide to the Isabella Beecher Hooker Project* (Hartford: Stowe-Day Foundation, 1979), 7.

12. Joseph S. Van Why and Earl French, eds., *Nook Farm* (Hartford: Stowe-Day Foundation, 1975), 40.

13. Vivian Gornick, *The Solitude of Self: Thinking about Elizabeth Cady Stanton* (New York: Macmillan, 2006), 7.

14. Ida Husted Harper, *The Life and Work of Susan B. Anthony* (Indianapolis: Bowen-Merrill Co., 1898), 535.

15. I. Harper, *The Life and Work*, 536.

16. Barbara Goldsmith, *Other Powers: The Age of Suffrage, Spiritualism, and the Scandalous Victoria Woodhull* (New York: Harper Perennial, 1999), 4.

17. Goldsmith, *Other Powers*, 5–6.

18. "Victorian Martin, Suffragist, Dies" (June 11, 1927), *New York Times* online, www.nytimes.com/learning/general/onthisday/bday/0923.html.

19. Carol Farley Kessler and Charlotte Perkins Gilman, *Charlotte Perkins Gilman: Her Progress toward Utopia, with Selected Writings* (Syracuse: Syracuse University Press, 1995), 24.

20. Kessler, *Charlotte Perkins Gilman*, 107.

21. Dagmar Hecher, *The Woman in the American Family* (Munich: GRIN Verlag, 2006), 1.

22. Boydston, *The Limits of Sisterhood*, 358.

23. Norman Bolotin and Christine Laing, *The World's Columbian Exposition: The Chicago World's Fair of 1893* (Champaign: University of Illinois Press, 2002), vii.

24. Chaim M. Rosenberg, *America at the Fair: Chicago's 1893 World's Columbian Exposition* (Chicago: Arcadia Publishing, 2008), vi.

25. David J. Bertuca, Donald K. Hartman, and Susan M. Neumeister, *The World's Columbian Exposition: A Centennial Bibliographic Guide* (Westport, CT: Greenwood Publishing Group, 1996), 306.

26. Marjorie Warvelle Bear, *A Mile Square of Chicago* (Oak Brook, IL: TIPRAC, 2007), 54.

27. Stanley Waterloo and John Wesley Hanson Jr. *Famous American Men and Women* (New York: Wasbash Publishing, 1896), 328.

28. Patricia Ward D'Itri, *Cross Currents in the International Women's Movement, 1848–1948* (Madison, WI: Popular Press, 1999), 77.

29. D'Itri, *Cross Currents*, 77.

30. Ibid., 78.

31. Ishbel Ross, *Silhouette in Diamonds: The Life of Mrs. Potter Palmer* (New York: Harper, 1960), 66.

32. Ibid., 67.

33. Ibid., 67.

34. Ibid., 68.

35. Tracey Jean Boisseau, Abigail M. Markwyn, and Robert Rydell, *Gendering the Fair: Histories of Women and Gender at World's Fairs* (Champaign: University of Illinois Press, 2010), 109.

36. Reid Neilson, *Exhibiting Mormonism: The Latter-Day Saints and the 1893 Chicago World's Fair* (New York: Oxford University Press, 2011), 100.

37. Neilson, *Exhibiting Mormonism*, 8.

38. Rita K. Gollin, *Annie Adams Fields: Woman of Letters* (Amherst: University of Massachusetts Press, 2002), 176.

39. David S. Reynolds, *Mightier than the Sword: "Uncle Tom's Cabin" and the Battle for America* (New York: W. W. Norton & Co., 2012), 201.

40. Reynolds, *Mightier than the Sword*, 202–3.

41. Eugene A. Hecker, *A Short History of Women's Rights* (Fairford, UK: Echo Library, 2007), 89.

42. I. Harper, *The Life and Work*, 537.

43. B. White, *The Beecher Sisters*, 315.

44. *Hartford Courant*, October 3, 1893.

45. William Gillette, *America's Sherlock Holmes* (Bloomington, IN: Xlibris Corp., 2011), 224.

46. Ron Powers, *Mark Twain: A Life* (New York: Simon & Schuster, 2005), 559.

47. Van Why, *Nook Farm*, 24–25.

48. B. White, *Nook Farm*, 315.

49. Debby Applegate, *The Most Famous Man in America: The Biography of Henry Ward Beecher* (New York: Doubleday, 2006), 469.

50. B. White, *The Beecher Sisters*, 316.

51. Susan Belasco, ed., *Stowe in Her Own Time: A Biographical Chronicle of Her Life,*

Drawn from Recollections, Interviews, and Memoirs by Family, Friends, and Associates
(Iowa City: University of Iowa Press, 2009), 253.

52. Boydston, 300.

12. THE END, AND A LEGACY

1. National American Woman Suffrage Association, *Proceedings of the Thirty-Second Annual Convention of the National American Woman Suffrage Association* (Washington, DC: The Association, 1900), 63.

2. Ibid., 63.

3. Barbara Sicherman and Carol Hurd Green, *Notable American Women: The Modern Period: A Biographical Dictionary* (Boston: Harvard University Press, 1980), 4: 380.

4. Carol Kort and Liz Sonneborn, *A to Z of American Women in the Visual Arts* (New York: Infobase Publishing, 2002), 110.

5. Katherine H. Adams and Michael L. Keene, *Alice Paul and the American Suffrage Campaign* (Champaign: University of Illinois Press, 2008), 149.

6. Hamlin Hill, *Mark Twain: God's Fool* (Chicago: University of Chicago Press, 2010), 34.

7. Sara A. Francis Underwood, *Automatic or Spirit Writing, with Other Psychic Experiences* (Chicago: T. G. Newman, 1896), 12.

8. "Biography Sketch of John Hooker," *Memorials of Connecticut Judges and Attorneys as Printed in the Connecticut Reports*, vol. 73, 745–6.

9. "The Death of John Hooker," *Hartford Courant*, February 13, 1901.

10. Ibid.

11. Barbara A. White, *The Beecher Sisters* (New Haven: Yale University Press, 2003), 242.

12. Ida Husted Harper, ed., *The History of Woman Suffrage: 1900–1920* (Fowler and Wells, 1922), 453.

13. I. Harper, ed., *The History of Woman Suffrage*, 69.

14. Jeanne Boydston, Mary Kelley, and Anne Throne Margolis, *The Limits of Sisterhood: The Beecher Sisters on Women's Rights and Woman's Sphere* (Chapel Hill: University of North Carolina Press, 1988), 331–32.

15. I. Harper, ed., *The History of Woman Suffrage*, 69.

16. Samuel Agnew Schreiner, *The Passionate Beechers: A Family Saga of Sanctity and Scandal That Changed America* (Hoboken, NJ: John Wiley & Sons, 2003), 352.

17. Suzanne O'Dea Schenken, *From Suffrage to the Senate, A–M* (Santa Barbara, CA: ABC-CLIO, 1999), 1: 42.

18. Anne Throne Margolis and Margaret Granville Mair, eds., *Guide to the Isabella Beecher Hooker Project* (Hartford: Stowe-Day Foundation, 1979), 7.

19. Jesse Lyman Hurlbut, *The Story of Chautauqua* (New York: G. P. Putnam's Sons, 1921), 112.

20. *The Congregationalist and Christian World*, vol. 93 (Pilgrim Press, 1908), 410.

21. I. Harper, ed., *The History of Woman Suffrage*, 71.

INDEX

Page numbers in *italics* indicate illustrations. Married women are listed under their married surnames unless they are generally known by their maiden names.

Smith, Julia and Abby, 138–39, 163

spirit writing, 167–73, 177–78

Spiritualism: abolitionism and suffragism, relationship to, 51; author's present-day exploration of, 52–54, 141–44; belief system of, 51–52; Charles Beecher and, 112, 149; death of Mary Hooker Burton and, 148–49, 169, 171, 173; Henry Ward Beecher and, 127, 151, 156; Hooker mansion séances, 59, 134; John Hooker's involvement in, 133–34, 149–50; late-life dependence of IBH on, 167–73, 175; mother of IBH and, 16, 50, 132, 150; in nineteenth-century America, 49–51, 133; religious beliefs of IBH and, 107; supposed insanity of IBH and, 141; Tilton-Beecher scandal and interest of IBH in, 132–34, 138; will of IBH, trial over, 177–78; of Woodhull, 115, 125

Stanton, Elizabeth Cady: abolitionist movement, 48–49, 86, 93; on Christianity and suffrage, 106; death of, 175; Dickinson, Anna, on, 82; on divorce, 96, 99, 107, 109, 111, 155; Harriet Beecher Stowe and Byron scandal, 100; husband and children of, 48, 90, 139; IBH and, viii, x, 93, 94, 95, 98–99, 100, 103, 104, 106, 107, 109, 111, 112, 120, 130–31, 145, 146; John Hooker and, 107, 111; on McFarland scandal, 109; in *My Wife and I* (Harriet Beecher Stowe), 123; racist, use of, 77–78, 89–90, 93; recognition by suffragist movement, 174; "The Solitude of Self" (1892), 158–59; suffragist activities of, 45, 77–78, 93–94, 97–98, 101–3, 121, 138, 146, 150, 155; on Tilton-Beecher scandal, 130–31; Woodhull and, 117, 119, 120, 131

Stearnes, Sara Burger, 118

Stone, Lucy, 78, 88, 94, 97–98

Stowe, Calvin (husband), 25, 28, 46, 86, 109, 163

Stowe, Harriet Beecher (half-sister of IBH): birth and childhood, 11; birth, childhood, and education, 6, 8, 12; brothers' opinions of, 56; Byron scandal and, 99–100, 122, 123; Catharine Beecher and, 66, 68; children of, 42, 62, 100, 112, 176; *Christian Union* and, 108–9; on Cincinnati move, 21; commemoration of, 162, 163–65; dementia and death of, 163; in Florida, 100; Lincoln and, 88; marriage of, 25, 28, 46, 86, 163; in Nook Farm, Hartford, 58, 69, 71; obituaries comparing IBH to, 176; sanity of IBH, questions regarding, 124; on slavery and abolitionism, viii, 63, 66–67, 96, 100; Spiritualism and, 51; stepmother and, 9–10, 11, 19; suffragist movement and, 95, 98, 99–100, 102, 107, 123–24; as teacher, 26, 28; Tilton-Beecher scandal and, 128, 129, 131, 145; Woodhull and, 116, 117, 123–24, 128

Stowe, Harriet Beecher, works of: historical novel, plans for, 60; *Lady Byron Vindicated*, 99–100, 122, 123; *My Wife and I,* 123–24, 173; *Uncle Tom's Cabin* (1852), vii, viii, 56, 60–63, 66–67, 68, 77, 88, 99, 165

suffragist movement: abolitionist movement and, 23, 48–49, 77–78, 86, 89, 90; African American suffrage and, 75, 93–96, 110; Alice Hooker mocking, 91–92; avowed racist used by, 77–78, 89; Beecher family views on, 65, 75–76, 80, 95–96, 98, 101–4, 107, 113–14, 122, 123–24; constitutional amendment on women's suffrage, 96–98, 103, 121, 138–39, 150, 154, 173–74; cult of domesticity and "true womanhood" arising at same time as, 73; free love

Garnet Books

SUSAN CAMPBELL is the author of the memoir *Dating Jesus: Fundamentalism, Feminism, and the American Girl,* winner of the 2010 CT Book Award for Memoir, and coauthor of *Connecticut Curiosities: Quirky Characters, Roadside Oddities & Other Offbeat Stuff.* She has appeared on CBS *Sunday Morning,* the BBC, and WNPR. Her column about the March 1998 shootings at the Connecticut Lottery headquarters in Newington was part of the Hartford *Courant*'s Pulitzer Prize–winning coverage of the tragedy. She lives in East Haven, Connecticut.